AN INTRODUCTION TO ARAMAIC

SOCIETY OF BIBLICAL LITERATURE
Resources for Biblical Study

Edited by
Marvin A. Sweeney

Number 38
AN INTRODUCTION TO ARAMAIC
by
Frederick E. Greenspahn

AN INTRODUCTION TO ARAMAIC

by
Frederick E. Greenspahn

Society of Biblical Literature
Resources for Biblical Study

Scholars Press
Atlanta, Georgia

AN INTRODUCTION TO ARAMAIC

by
Frederick E. Greenspahn

Copyright © 1999 by the Society of Biblical Literature

Funerary Inscription of Uzziah, Jerusalem, 1st Century BCE–1st Century CE is used with the permission of the Israel Museum, Jerusalem.

Dolerite wall relief from Sinjerli (Sam'al) showing King Barrekib on his throne with a scribe. Aramean c. 750 BCE. Vorderasiatisches Museum, Staatliche Museen, Berlin, Germany. Used with permission of Foto Marburg/ Art Resource, NY.

Library of Congress Cataloging-in-Publication Data
Greenspahn, Frederick E., 1946–
    An introduction to Aramaic / by Frederick E. Greenspahn.
        p.   cm. —(Resources for biblical study ; no. 38)
    Includes bibliographical references.
    ISBN 0-7885-0463-0 (pbk. : alk. paper)
    1. Aramaic language. 2. Bible. O.T.—Language, style.
I. Title. II. Series.
PJ5211.G74   1998
492'.29—dc21   98-17632
                                    CIP

08 07 06 05 04 03 02 01   5 4 3 2

Printed in the United States of America
on acid-free paper

CONTENTS

FOREWORD

This book is intended for students who are just beginning to study Aramaic. Seldom is it the language's inherent value which attracts such individuals; more often, they are motivated (if not always directly) by an interest in the Bible, although some may want to explore early Judaism or Christianity as well. This fact has several fairly obvious corollaries for a book such as this. First, it means that those using it already have some familiarity with Hebrew, typically biblical Hebrew. At the same time, however, that knowledge is probably rudimentary, given the stage at which most students are encouraged, or expected, to learn Aramaic. Finally, it suggests that students are likely to proceed to other Aramaic texts or other Semitic languages, whether they realize it yet or not. In other words, although biblical Aramaic is usually introduced as an end in itself, it most often functions as a bridge between the Hebrew Bible and some other, related area.

This text tries to take these facts seriously. Recognizing students' existing knowledge and motivation, it treats Aramaic as if it were a dialect of Hebrew, without trying to cover all of the language's depth and richness. This is a widespread, if seldom acknowledged, approach with a long pedigree. The fourteenth century grammarian Profiat Duran described Aramaic as "the Holy Tongue corrupted" (לשון הקדש שנשתבש).* That, however, is a patently inaccurate and very unfair way to characterize an independent language that has produced several quite separate bodies of literature, each historically and linguistically important in its own right.

Our only justification for this approach is pedagogic utility. Indeed, pedagogic considerations have governed most of the presentation here, which has been kept as non-technical as possible. Thus verb, noun, and pronoun charts include hypothetical forms (unmarked) on the premise that students will find it easier to learn patterns as a whole without trying to distinguish attested from theoretical forms or to remember where direct evidence is lacking. Where several alternative forms exist, only one is presented. The selection of these preferred forms has frequently been difficult, especially in cases of *ketîv* and *qerê*, where the problem of deciding whether it is pre-Christian or masoretic Aramaic that is being taught had to be con-

---

Ma'aseh Efod, ed. J. Friedländer and J. Kohn (Vienna: Haltswarte, 1865) p. 40.

fronted. Our decisions have been somewhat eclectic. Thus the second person masculine singular pronoun is presented as אַנְתָּ, in conformity with the *qerê*, rather than the presumably earlier *ketîv* אַנְתָּה, while proper names have been presented exactly as they occur in the standard *Biblia Hebraica Stuttgartensia*; thus דָּנִיֵּאל, despite the obvious anomaly in the placement of the vowel. In order to ensure the consistency of what students encounter, the biblical text has occasionally been normalized to fit the regular patterns taught in the grammar. Students may, therefore, wish to read the original exactly as it appears in the Bible after finishing this course.

Pedagogical concerns have also affected terminology. Thus the conjugations are identified as G, D, and H in order to facilitate comparison among Semitic languages, which would be complicated by terms such as *peʿal*, *paʿʿel* and *hafʿel*, which are appropriate for Aramaic alone.

A word about the terms "conjugation" and "tense" is also in order. The nature of the phenomena which these terms designate is enmeshed in difficult technical issues. We have chosen to use terms that are likely to be familiar from the study of other languages, letting instructors choose whether to describe the problems involved or to leave that for some later stage of study. Similarly, the periodization presented in chapter 2 is only one of several that are possible. Since any such scheme is inherently arbitrary and heuristic, a straightforward one that would facilitate clarity was selected.

It should by now be obvious that this is not intended to be a reference work, although paradigms and a glossary are included at the end. There is already an abundance of advanced and technically proficient resources for those who choose to continue beyond the introductory level. This book is meant to help students take advantage of those tools. It has, therefore, been constructed as a kind of workbook, organized around the Aramaic passages from the Bible. These are at first simplified and abridged, in order to keep the quantity of new vocabulary to within manageable proportions. Daniel 7, the last biblical passage in Aramaic, is read exactly as it occurs in the Bible (chapter 27).

Each chapter introduces a grammatical feature. Vocabulary has been coordinated with the biblical passages and divided into important (recurring) and reference sections — though both are included in the glossary at the end. (The glossary is not a complete lexicon of biblical Aramaic, but contains only words actually used in the passages which appear in this book; for that reason, it also includes the handful of Hebrew terms that occur in some of the late texts presented in the readings.) Both grammar and vocabulary are reviewed in practice exercises.

While there is much about this presentation of the material that may appear idiosyncratic, I am deeply aware of my debt to many scholars whose knowledge and experience of Aramaic far exceeds my own. Experienced teachers will likely recognize the influence of

Ethelyn Simon, Irene Resnikoff, and Linda Motzkin's *The First Hebrew Primer* (3d edition, Oakland, CA: EKS Publishing Co, 1992), Isaac Jerusalmi's *The Aramaic Sections of Ezra and Daniel* (Cincinnati: Hebrew Union College-Jewish Institute of Religion, 1972), and Ehud ben Zvi, Maxine Hancock, and Richard Beinert's *Readings in Biblical Hebrew, An Intermediate Textbook* (New Haven: Yale University Press, 1993), a debt gratefully acknowledged. The grammar draws heavily on Franz Rosenthal's *A Grammar of Biblical Aramaic* (Wiesbaden: Otto Harrasowitz, 1963) and Hans Bauer and Pontus Leander's *Grammatik des Biblisch-Aramäische* (Halle/Saale: Max Niemayer Verlag, 1927). Rather than supplanting these valuable tools, this book is intended to prepare students to use them easily and profitably. Like training wheels, the surest sign of its success will be when it is no longer necessary. For students to outgrow it will, therefore, be a source of pleasure rather than evidence of its inadequacy. Indeed, after finishing this course, students should be encouraged to acquire other tools, primarily Rosenthal's *Grammar*, which is in English and in print.[*]

Several individuals contributed to this project in a variety of ways. Marvin Sweeney and David Petersen had the confidence to propose that I undertake it in the first place. Barbara Beckman helped with technical elements of preparing the manuscript, while Jeanne Abrams and Diane Rutter provided a supportive environment. Paul Kobelski and Maurya Horgan shared their skill and creativity to bring that manuscript to final form. Paul Flesher, Peter Miscall, Gary Rendsburg, and Seth Ward reviewed an earlier draft, rooting out errors and proposing improvements, while David Ackerman, Scott Althof, Susan Brayford, Gary Collier, Brandon Fredenberg, Arlene Lance, Joy Lapp, Gilberto Lozano, Aquiles Martinez, Andrew Tooze, and David Valeta shared students' perspectives. For all of these contributions I am deeply grateful. In the end, however, the decision of how to use the information they so generously shared was my own along with responsibility for the finished product, which often, but not always, followed their suggestions. I hope it will provide a straightforward introduction to a subject rarely begun in a simple way and a coherent enough presentation to kindle interest in proceeding further.

---

[*]Other grammars which might be helpful are Alger F. Johns, *A Short Grammar of Biblical Aramaic* (Berrien Springs, MI: Andrews University Press, 1972) and Elisha Qimron, דקדוק הארמית המקראית (Beer Sheba: Ben-Gurion University of the Negev Press, 1990).

Chapter 1

INTRODUCTION

What is Aramaic and why should you learn it? Although the Aramaic language is not as familiar as French or Hebrew so that its importance may not appear self-evident, it is as old as the Bible. In fact, the language's name first appears in the Bible (Ezra 4:7, Daniel 2:4, 2 Kings 18:26 = Isaiah 36:11); other ancient sources call it Chaldean or Syrian. The language is named after the ancient Arameans, among whom it originated; they lived in what is today Syria at the same time that the Israelites were establishing themselves in Canaan. Their language spread, eventually becoming *the* language of government and international communication throughout the Near East, from about the time of the Babylonians, who destroyed the Jerusalem temple in the sixth century B.C.E., and continued to be widely used even after the coming of the Greeks until the Arab conquest in the seventh century, long after the Arameans themselves had disappeared.

Strangely, the best known writings in Aramaic were produced by other peoples. According to Jewish tradition it was spoken by Adam (*b. Sanhedrin* 38b), and was probably the native language of Jesus, of numerous talmudic rabbis, and of the third century religious innovator Mani, the founder of what we call Manicheanism. Moreover, a formidable body of literature, including many formative texts of both Judaism and Christianity, were written in or influenced by Aramaic. Aramaic was also used by the Nabateans, an Arab desert people who flourished around the time of Jesus, the later Syrian church, and the Mandeans, a gnostic sect that originated close to two thousand years ago in what is today southern Iraq. It continues to be used as a spoken language to the present day, albeit only in small pockets of Syria, Iraq, and Iran, as well as among Jews and Christians who have migrated to Israel and the United States from these regions.

Today few people study Aramaic because they are interested in the Arameans. Most are motivated by the fact that parts of the Bible are written in Aramaic, specifically major sections of the books of Ezra (4:6–6:18 and 7:12–26) and Daniel (2:4–7:28), as well as one sentence in Jeremiah (10:11) and two words in Genesis (31:17). In order to read the entire "Hebrew" Bible in the original, then, one must know Aramaic.

With only some 200 verses of the Bible in Aramaic, there would be little reason to learn the dialect for that reason alone. However, mastering this limited body of material can open the door to a wide range of possibilities.

Because Aramaic was a dominant language among the Jews of first century Palestine, a wealth of important texts are written in it. Although Jesus' teachings survive only in the Greek New Testament, the Gospels provide ample evidence of Aramaic traditions surrounding him, and the language's influence can be felt in several other passages as well. Being familiar with Aramaic can, therefore, deepen your appreciation of the New Testament. Extensive bodies of both Jewish and Christian literature are also written in Aramaic. Among these are several of the Dead Sea Scrolls, many rabbinic texts, including parts of both talmuds and various midrashim, a substantial number of ancient Jewish Bible translations, called targumim, masoretic notes to the biblical text, and legal and mystical works from as late as the eighteenth century. Within Christian tradition, important writings from the Syrian church, including the Peshitta translation of the Bible, are written in a dialect of Aramaic known as Syriac. In order to provide a taste of the riches which await those who have mastered Aramaic, a small selection from some of these has been included in the final chapters of this book.

Learning Aramaic can also be a first step into the Semitic family of languages as a whole, for those who choose to explore some of its other members. Familiarity with these languages can illuminate elements of biblical Hebrew by providing greater perspective than is possible from knowledge of Hebrew alone, much as we can see things better with two eyes than is possible with only one. For example, it can sensitize us to what might otherwise seem ordinary and unremarkable features of Hebrew, ranging from its system of "tenses" to the existence of internal passives and the changing function of the participle. Indeed, because they belong to the same Northwest branch of the Semitic language family, Aramaic can be a relatively easy second language to learn and a particularly useful way to achieve a deeper understanding of Hebrew itself, offering insights into the nuances of individual Hebrew words and alerting us to differing styles within the Bible. It will, for example, make us aware of "Aramaisms" not only in late passages, such as the books of Esther or Chronicles where one would expect them, but also in earlier parts of the Bible, such as the song of Deborah (Judges 5). These characteristics have even led some scholars to speculate that certain books of the Bible were originally written in Aramaic and only later translated into Hebrew. The knowledge you are about to gain will, therefore, open the door to an entirely new world, one which is interesting and rewarding in its own right.

Because most people who undertake the study of Aramaic are motivated by their interest in the Bible, we will presume that you already have a working knowledge of biblical Hebrew. Since Hebrew and Aramaic share many words, this is a substantial advantage, because it means that you already have an extensive Aramaic vocabulary and understand a variety of Aramaic grammatical principles without even knowing it. For example, many of the following Aramaic words are, undoubtedly, already familiar:

fall . . . . נפל	consider . . . . . . חשב	father . . . . אַב
lift up . . . . נשא	seal . . . . חתם	stone . . . . אֶבֶן
give . . . . נתן	dew . . . . טַל	brother . . . . אַח
end . . . . סוֹף	hand . . . . יָד	after . . . . אַחֲרֵי
until . . . . עַד	know . . . . ידע	eat . . . . אכל
still . . . . עוֹד	day . . . . יוֹם	these . . . . אֵלֶּה
bird . . . . עוֹף	be able . . . . . . יכל	say . . . . אמר
eye . . . . עַיִן	sea . . . . יָם	four . . . . אַרְבַּע
on . . . . עַל	add . . . . יסף	in . . . . בְּ
Most High . . . . עֶלְיוֹן	like, as . . . . כְּ	between . . . . . . בֵּין
with . . . . עִם	all . . . . כל	house . . . . בַּיִת
people . . . . עַם	thus . . . . כֵּן	build . . . . בנה
answer . . . . ענה	write . . . . כתב	bless . . . . ברך
open . . . . פתח	to . . . . לְ	reveal . . . . גלה
rise . . . . קוּם	heart . . . . . לֵב (לְבַב)	bear . . . . דֹּב
buy . . . . קנה	wear . . . . לבש	judgment . . . . . . דִּין
call . . . . קרא	scroll . . . . מְגִלָּה	resemble . . . . . דמה
draw near . . . . קרב	what . . . . מָה	he . . . . הוּא
battle . . . . קְרָב	be full . . . . מלא	be . . . . הוה
horn . . . . קֶרֶן	word . . . . מִלָּה	she . . . . הִיא
wind . . . . רוּחַ	king . . . . מֶלֶךְ	go . . . . הלך
height . . . . רוּם	queen . . . . . . מַלְכָּה	and . . . . וְ
ask . . . . שאל	from . . . . מִן	time . . . . זְמָן
praise . . . . שבח	count . . . . מנה	see . . . . חזה
dwell . . . . שכן	(D—appoint)	live . . . . היה
send . . . . שלח	meal offering . . מִנְחָה	strength . . . . . . חַיִל
hear . . . . שמע	bed . . . . מִשְׁכָּב	wisdom . . . . . חָכְמָה
be low . . . . . . שפל	prophesy . . . . . נבא	be gracious . . . . חנן
drink . . . . שתה	prophecy . . . . נְבוּאָה	magician . . . . . חַרְטֹם

You are also already familiar with the outline of Aramaic grammar, whether you have studied it or not. For example, Aramaic verbs are built on 3-letter roots, which can be conjugated in several different patterns, including one in which the middle letter is marked with a *dagesh* (doubled), just like Hebrew's *pi'el*, and another characterized by a prefixed ה, like the *hif'il*.

We will, therefore, take advantage of your Hebrew background, rather than trying to introduce everything you would need to learn if you were studying Aramaic from scratch. Aramaic phenomena will often be explained in terms of their Hebrew counterparts. We will not, for example, describe the alphabet, since biblical Aramaic is written with the same script and follows several of the same principles (e.g., the use of *dagesh lene* in the letters בג"ד כפ"ת) as biblical Hebrew.

However useful it may be to treat Aramaic as a dialect of Hebrew, we need to remember that it is really a separate language. This approach can, therefore, create problems. Chief among these is the fact that the vowels, on which so much of biblical grammar centers, were added by the Masoretes over a thousand years after the biblical books had themselves been written. We should, therefore, at least wonder how reliable a guide they are to ancient Aramaic usage. Of course, that is a problem for the study of biblical Hebrew as well; indeed, since the Masoretes wrote their own notes in Aramaic, they may have been more familiar with Aramaic grammar than with Hebrew and, therefore, imposed some of its principles onto the Hebrew sections of the Bible.

Because of our presumption that your reason for learning Aramaic is based in the Bible, its Aramaic passages will be used as the focus of our study, with sample readings included in each chapter. These have been edited in order to progress from relatively simple to more complex usage, until the last chapter of biblical Aramaic (Daniel 7) will be read exactly as it appears in the Bible. Because our focus will be on grammar and vocabulary, you should turn to the standard commentaries for historical and exegetical questions. The most useful ones on Ezra are those by Loring Batten (International Critical Commentary), Jacob Myers (Anchor Bible), and H. G. M. Williamson (Word Biblical Commentary); and for Daniel, those of James Montgomery (International Critical Commentary), John Collins (Hermeneia), and Louis Hartman and Alexander DiLella (Anchor Bible). Since only part of Ezra and Daniel are in Aramaic,* it would be helpful to read the preceding (Hebrew) sections (Ezra 1:1–4:7), at least in English, before beginning with the Aramaic in chapter 3 of this book.

---

*This strange phenomenon is discussed in many of the standard introductions to the Bible, such as Otto Eissfeldt, *The Old Testament, An Introduction* (New York: Harper and Row, 1965) pp. 516–17, 543, and 551.

Chapter 2

A BRIEF HISTORY OF ARAMAIC

The term "Aram" was used in place names almost four thousand years ago; the book of Genesis mentions places called Paddan-Aram and Aram-Naharaim. However, there are no references to the Aramean people themselves until the eleventh century, when the Assyrian ruler Tiglath Pilesar I encountered them on military expeditions along the Euphrates. They had apparently established small, independent kingdoms, primarily in Syria, but extending as far east as the Persian Gulf. One Aramean ruler, named Adad-apla-iddina, even seized the Babylonian throne before coming under attack from other Arameans.

The Bible describes close connections between Israel's patriarchs and Aram, where they "returned" from time to time (Genesis 24:1–10, 28:1–5), usually to find suitable wives. Deuteronomy even refers to the Israelites as being descended from "a wandering Aramean" (26:5) in a passage traditionally linked to Jacob, whose father-in-law Laban is called an Aramean in Genesis 31:20. Although scholars are not certain about the historical reliability of biblical statements about the patriarchs, such passages do demonstrate that the Israelites believed they were related to the Arameans.

During the period of Israel's monarchy, the Aramean kingdoms of Zobah and Damascus jockeyed with Israel for power and preeminence. The Bible reports that David defeated Hadadezer, the ruler of Zobah (2 Samuel 8:3–10), and that Solomon battled with Rezon, who had fled from Zobah and become king in Damascus (1 Kings 11:23–25).

After the Israelite kingdom split near the end of the 10th century, regional control passed back and forth between the now-divided kingdoms of Israel and Judah and the Arameans, depending most often on whether the Israelite kingdoms were united or not. Sometimes they were subordinate to the Aramaeans (1 Kings 15:8–20, 20:34, 2 Kings 10:32, 12:17, 13:7,22); at others, they were dominant (1 Kings 20:34, 2 Kings 13:25). In the ninth century, an alliance linking Damascus and Hamath with the Northern Kingdom as well as nine other countries was able to withstand the powerful Assyrian ruler Shalmaneser III (853 B.C.E.); a decade later, the coalition fell apart and these same nations were defeated (841 B.C.E.).

In the middle of the eighth century, Damascus entered into another alliance with Northern Israel, this time including the Phoenicians of Tyre. They tried to gain Judean support, but the king of Judah turned instead to Assyria, which was more than willing to intervene. As a result, the Aramean states were conquered by Tiglath-Pileser III, who claims to

5

have destroyed "592 towns . . . of the sixteen districts of the country of Damascus."* He put several Aramean kingdoms under direct Assyrian control, including ultimately Damascus itself. The Arameans' political power thus came to an end; however, their language survived, ironically achieving a far wider presence than the people among whom it had originated.

Aramaic is usually divided into several dialects, organized according to chronological and geographic principles. Although several systems have been proposed for doing this, each with its own idiosyncrasies, their general structures are quite similar.

Our earliest evidence of Aramaic comes from the Aramaic kingdoms just described. These are said to be written in "Old" or "Ancient" Aramaic. Among them are several inscriptions from northern Syria (mostly near the town of Aleppo) that were written early in the first millennium B.C.E. (probably between the tenth and the seventh centuries). The language of these texts shares a variety of features with Hebrew, suggesting that the division between the Aramaic and the Canaanite (Hebrew and Phoenician) branches of Northwest Semitic was relatively recent. A sample of an Aramaic text from this period will be read in chapter 28.

The next period of Aramaic is dominated by what is called Official, Imperial, or Standard Literary Aramaic because it served as the official administrative language of the Persian empire from the sixth to the fourth centuries, although it may have begun to spread somewhat earlier, under the Assyrians and Babylonians. This is also the dialect found in the Bible, although some scholars assign the book of Daniel to a later category.

Several ancient sources document the growing prevalence of Aramaic. The Bible reports a request by Judean leaders that the Assyrian army, which was besieging Jerusalem near the end of the eighth century, use Aramaic so that the people would not understand what they were saying (2 Kings 18:26 = Isaiah 36:11), suggesting that the leaders of the time were familiar with it. A century later, when a Philistine ruler sought assistance from the Egyptian Pharaoh, he wrote in Aramaic, demonstrating that the language had already achieved a significant role in international communication.**

After Judah fell to the Babylonian emperor Nebuchadnezzar, the Jews adopted the Aramean form of what had originally been the Phoenician alphabet. (It is important to distinguish between a language and a script; one could, for example, theoretically write English using the Hebrew, Cyrillic or Japanese scripts, or any other alphabet for that matter. Some Aramaic texts were written in Egyptian [demotic] and cuneiform scripts.) Interestingly, derivatives of the older script were still used by Jews from time to time, as in coins produced by the Maccabees and the later rebel leader Bar Kochba as well as some of the Dead Sea Scrolls.

---

* James Pritchard, *Ancient Near Eastern Texts Relating to the Old Testament* (Princeton, NJ: Princeton University Press, 1969) p. 283.

** See Bezalel Porten, "The Identity of King Adon," *Biblical Archaeologist* 44 (1981) 36–52; the role of Aramaic is comparable to that of Akkadian in the fourteenth-century correspondence between Egypt and its Canaanite subordinates from Tell el-Amarna.

The Arab tribe known as the Nabateans also used an alphabet that was based on the older letters, as do the Samaritans to the present day.

When Persia, which defeated Babylonia in 539, adopted Aramaic for official administrative purposes, the language's importance grew dramatically. Eventually, the Persian empire stretched from Egypt to India, ensuring Aramaic's widespread use and prominence. Official sponsorship also created a kind of standardization, something which did not begin to wane until the encroachment of Greek under Alexander the Great and then, many centuries later, Arabic.

Among those who returned from the Babylonian exile, familiarity with Aramaic was no longer limited to the leaders of Judea. In addition to the extensive sections of Daniel and Ezra which are written in Aramaic, its influence can be felt in Hebrew books of the Bible which were composed after the exile. Some scholars have even understood Nehemiah 8:8 to suggest that the Jews of this period needed to have their scriptures translated into Aramaic.

Aramaic continued unchallenged among Jews until the coming of the Greeks. It was particularly prevalent in Palestine during the time of Jesus, a period for which we use the term "Middle" Aramaic. Since the Persian empire, which had been responsible for the language's earlier uniformity, no longer existed, it is not surprising that regional variation begins to be apparent at this time (note the reference to Peter's distinctive accent in Matthew 26:73). These include the dialects attested in the Dead Sea Scrolls (see chapter 30) and the New Testament, as well as that in use among the Arab tribes known as Nabateans. The earliest layers of the targumim to the Pentateuch (Onkelos) and the Prophets (Jonathan) also probably date from this period. Other dialects are known from Palmyra (biblical Tadmor) and Edessa in Syria, and Hatra, which is in Mesopotamia.

The title "Late" Aramaic is used for material written between the second and the ninth (or possibly later) centuries C.E. From Palestine come a wide range of Jewish sources, including the Palestinian Talmud, midrashim, and several targumim (see chapters 31 and 32). Other writings from this region are by Christians (presumably converts from Judaism) and Samaritans. In the east, one finds Babylonian Jewish (for the Babylonian Talmud), Mandaic, and Syriac texts, with the latter divided into eastern and western dialects.

Finally, there is "Modern Aramaic," which is spoken in several villages near Damascus, the largest of which is Ma'lula, as well as among Christians in southeastern Turkey (near Tur ʿAbdin), Mandeans in southern Iraq, and Jews and Christians from Iraqi and Iranian Kurdistan, virtually all of whom have now migrated to Israel and the United States.

Thus, the Aramaic language has outlived the people whose name it bears, with a rich and extensive literature created by several different communities. Indeed, the language's very survival is the result of its having been adopted, for various purposes, by several different peoples who created with it a substantial body of documents that have played an important historical role.

Chapter 3

THE ARAMAIC LANGUAGE

Because they are both members of the Northwest branch of the Semitic language family, Aramaic and Hebrew have many words in common, as we saw in Chapter 1. Further evidence of this can be seen by comparing Jesus' words on the cross as presented by the Gospels of Matthew and Mark with the Psalm verse from which they were taken:

ηλι ηλι λεμα σαβαχθανι   (Matthew 27:46)

ελωι ελωι λαμα σαβαχθανι   (Mark 15:34)

אֵלִי אֵלִי לָמָה עֲזַבְתָּנִי   (Psalm 22:1[2])

Although the first three words in these passages are virtually identical,[*] the difference in the last word of the quote demonstrates that the Gospels are not reporting a Hebrew tradition, since there is no Hebrew word which might be represented by σαβαχθανι. Such a word does, however, exist in Aramaic, where שבק means "abandon," just like the Hebrew עזב; indeed, the ancient Aramaic translation (targum) of Psalm 22 uses שבק to translate עזב in this very passage.

The striking similarity between the first three words in both Gospel accounts and their Hebrew equivalent demonstrates how close Hebrew and Aramaic really are. Even the structure of the final verb is essentially the same, once one accounts for their different roots (עזב instead of שבק); that is to say that in each text the verb's root consonants are separated by the vowel *a* and followed by *ta* (the second person masculine singular suffix) and then *ni* (for the first person singular direct object).[**]

The Hebrew Bible contains one Aramaic sentence outside the books of Daniel and Ezra. It is found in Jeremiah 10:11:[***]

---

[*] The transliteration of the New Testament passages is *eli eli lema sabakthani* (Matthew) and *eloi eloi lama sabakthani* (Mark).

[**] Vowel differences in the first three words as presented by Matthew and Mark may reflect characteristically Aramaic features — the reduction of originally pretonic short vowels (see chapter 5), here Hebrew לָמָה = Aramaic לְמָה, and the 3d person masculine singular pronominal suffix הִ‑וֹ (see chapter 13).

[***] As one might imagine, the existence of this one Aramaic sentence has raised a host of questions in the minds of biblical scholars, many of whom have theorized that it is a gloss which was introduced into the text by mistake.

כִּדְנָה תֵּאמְרוּן לְהוֹם אֱלָהַיָּא דִּי שְׁמַיָּא וְאַרְקָא לָא עֲבַדוּ
יֵאבַדוּ מֵאַרְעָא וּמִן תְּחוֹת שְׁמַיָּא אֵלֶּה.

A close look at this verse demonstrates many similarities with Hebrew:

כִּדְנָה תֵּאמְרוּן לְהוֹם

דְּנָה — כְּ + דְּנָה is equivalent to Hebrew זֶה.

כְּ — means "like" or "as" in Aramaic, just as it does in Hebrew.

אמר — is a very common verb in biblical Hebrew, where it means "say." The -תֵּ pre-fix and ־וּ suffix indicate that the word is imperfect, 2d person, masculine plur-al (plural suffixes often have a final ־ן in Aramaic, as sometimes occurs in bib-lical Hebrew), so that the whole form means "you shall say."

לְהוֹם — =Hebrew לָהֶם

Thus, the phrase כִּדְנָה תֵּאמְרוּן לְהוֹם ("thus shall you say to them") corresponds to the Hebrew כֹּה תֹאמְרוּ לָהֶם.

אֱלָהַיָּא דִּי שְׁמַיָּא וְאַרְקָא לָא עֲבַדוּ

Most of these words are very similar to Hebrew:

אֱלָהַיָּא = אֱלֹהִים
שְׁמַיָּא = שָׁמַיִם
לָא = לֹא

The root עבד also occurs in Hebrew, although its meaning "serve" is inappropriate here; the meaning is clearly "make" (i.e. עשׂה).

Since דִּי means "which" or "who," this phrase can be recognized as corresponding to the Hebrew: . . . . וְ (אֵת) הַשָּׁמַיִם (הָ)אֱלֹהִים אֲשֶׁר לֹא עָשׂוּ.

The context clearly requires that the next word (אַרְקָא) be equivalent to Hebrew הָאָרֶץ.

Notice the Aramaic ending ־ָא on אֱלָהַיָּא, שְׁמַיָּא and אַרְקָא where Hebrew uses a pre-fixed הַ־. Thus the whole phrase means "the gods which did not make the heavens and the earth."

יֵאבַדוּ מֵאַרְעָא וּמִן תְּחוֹת שְׁמַיָּא אֵלֶּה

Every word in this section has an exact Hebrew equivalent, so it is easily translated as:

יֹאבְדוּ מִן הָאָרֶץ וּמִ(ן)תַּחַת הַשָּׁמַיִם (הָ)אֵלֶּה

(shall perish from the earth and from under these heavens)

Notice how this phrase uses אַרְעָא where the earlier part of the verse had אַרְקָא as the equivalent to the Hebrew אֶרֶץ.[*]

VOCABULARY

You will need the following vocabulary to understand the simplified version of Ezra 4:8-11 that is given below. Before reading that, it would be a good idea to read the preceding sections of Ezra (1:1-4:7) either in the original Hebrew or in English translation.

To Be Learned		*Reference*	
letter	אִגְּרָה	perish	אבד
the letter	אִגַּרְתָּא	these	אֵלֶּה
God (אֱלָהַיָּא)	אֱלָהּ	say	אמר
which, that, of	דִּי	earth	אַרְעָא
this	דְּנָה	earth	אַרְקָא
write	כתב	and	וְ-
to	לְ-	from	מִן
to them	לְהוֹם	do, make	עבד
king	מֶלֶךְ	heaven	שְׁמַיָּא
the king	מַלְכָּא	under	תְּחוֹת
the scribe	סָפְרָא		
on, to, against, concerning	עַל		
send	שׁלח		

---

* See page 14 below.

FROM THE BIBLE (Ezra 4:8–11)

רְחוּם וְשִׁמְשַׁי סָפְרָא כְּתַבוּ אִגְּרָה חֲדָה עַל יְרוּשְׁלֶם לְאַרְתַּחְשַׁשְׂתְּא מַלְכָּא.

דְּנָה אִגַּרְתָּא דִּי שְׁלַחוּ עַל אַרְתַּחְשַׁשְׂתְּא מַלְכָּא.

Proper Nouns

אַרְתַּחְשַׁשְׂתְּא — Artaxerxes, the Persian king (ruled 465–425 B.C.E.), who appointed Nehemiah governor of Jerusalem; either he or Darius' son Artaxerxes II (ruled 404-359 B.C.E.) authorized Ezra's mission to Jerusalem. The Bible also spells the name as אַרְתַּחְשַׁסְתְּא and אַרְתַּחְשַׁשְׂתְּא (e.g., Ezra 4:7 and 7:12).

יְרוּשְׁלֶם — Jerusalem, where the Judeans who had returned from Babylonian exile had settled. Although the city's name has come to be spelled יְרוּשָׁלַיִם in Hebrew, it appears without a י in the Bible (see p. 43 below).

רְחוּם וְשִׁמְשַׁי — Officials in Persia's Trans-Euphrates province.

EXERCISES

The following Aramaic sentences use vocabulary that should be familiar from biblical Hebrew (the vowels may be somewhat different). Read each sentence out loud and translate it into English:

(1) סָפְרָא כְּתַב אִגַּרְתָּא לְהוֹם.

(2) אֱלָהַיָּא עֲבַד שְׁמַיָּא.

(3) אֲמַר מַלְכָּא עַל יְרוּשְׁלֶם. . . .

‫(4) מַלְכָּא שְׁלַח אִגַּרְתָּא לְסָפְרָא.‬

‫(5) אֲמַר אֱלָהַיָּא מִן שְׁמַיָּא.‬

‫(6) אֲבַד סָפְרָא דְּנָה תְּחוֹת אַרְעָא.‬

‫(7) אֱלָהַיָּא אֲמַר דִּי אַרְעָא לְמַלְכָּא.‬

Chapter 4

CONSONANTS

Although some Aramaic dialects, such as Syriac and Nabatean, have their own scripts, the Aramaic sections of the Bible are written with the same alphabet as its Hebrew passages. Therefore, you already know how to read biblical Aramaic. And since Aramaic belongs to the same Northwest group of the Semitic family of languages as does Hebrew, these two languages have a goodly number of words in common, so that your knowledge of Hebrew provides a substantial Aramaic vocabulary as well. However, the number of these words can be easily multiplied.

The consonantal alphabet used for both Hebrew and Aramaic was probably invented by the Phoenicians, but it did not fit either language perfectly, since both originally had more sounds than the number of Phoenician letters. (English has the same problem, since our 26 letter alphabet, which also derives from the Phoenicians, does not have enough symbols to represent all the sounds we use. That is why we have to use pairs of letters, such as *sh* and *th*, for some sounds.) For Hebrew and Aramaic, certain individual letters were used to represent what were originally different sounds; however, the two languages sometimes use different letters for what were originally the same sounds. Words that look different in Hebrew and Aramaic may, therefore, actually be historically related.

An example of this involves the letter שׁ, which Hebrew uses for what were originally two different sounds — *sh* and *th* (as in English "thin"). The first of these quite separate consonants occurs in the word שׁלח ("send"), while the second was in the Hebrew word ישׁב ("sit, dwell"). However, Aramaic uses שׁ only for words which originally included *sh*, representing the *th* sound with the letter ת, which it also uses for the sound *t*, as does Hebrew. Thus, שׁלח and כתב ("write") are found in both languages, whereas Aramaic has יתב for the Hebrew word ישׁב.

Semitic	Hebrew	Aramaic	
sh	שׁ שׁלח	שׁ שׁלח	(send)
th	שׁ ישׁב	ת יתב	(dwell)
t	ת כתב	ת כתב	(write)

A similar phenomenon occurs with the letters ד and ז. In Hebrew ז is used both for the sound *z* (as in the word זֶרַע, which means "seed") and for a letter that was once pronounced as *ḏ* (like the *th* in "than"), which occurs in the word זֶבַח ("sacrifice"). However, Aramaic uses ז only for the *z* sound, whereas *ḏ* is represented with the letter ד, which both languages also use for the sound *d*. Thus, the Hebrew word זֶרַע corresponds to זְרַע in Aramaic, but the Aramaic cognate of the Hebrew word זֶבַח is דְּבַח.

Semitic	Hebrew	Aramaic	
z	ז זֶרַע	ז זְרַע	(seed)
ḏ	ז זֶבַח	ד דְּבַח	(sacrifice)
d	ד ידע	ד ידע	(know)

A final example of this phenomenon involves the letter צ, which Hebrew uses for what were originally *three* different sounds: (1) *ṣ*, as in the word צֶלֶם ("image"), (2) *ṭ* (sometimes represented as *ḍ* or *ẓ*), as in קַיִץ ("summer"), and (3) *ḍ*, as in אֶרֶץ ("land"). However, Aramaic represents these with three different consonants — צ, ט, and ע.[*] Therefore, the Hebrew word צֶלֶם is צְלֵם in Aramaic, but קַיִץ occurs as קַיִט, and אֶרֶץ as אֲרַע.

Semitic	Hebrew	Aramaic	
ṣ	צ צֶלֶם	צ צְלֵם	(image)
ṭ	צ קַיִץ	ט קַיִט	(summer)
ḍ	צ אֶרֶץ	ע אֲרַע	(earth)

The following chart summarizes these equivalences according to which letter is used in Aramaic. Being familiar with them will make it possible to recognize many Aramaic words that do not look exactly like their Hebrew counterparts.

---

[*] This last consonant is sometimes represented with a ק, as in the form אַרְקָא, which occurs alongside אַרְעָא in Jeremiah 10:11 (see p. 10) and in early inscriptions (see p. 168).

Aramaic	Hebrew	Semitic
	ד	*d*
ד		
	ז	*ḏ*
ז	ז	*z*
	ט	*ṭ*
ט		
	צ	*ṭ* / *ḏ* / *ẓ*
ע	ע	ʿ or *ġ*
ק/ע	צ	*ḍ*
שׂ	שׂ	*š*
	שׁ	*ṯ*
ת		
	ת	*t*

Other historical-linguistic processes can help in recognizing more word relationships. For example, many Semitic languages form nouns by adding an initial ("prosthetic") א to a three letter root. Thus the number "four" (אַרְבַּע) has four letters in both Hebrew and Aramaic; however, its root is actually רבע, as can be seen from the ordinal רְבִיעִי ("fourth"). Similarly, the word for "arm" exists in two forms, both in Hebrew (זְרוֹעַ and אֶזְרוֹעַ) and in Aramaic (דְּרָע and אֶדְרָע). This principle accounts for the relationship between the Hebrew word חִדָה and the Aramaic אֲחִידָה, both of which mean "riddle." Conversely, the Aramaic word חַד ("one") corresponds to the Hebrew אֶחָד.

Less certain is the relationship between the word אָע, which means "tree" in biblical Aramaic, and its apparent Hebrew cognate עֵץ. The original root was presumably ʿḍ, which came to be עֵץ in Hebrew and is represented as עק in several fifth century Aramaic documents (see p. 178). It should be עע in biblical Aramaic, but the first ע apparently dissimilated to an א in order to avoid having two identical consonants next to each other.

VOCABULARY

To Be Learned		*Reference*	
we	אֲנַחְנָה	there is	אִיתַי
in	בְּ־	tax	בְּלוֹ
build	בנה	search	בקר
participle (m pl)	בָּנַיִן	*impf 3 ms*	יְבַקַּר
passive impf 3fs	תִּתְבְּנֵא	if	הֵן
that	דָּךְ	memoranda	דָּכְרָנַיָּה
know	ידע	be	הוה
passive participle	יְדִיעַ	*imf 3ms*	לֶהֱוֵא
causal pfct (1 pl)	הוֹדַעְנָא	portion	חֲלָק
causal ptcl (m pl)	מְהוֹדְעִין	to you	לָךְ
now	כְּעַן	find	שכח
not	לָא	*causal impf 2 ms*	תְּהַשְׁכַּח
rebellious *(fs)*	מָרָדְתָּא	שלה *perfect 3 m pl*	שְׁלַחְנָא
give	נתן		
imperfect (3 m pl)	יִנְתְּנוּן		
the city	קִרְיְתָא		

FROM THE BIBLE (Ezra 4:12–16)

יְדִיעַ לֶהֱוֵא לְמַלְכָּא דִּי יְהוּדָיֵא דִּי יְרוּשְׁלֶם קִרְיְתָא מָרָדְתָּא בָּנַיִן. כְּעַן יְדִיעַ לֶהֱוֵא

לְמַלְכָּא דִּי הֵן קִרְיְתָא דָךְ תִּתְבְּנֵא בְּלוֹ לָא יִנְתְּנוּן. עַל דְּנָה שְׁלַחְנָא וְהוֹדַעְנָא לְמַלְכָּא

דִּי יְבַקַּר בִּסְפַר דָּכְרָנַיָּא   וּתְהַשְׁכַּח דִּי קִרְיְתָא דָךְ קִרְיָא מָרָדָא. מְהוֹדְעִין אֲנַחְנָה

לְמַלְכָּא דִּי הֵן קִרְיְתָא דָךְ תִּתְבְּנֵא חֲלָק בַּעֲבַר נַהֲרָא לָא אִיתַי לָךְ:

Note: תָא- is a feminine suffix; thus both קִרְיָא מָרָדָא and קִרְיְתָא מָרָדְתָּא mean "rebellious city."

Proper Nouns

יְהוּדָיֵא — (the) Judeans

עֲבַר־נַהֲרָא — Trans-Euphrates, one of the Persian Empire's several major provinces (satrapies); it stretched along the Mediterranean coast, west (and south) of the Euphrates River, and included the land of Judah (יְהוּד).

EXERCISES

Write the following Aramaic words next to their Hebrew cognates:

שֵׁת (six)	חֲדַת (new)	אֶדְרָע (arm)
תוּב (return)	יָעַט (advise)	אֲחִידָה (riddle)
תּוֹר (ox)	יְתַב (sit, dwell)	אִיתַי (there is)
תְּלַג (snow)	כִּדְבָה (lie)	אֲרַע (land)
תְּלָת (three)	נְטַר (guard)	דְּבַח (sacrifice)
תְּקֵל (unit of weight)	קַיִט (summer)	דְּהַב (gold)
		דִּכְרָן (memorandum)

_____ נְצַר		_____ יֵשׁ	
_____ שָׁלוֹשׁ		_____ שֶׁלֶג	
_____ כָּזָב		_____ קַיִץ	
_____ יָעַץ		_____ שֶׁקֶל	
_____ זְרוֹעַ		_____ זִכָּרוֹן	
_____ יָשַׁב		_____ שׁוֹר	
_____ זָהָב		_____ חִדָה	
_____ אֶרֶץ		_____ חָדָשׁ	
_____ זֶבַח		_____ שׁוּב	
		_____ שֵׁשׁ	

Translate into English:

(1) אֲנַחְנָה בָּנַיִן קִרְיְתָא.

(2) סָפְרָא שְׁלַח אִגַּרְתָּא דָךְ.

(3) תְּהַשְׁכַּח אֱלָהַיָּא בִּירוּשְׁלֶם מָרָדְתָּא.

(4) לָא אִיתַי חֲלָק לְהוֹם בַּעֲבַר־נַהֲרָה.

(5) כְּעַן יְדִיעַ דִי יִנְתְּנוּן יְהוּדָיֵא בְּלוֹ לְמַלְכָּא.

(6) רְחוּם כְּתַב דָּכְרָן דְּנָה.

Chapter 5

VOWELS

The Hebrew Bible was originally written with only consonants. The Masoretes, who added the vowels, used essentially the same system for both the Hebrew and the Aramaic sections; however, the vowel systems are not completely identical. For example, the composite *sh'va* is not limited to guttural letters as it is in Hebrew, but also appears before and after the letters ק and ג and before ל, נ, and ר, as can be seen in the following words:

גְּלִי   מַדְּקָה

בְּנַיְתַהּ   קֳדָם

צִפֳּרֵי   סֲגַר

Other differences between Hebrew and Aramaic involve the way each of them treats certain vowels:

(1) The Canaanite Shift (*ā* > *ō*) — long *a* usually became long *o* (*ō*) in some Northwest Semitic languages, including Hebrew. However, Aramaic belongs to a non-Canaanite group of languages, in which the original vowel (*ā*) is retained. A familiar example is the Hebrew word שָׁלוֹם. Both vowels in this word were once pronounced *a*, but the second one was long (the Arabic word is *salām*). In the Canaanite branch, that vowel became *ō*, but not in Aramaic, where the word is, therefore, pronounced שְׁלָם. The following words provide several other examples:

Aramaic		*Hebrew*
אֱנָשׁ	(man)	אֱנוֹשׁ
דָּר	(generation)	דּוֹר
טָב	(good)	טוֹב
לָא	(not)	לֹא
עָלַם	(eternity)	עוֹלָם
קָל	(sound)	קוֹל

(2) Reduction of Short Vowels — short vowels that occur in syllables immediately prior to the accent become long in Hebrew but are reduced in Aramaic. That is why the first syllable of שָׁלוֹם has a *qameṣ* (*ā*) in Hebrew, but a *sh'va* (שְׁלָם) in Aramaic. Other Aramaic words reflect this same principle:

19

Aramaic		Hebrew
מְאָה	(hundred)	מֵאָה
נְבִיא	(prophet)	נָבִיא
עֲתִיד	(ready)	עָתִיד

Both of these principles can be seen by comparing the Aramaic word for "three" (תְּלָת) with its Hebrew equivalent (שָׁלוֹשׁ), in which the first vowel, which was originally a short *a* preceding the accent, has become a *sh'va* in Aramaic but a long *a* in Hebrew while the second vowel, which was originally a long *a,* has shifted to *ō.* Notice also the equivalence of Hebrew שׁ and Aramaic ת.

(3) Segolate nouns — Many Hebrew nouns with the accent on their first syllable and a *segol* in the second (e.g., מֶלֶךְ, סֵפֶר, and קֹדֶשׁ) developed out of words that were originally mono-syllabic (i.e. קֹדְשׁ סֵפְר, מַלְךְ). In Aramaic these usually have only one full vowel, but it is found under the *second* consonant. (As in Hebrew, it often shifts to *a* when there is a guttural or ר nearby.)

Aramaic		Hebrew
לְחֶם	(meal)	לֶחֶם
צְלֵם	(statue)	צֶלֶם
תְּקֵל	(unit of weight)	שֶׁקֶל
כְּסַף	(silver)	כֶּסֶף
פְּשַׁר	(interpretation)	פֵּשֶׁר
נְשַׁר	(eagle)	נֶשֶׁר
עֲמַר	(wool)	צֶמֶר
תְּלַג	(snow)	שֶׁלֶג
סְפַר	(book)	סֵפֶר
שְׁבַט	(tribe)	שֵׁבֶט
רְגַז	(anger)	רֹגֶז
זְרַע	(seed)	זֶרַע
*בְּעֵל	(master)	בַּעַל

---

* For the vocalization of this form, compare its Akkadian cognate *bēlu*, in contrast to the Hebrew בַּעַל.

In Aramaic, as in Hebrew, the original vowel often returns when a suffix is added:

e.g., כַּסְפָּא — the silver

סִפְרִין — documents

פִּשְׁרֵהּ — its interpretation

VOCABULARY

To Be Learned		*Reference*	
then	אֱדַיִן	go (G)	אזל
stop	בטל	*pf 3 m pl*	אֲזַלוּ
G (intrans) pf 3fs	בְּטֵלַת	be	הוה
D (trans) pf 3 pl	בַּטִּלוּ	G pf 3 m pl	הֲווֹ
D (trans) inf	לְבַטָּלָה	day	יוֹמָת
house	בַּיִת	dwell (G)	יתב
master	בְּעֵל	G ptcpl m pl	יָתְבִין
them	הִמּוֹ	G inf of בנה	מִבְנֵא
decree	טְעֵם	kings	מַלְכִין
do	עבד	after	מִן דִּי
Gt (passive) participle	מִתְעֲבֵד	rebellion	מְרַד
work, service	עֲבִידָה	letter	נִשְׁתְּוָנָא
eternity	עָלְמָא	message	פִּתְגָמָא
before	קֳדָם	is read	קֱרִי
before me	קֳדָמַי	issue	שׂים
peace	שְׁלָם	imv m pl	שִׂימוּ
strong	תַּקִּיף	remnant	שְׁאָר
m pl	תַּקִּיפִין	G pf 2 m pl of שלח	שְׁלַחְתּוּן

FROM THE BIBLE (Ezra 4:17–24)

פִּתְגָמָא שְׁלַח מַלְכָּא עַל רְחוּם בְּעֵל טְעֵם וְשִׁמְשַׁי סָפְרָא דִּי יָתְבִין בְּשָׁמְרָיִן וּשְׁאָר עֲבַר־

נַהֲרָה: שְׁלָם. וּכְעֶנֶת. נִשְׁתְּוָנָא דִּי שְׁלַחְתּוּן עֲלֶינָא מְפָרַשׁ קֱרִי קֳדָמָי. מְרַד מִתְעֲבֶד בְּקִרְיְתָא דָךְ מִן יוֹמָת

עָלְמָא וּמַלְכִין תַּקִּיפִין הֲווֹ עַל יְרוּשְׁלֶם. כְּעַן שִׂימוּ טְּעֵם לְבַטָּלָה מִבְּנֵא קִרְיְתָא דָךְ.

אֱדַיִן מִן דִּי נִשְׁתְּוָנָא דִּי אַרְתַּחְשַׁשְׂתְּא מַלְכָּא קֱרִי קֳדָם רְחוּם וְשִׁמְשַׁי סָפְרָא אֲזַלוּ

לִירוּשְׁלֶם עַל יְהוּדָיֵא וּבַטִּלוּ הִמּוֹ. בֵּאדַיִן בְּטֵלַת עֲבִידַת בֵּית אֱלָהָא דִּי בִּירוּשְׁלֶם.

Proper Nouns

שָׁמְרָיִן — Persian province in the central hill country; named after the capital of Israel's Northern Kingdom when it was conquered by the Assyrians in 721 B.C.E.

EXERCISES

Explain the *differences* between the following pairs of Hebrew and Aramaic cognates:

Aramaic	Hebrew		Difference
לָא	לֹא	(not)	_____
עֲמַר	צֶמֶר	(wool)	_____
דָּא	זוֹ	(this)	_____
אֶדְרָע	אֶזְרֹעַ	(arm)	_____
תְּלַג	שֶׁלֶג	(snow)	_____
שָׁפְטִין	שׁוֹפְטִים	(judges)	_____
נְהַר	נָהָר	(river)	_____
תּוּב	שׁוּב	(return)	_____
נְחָשׁ	נָחָשׁ	(copper)	_____

Aramaic	**Hebrew**		**Difference**
שֵׁת	שֵׁשׁ	(six)	_____
סָפַר	סוֹפֵר	(scribe)	_____
נְשִׁין	נָשִׁים	(women)	_____
חֲדַת	חָדָשׁ	(new)	_____
שְׂעַר	שֵׂעָר	(hair)	_____
חֲבַר	חָבֵר	(companion)	_____
דְּהַב	זָהָב	(gold)	_____
עֲשַׂר	עֶשֶׂר	(ten)	_____
אָת	אוֹת	(sign)	_____
תבר	שׁבר	(break)	_____
עָלַם	עוֹלָם	(eternity)	_____

Translate into English:

(1) כְּתַב בְּעֵל עָלְמָא אִגְּרָה לְמַלְכִין תַּקִּיפִין.

(2) אֲנַחְנָא בָּנַיִן בֵּית בְּקִרְיְתָא מָרָדְתָּא.

(3) אֱדַיִן הִמּוֹ בַּטִלוּ מִבְנֵה דְּנָה בִּירוּשְׁלֶם.

(4) שִׂימוּ טְעֵם קֳדָם סָפְרָא מִן דִּי נִשְׁתְּוָנָא קֱרִי.

(5) כְּעַן לָא יִנְתְּנוּן עֲבִידָה עַל יְהוּדָיֵא.

(6) מַלְכַיָּא תַּקִּיפַיָּא אֲזַלוּ עַל קִרְיְתָא.

(7) טְעֵם אֱלָהָא קֱרִי קֳדָם בְּעֵל.

(8) אֱדַיִן אֲמַר שִׁמְשַׁי לְבַטָּלָה מִבְּנֵה בַּיְתָא.

(9) הִמּוֹ עֲבַדוּ מְרַד בִּירוּשְׁלֶם.

(10) שִׂימוּ שְׁלָם לְהוֹם מִן עָלְמָא.

(11) אֲנַחְנָא מְהוֹדְעִין לְסָפְרָא דִּי בְּטֵלַת עֲבִידַת בַּיְתָא דִּי מַלְכָּא.

Chapter 6

NOUNS, DEFINITE ARTICLE

Nouns behave much the same way in Aramaic as they do in Hebrew: They can be masculine or feminine, absolute or construct, singular or plural (or dual). However, Aramaic nouns are unique in two, nearly ubiquitous features.

(1) Alongside the absolute and construct, Aramaic has a third "state," called "determined." This form typically ends with אָ-, although it is occasionally spelled with the letter ה. It functions much like the definite article in Hebrew (-הַ); that is to say, words with the determinative ending אָ- can be translated "the . . ." (In some later dialects of Aramaic this determined form of the noun became the normal one and thereby lost its connotation of definiteness.)

Although there is nothing *formally* comparable to the determined suffix אָ- in biblical Hebrew, it does exist in a word which occurs several times in the New Testament and has become standard in modern Hebrew. In Mark 14:36, Jesus refers to God as αββα.* This is obviously the determined form of the noun אַב ("father"), which has survived into modern Hebrew, where it and its feminine counterpart אִמָּא serve as familiar forms, equivalent to the English "Daddy" and "Mommy."

(2) Masculine plural forms usually end with ן-, rather than the ם- that is familiar in Hebrew. In fact, the Hebrew Bible contains many masculine forms that end with ן. Before either Aramaic or Hebrew had reached the stage with which we are familiar, masculine plural forms were apparently marked with ִי-. Later, Hebrew and Aramaic added different consonants to this original suffix. As a result, masculine plural nouns usually end with ִין- rather than ִים- as they do in Hebrew.

Aramaic's added ן can also be found on verbs, most notably in the imperfect:

---

* Contrast the parallel passages Matthew 26:39 and Luke 22:42; but see Romans 8:15 and Galatians 4:6. This is the source of our own English term "Abbot."

	Aramaic	**Hebrew**
2d feminine singular	תִּכְתְּבִין	תִּכְתְּבִי
2d masculine plural	תִּכְתְּבוּן	תִּכְתְּבוּ
2d feminine plural	תִּכְתְּבָן	תִּכְתֹּבְנָה
3d masculine plural	יִכְתְּבוּן	יִכְתְּבוּ
3d feminine plural	יִכְתְּבָן	תִּכְתֹּבְנָה

The resulting noun patterns are:

		masculine	*feminine*
singular	absolute	מֶלֶךְ	מַלְכָּה *
	construct	מֶלֶךְ	מַלְכַּת
	determined	מַלְכָּא	מַלְכְּתָא
plural	absolute	מַלְכִין	מַלְכָן
	construct	מַלְכֵי	מַלְכָת
	determined	מַלְכַיָּא	מַלְכָתָא

Notice the תָ - ending on the construct and determined forms of the feminine plural. This corresponds to Hebrew's feminine plural suffix וֹת-. (Remember that long *ā* becomes long *ō* in Hebrew.)

Not all nouns fit these patterns perfectly. As in any language, Aramaic has some irregular forms. These include plurals which do not seem to match their singulars, whether in form or in gender:

נָשִׁין "women" (The Bible does not include a singular form, but compare Hebrew אִשָּׁה, for which the plural is נָשִׁים.)

אֲבָהָן "fathers" (This form is inferred from the construct אֲבָהָת, which can be compared to the Hebrew plural אָבוֹת.)

שְׁמָהָן "names," judging from the construct שְׁמָהָת (cf. Hebrew שֵׁמוֹת).

Similarly, the word for "great" (רַבְרְבָן) is an expanded form of רַב (cf. רַבְרְבָנִים, "chiefs").

---

* In the Bible, the feminine suffix ה- is sometimes spelled with an א, just as the determined suffix א- is sometimes spelled with a ה. Notice the inconsistent use of *dagesh*, which occurs in the כ of singular but not the plural forms of both masculine and feminine.

Like Hebrew, Aramaic also has dual forms, although there are not many examples in the Bible. Perhaps some dual forms are indistinguishable from the plural so that we cannot identify them. However, those that can be recognized resemble their Hebrew equivalents, except for the no-longer surprising presence of ן- where Hebrew has ם-:

e.g.,   יְדַיִן   (2 hands)

מָאתַיִן   (200)

VOCABULARY

To Be Learned		*Reference*	
say	אמר	god	אֱלָהּ
participle (m pl)	אָמְרִין	their gods	אֱלָהַם
he came	אֲתָא	was (*G pf 3fs of* הוה)	הֲוָת
son	בַּר	thus	כֵּן
man (*pl.* גֻּבְרִין)	גְּבַר	to you	לְכֹם
and	וְ/וּ	build (*G infinitive*)	מִבְנֵא
who	מַן *	prophesy (Dt הִתְנַבִּי)	נבא
governor	פֶּחָה	prophet	נְבִיא
arise (G)	קוּם	eye	עַיִן
perfect 3 m pl	קָמוּ	on them	עֲלֵיהוֹן
issue (an order)	שִׂים		
G pf 3 ms	שָׂם		
name (*pl.* שְׁמָהָת)	שֵׁם		

FROM THE BIBLE (Ezra 5:1–5)

וְהִתְנַבִּי חַגַּי וּזְכַרְיָה בַר עִדּוֹא נְבִיאַיָּא עַל יְהוּדָיֵא דִּי בִיהוּד וּבִירוּשְׁלֶם בְּשֻׁם אֱלָהּ

יִשְׂרָאֵל עֲלֵיהוֹן. בֵּאדַיִן קָמוּ זְרֻבָּבֶל בַּר שְׁאַלְתִּיאֵל וְיֵשׁוּעַ בַּר יוֹצָדָק לְמִבְנֵא בֵּית

אֱלָהָא דִּי בִירוּשְׁלֶם. אֲתָא עֲלֵיהוֹן תַּתְּנַי פַּחַת עֲבַר נַהֲרָה וּשְׁתַר־בּוֹזְנַי וְכֵן אָמְרִין

לְהֹם: מַן שָׂם טְעֵם בַּיְתָא דְנָה לְמִבְנֵא? מַן שְׁמָהָת גֻּבְרַיָּא דִּי דְנָא בָּנַיִן?

וְעֵין אֱלָהֲהֹם הֲוָת עַל יְהוּדָיֵא וְלָא בַטִּלוּ הִמּוֹ.

---

* In Exodus 16:15 this word is the basis for a pun with the Hebrew word מָן, meaning "manna."

Proper Nouns

זְכַרְיָה בַּר עִדּוֹא — A Judean prophet of priestly descent during the reign of Darius I (521–486 B.C.E.), who encouraged the reestablishment of the kingdom.

זְרֻבָּבֶל בַּר שְׁאַלְתִּיאֵל — Grandson of Judah's king Jehoiachin, who was appointed governor by the Persians and led a group of exiles back to Judah, where he was viewed by some Judeans with messianic fervor.

חַגַּי — Prophesied to those who had returned to Judah in 520 on the importance of rebuilding the Temple

יְהוּד — Province of Persian empire, centered in Jerusalem

יִשְׂרָאֵל — Still used after the exile to refer to the ethnicity of the people chosen by God

יֵשׁוּעַ בַּר יוֹצָדָק — (Called יְהוֹשֻׁעַ in Haggai and Zechariah) — descendant of Seriah, a leading priest who was killed when the Babylonians conquered Jerusalem and whose son Jozadak was taken into exile; he returned to Judah in 520 with Zerubbabel, alongside of whom he played a major role in the reestablishment of sacrifice

שְׁתַר־בּוֹזְנַי — Persian official

תַּתְּנַי — Persian governor of Trans-Euphrates under Darius I

EXERCISES

Fill in the blank with the Aramaic translation of the parenthesized words:

(1) יְהָדָיֵא בָּנַיִן בֵּית _____ (of a king).

(2) _____ (scribe) דְּנָה כְּתַב אִגַּרְתָּ.

(3) _____ (the names of) גֻּבְרַיָּא.

Fill in the following charts with the noun forms given below:

רֵאשִׁי, רֵאשָׁא, רֵאשׁ, רֵאשַׁיָּא, רֵאשִׁין

	absolute	construct	determined
Singular			
Plural			

נְבִיא, נְבִיאַיָּא, נְבִיאִין, נְבִיאָא

	absolute	construct	determined
Singular			
Plural			

סִפְרִין, סִפְרֵי, סִפְרַיָּא, סִפְרָא, סְפַר

	absolute	construct	determined
Singular			
Plural			

עֲבִידַת, עֲבִידָת, עֲבִידָן, עֲבִידְתָא, עֲבִידָה, עֲבִידָתָא

	absolute	construct	determined
Singular			
Plural			

קִרְיַת, קִרְיָתָא, קִרְיָן, קִרְיָה, קִרְיָתָא, קִרְיָת

	absolute	construct	determined
Singular			
Plural			

אֱלָהִי, אֱלָהַיָּא, אֱלָהָא, אֱלָהִין, אֱלָה

	absolute	construct	determined
Singular			
Plural			

סָפְרָא, סָפֵר, סָפְרִין, סָפְרַיָּא, סָפְרֵי

	absolute	construct	determined
Singular			
Plural			

Translate into Aramaic:

(1) The scribe wrote the name of the men.

(2) The prophets of Israel arose before the kings.

(3) They sent the letter to Trans-Euphrates.

(4) God came to Israel.

(5) They are building the city of Jerusalem

(6) A master issued a decree.

(7) We informed the men of the city.

(8) Who are the governors of Judah and Samaria?

Chapter 7

THE VERB SYSTEM

Verbal systems are a prominent feature of most languages and provide a particularly useful way to classify them. Semitic verbs are based on three-letter roots, which can be conjugated in several different ways. Hebrew is usually said to have 7 of these conjugations (בִּנְיָנִם)—*qal, nifʿal, piʿel, hifʿil, puʿal, hofʿal*, and *hitpaʿel*. In order to facilitate comparisons with other languages, these are identified here with single letters, which reflect their characteristic features: *Qal* is called G for the German *Grundstamm*, which means "basic conjugation," as does the Hebrew term *qal*. *Piʿel* is designated D for its doubled middle letter. The *hifʿil* will be called H, and the *nifʿal* (which does not exist in Aramaic) N in recognition of the letter which is prefixed to each.

This scheme of 7 separate conjugations is somewhat artificial. In the first place, several of these conjugations are actually related to each other. These include the *puʿal* and the *hofʿal*, which are patently variations (sometimes called internal passives) of the *piʿel* and *hifʿil*, with which they are identical except for their *u-a* vowel pattern, which shifts the meaning from active to passive.* (Significantly, Hebrew's *qal* passive participle, e.g., כָּתוּב, also uses *a* and *u* vowels.)

The *hitpaʿel* (here designated Dt) is built on the *piʿel*, as can be seen from the fact that its middle root letter is doubled. The prefix הִתְ- conveyed a reflexive meaning and was not necessarily limited to a *piʿel* base, as can be seen from other Semitic languages.** The Bible preserves a handful of Hebrew words in which this prefix was added to *qal* forms (הִתְפָּקֵד in Judges 20:15,17, 21:9; note the passive forms beginning with with הָתְ- in Numbers 1:47 and 2:33).

At the same time that several of these standard seven conjugations appear to be related to one another, there are conjugations that this list does not include. Thus Gesenius' Hebrew grammar lists *pôʿēl, paʿlēl, pěʿalˢal, pilpēl, tifˢēl*, and *šafˢel*.***

---

* The Hebrew *qal* probably had an internal passive, too; for the evidence, see *A Grammar of Biblical Hebrew* by Paul Joüon and T. Muraoka (Rome: Pontifical Biblical Institute, 1991) §58, pp. 166–68.

** Although Aramaic is the only Semitic language in which a *t* can be added to the H conjugation, several languages which form their causatives with שׁ have it (including Hebrew הִשְׁתַּחֲוָה); see Sabatino Moscati, *An Introduction to the Comparative Grammar of the Semitic Languages* (Wiesbaden: Otto Harrassowitz, 1969) §16.17–23, pp. 127–30.

*** A. E. Cowley, *Gesenius' Hebrew Grammar* as edited and enlarged by the late E. Kautzsch (2d English edition, Oxford: Clarendon Press, 1910) §55, pp. 151–54.

Because Aramaic belongs to the same Northwest group of the Semitic language family as does Hebrew, its verbal system is essentially the same and can be characterized with the following pattern:

		Passive	Prefixed t
G	*peʿal*	*peʿil*	Gt—*hitpeʿel*
D	*paʿʿel*	*puʿʿal*	Dt—*hitpaʿʿel*
H	*hafʿel*	*hofʿal*	Ht—*hitapʿel* (not in biblical Aramaic)
N	not in Aramaic		

As in Hebrew, each Aramaic conjugation comprises two major tenses, one of which generates its various forms with a series of suffixes (the perfect), while the other uses primarily prefixes (the imperfect). Each also has imperative, infinitive, and participial forms.

VOCABULARY

To Be Learned		*Reference*	
go	אֲזַל	we said	אֲמַרְנָא
G pf 1 pl	אֲזַלְנָא	also	אַף
those	אִלֵּךְ	everything	כֹּלָּא
interior	גַּו	write (G)	כְּתַב
3 ms (him, his) suffix	הֵ-	*passive participle*	כְּתִיב
3 m pl (they, them) suffix	הֹם-	*imf 1 pl*	נִכְתֻּב
2mpl (you, your) suffix	כֹם-	let it be *(imf 3 ms)*	לֶהֱוֵה
colleague *(plural* כְּנָוָת*)*	כְּנָה	elder	שָׂב
province	מְדִינָה	ask	שְׁאֵל
head	רֵאשׁ		
great	רַב		

FROM THE BIBLE (Ezra 5:6–10)

אִגַּרְתָּא דִּי שְׁלַח תַּתְּנַי פַּחַת עֲבַר־נַהֲרָה וּשְׁתַר־בּוֹזְנַי וּכְנָוָתֵהּ דִּי בַּעֲבַר־נַהֲרָה עַל

דָּרְיָוֶשׁ מַלְכָּא וְכִדְנָה כְּתִיב בְּגַוֵּהּ: לְדָרְיָוֶשׁ מַלְכָּא שְׁלָמָא כֹלָּא. יְדִיעַ לֶהֱוֵא לְמַלְכָּא

דִּי אֲזַלְנָא לִיהוּד מְדִינְתָּא לְבֵית אֱלָהָא רַבָּא. אֱדַיִן שְׁאֵלְנָא לְשָׂבַיָּא אִלֵּךְ אֲמַרְנָא

לְהֹם: מַן שָׂם לְכֹם טְעֵם בַּיְתָא דְנָה לְמִבְנְיָה. וְאַף שְׁמָהָתְהֹם שְׁאֵלְנָא לְהֹם

דִּי נִכְתֻּב שֻׁם גֻּבְרַיָּא דִּי בְרָאשֵׁיהֹם.

Proper Names

דָּרְיָוֶשׁ — Darius I conquered Persia after the death of Cambyses II and reigned from 522 to 486 B.C.E.

EXERCISES

Identify the major conjugation (G, D, or H) to which the following Aramaic verbs belong:

הִתְקְטָלָה _____	נַחֲוֵא _____	אָכְלָה _____
מְהֵימַן _____	סָגְדִין _____	הַדְרֵת _____
מִתְכַּנְּשִׁין _____	בְּנַס _____	הוּבַד _____
מִתְנַשְּׂאָה _____	הַרְגִּזוּ _____	הָחָרְבַת _____
יְבַקַּר _____	הֶעְלוּ _____	יִשְׁאֲלֶנְכוֹן _____
תִּקְנֵא _____	הַשְׁכַּחַת _____	בְּטֵלַת _____
רְשַׁמְתָּ _____	תִּתְרְמוֹן _____	הַשְׁפֵּלְתְּ _____
הִתְרְחִצוּ _____	נְפַלוּ _____	מַלִּל _____
מְהַלְּכִין _____	הִתְנַבִּי _____	שַׁבַּחֵת _____
אִתְעֲקַרוּ _____	בְּטִלוּ _____	חֲשִׁיבִין _____
מְצַבְּעִין _____	מְהַעְדֵּה _____	אֶבְעֵה _____
	הִתְגְּזֶרֶת _____	

Translate into Aramaic:

(1) We went to the great province.

(2) They sent a letter to the house and to the men inside it.

(3) Now Darius is the head of these elders.

(4) The elders say that the decree is known to them.

(5) Let peace be over Jerusalem.

(6) Everything is written.

Chapter 8

G PERFECT

Not only are the Aramaic verb conjugations (G, D, and H) and tenses (perfect, imperfect, etc.) analogous to those of Hebrew, but the individual forms are also similar, once the various principles that have already been discussed are taken into account. For example, the perfect tense, which describes completed action, uses pronominal suffixes attached at the end of the verbal root. Moreover, although these suffixes are somewhat different from those in Hebrew (but not unrecognizably so), the pattern itself is built on the same (3d person, masculine singular) base—כְּתַב, with the accent on the final syllable as is usual in these languages. Because the short vowel in the first syllable precedes the accent, it is lengthened in Hebrew, resulting in the form כָּתַב, but reduced in Aramaic, yielding כְּתַב.

All the various perfect forms are built on this base. In a few cases the first two letters could both have *sh'va*s (i.e., -כְּתְ); since Aramaic will not tolerate two vocal *sh'va*s in a row any more than Hebrew, the first of these shifts to *ḥiriq* (i.e., -כִּתְ).*

Overall, the G perfect conjugation looks like this:

		Singular	*Plural*
1		כִּתְבֵת	כְּתַבְנָא
2	masculine	כְּתַבְתְּ (or כְּתַבְתָּ)	כְּתַבְתּוּן
	feminine	כְּתַבְתִּי	כְּתַבְתֵּן**
3	masculine	כְּתַב	כְּתַבוּ
	feminine	כִּתְבַת	כְּתַבָה***

---

* The same process is responsible for the Hebrew plural imperative שִׁמְרוּ, which results when the imperfect prefix is dropped from יִשְׁמְרוּ, and for the vocalization of prepositional prefixes attached to words beginning with *sh'va*, such as בִּסְפָרִים.

** Note that Aramaic uses different vowels for masculine and feminine forms of perfect verbs in the third (-הֹ/-הֵן) and second persons (-תְ/-תּוּן) and for possessive pronouns (-כֹ/-כֵן, see chapter 13), unlike Hebrew, which uses the same vowels in the second person (e.g., כְּתַבְתֶּם/תֶּן and סְפַרְכֶם/כֶן).

*** Sometimes the masculine form is used as a common plural.

36

The vowel under the second root letter (e.g., the *pataḥ* under the ת in many of the forms above) is called the "theme vowel" and is particular to specific roots. Examples of verbs with different theme vowels in the perfect include:

בְּטֵלַת	she stopped
שְׁאֵלְנָא	we asked
סְגֵד	he bowed down

VOCABULARY

To Be Learned		*Reference*	
earth	אַרְעָא	father	אַב
be	הוה / הוא	our ancestors	אֲבָהֳתַנָא
palace	הֵיכַל	these	אֵלֶּה
one	חַד	build	בנה
give	יהב	*passive participle*	בְּנֵה
G pf passive 3 pl	יְהִיבוּ	*infinitive*	לִבְנֵא
vessel	מָאן	*Gt (passive) imf 3 ms*	יִתְבְּנֵא
go out	נפק	exile	גלה
H (causal) pf 3 ms	הַנְפֵּק	*H (causal) pf 3 ms*	הַגְלִי
many	שַׂגִּיא	descend	נחת
heaven	שְׁמַיָּא	*H ("deposit") imv*	אֲחֵת
year	שְׁנָה	tear down (G)	סתר
		servant	עֲבֵד
		his servants	עַבְדוֹהִי
		people, nation	עַם
		former time	קַדְמָה
		anger (H)	רגז
		perfect 3 pl	הַרְגִּזוּ
		reply (H)	תוב
		they replied	הֲתִיבוּ

FROM THE BIBLE (Ezra 5:11–15)

הֲתִיבוּ: אֲנַחְנָא עַבְדוֹהִי דִי אֱלָהּ שְׁמַיָּא וְאַרְעָא וּבָנַיִן בַּיְתָא דִי הֲוָא בְנֵה מִקַּדְמַת דְּנָה

שְׁנִין שַׂגִּיאָן. הַרְגִּזוּ אֲבָהָתַנָא לֶאֱלָהּ שְׁמַיָּא וִיהַב הִמּוֹ לִנְבוּכַדְנֶצַּר מֶלֶךְ בָּבֶל כַּסְדָּיָה

וּבַיְתָה דְנָה סְתַר וְעַמָּה הַגְלִי לְבָבֶל. בִּשְׁנַת חֲדָה לְכוֹרֶשׁ מַלְכָּא דִי בָבֶל כּוֹרֶשׁ מַלְכָּא

שָׂם טְעֵם בֵּית אֱלָהָא דְנָה לִבְּנֵא וּמָאנַיָּא דִי בֵית אֱלָהָא דִי נְבוּכַדְנֶצַּר הַנְפֵּק מִן הֵיכְלָא

דִי בִירוּשְׁלֶם לְהֵיכְלָא דִי בָבֶל הַנְפֵּק הִמּוֹ כּוֹרֶשׁ מַלְכָּא מִן הֵיכְלָא דִי בָבֶל וִיהִיבוּ

לְשֵׁשְׁבַּצַּר וַאֲמַר: אֵלֶּה מָאנַיָּא אֶחֵת הִמּוֹ בְּהֵיכְלָא דִי בִירוּשְׁלֶם וּבֵית אֱלָהָא יִתְבְּנֵא.

Proper Names

- בָּבֶל — A central Mesopotamian city on the Euphrates, which established an empire in the sixth century that conquered Judah and destroyed Jerusalem, taking its leading citizens into exile.

- כּוֹרֶשׁ — Founder of Persian empire, which he ruled from 559–30 B.C.E.; he conquered Media, Lydia, and Babylonia (in 539 B.C.E.), granted the various nations under his control cultural autonomy, and, according to Herodotus, believed himself "more than a man" (1:204).

- כַּסְדָּי — Southern Mesopotamian region where the Babylonian empire was centered in the seventh and sixth centuries (for the spelling, see p. 70).

- נְבוּכַדְנֶצַּר — Chaldean ruler of Babylonian empire (605–562 B.C.E.), who conquered Jerusalem in 587.

- שֵׁשְׁבַּצַּר — Babylonian-born Judean who was appointed governor by Cyrus in 538 B.C.E. and returned to Jerusalem with the temple vessels.

EXERCISES

Conjugate the following verbs, all of which have a *pataḥ* theme vowel, in the G perfect:

		יתב	נטל
singular	1		
	2 m		
	2 f		
	3 m		
	3 f		
plural	1		
	2 m		
	2 f		
	3 m		
	3 f		

		רשם	שלח
singular	1		
	2 m		
	2 f		
	3 m		
	3 f		
plural	1		
	2 m		
	2 f		
	3 m		
	3 f		

Identify the form of the following G perfect verbs:

	Root	Person	Gender	Number
יְדַעְתָּ				
יְדְעֵת				
יְהַב				
כִּתְבְנָא				
כְּתַבוּ				
מְלַחְנָא				
נְטְרֵת				
נְפַל				
סְלֵקֵת				
עֲבַד				

Translate from Aramaic into English:

(1) אֲזַל מַלְכָּא קֳדָם קִרְיְתָא.

(2) אֲנַחְנָה יָדְעְנָא דִּי בְּעֵל עָלְמָא בִּירוּשְׁלֶם.

(3) כִּתְבֵת אִגְּרָה עַל בֵּית מַלְכָּא.

(4) אֱדַיִן שְׁלַח אֱלָהָא טְעֵם עַל מְדִינְתָּא דָּךְ.

(5) יְהַבְתְּ עַבְדִין שַׂגִּיאִין לְפֶחָה.

(6) אֲבָהָתָנָא נְתַנוּ מָאנַיָּא אִלֵּךְ לְכוֹרֶשׁ.

(7) רֵאשׁ הֵיכְלָא הֲוָא בִּשְׁמַיָּא.

(8) נְבוּכַדְנֶצַּר לָא הַנְפֵּק גֻּבְרַיָּא לְאַרְעָא.

(9) בַּיְתָא רַבָּא דֵּךְ יִתְבְּנֵה בִּשְׁנָה חֲדָה.

Chapter 9

G PARTICIPLE

Like the G perfect, Aramaic participles are morphologically and functionally similar to their Hebrew counterparts. In both languages they act like nouns. Moreover, they look very much alike, with Aramaic's active participle even vocalized like its Hebrew equivalent (כּוֹתֵב), except that the Hebrew $\bar{o}$, of course, appears as $\bar{a}$ in Aramaic. Thus:

		Masculine	*Feminine*
singular	absolute	כָּתֵב	כָּתְבָה
	construct	כָּתֵב	כָּתְבַת
	determined	כָּתְבָא	כָּתְבְתָא
plural	absolute	כָּתְבִין	כָּתְבָן
	construct	כָּתְבֵי	כָּתְבָת
	determined	כָּתְבַיָּא	כָּתְבָתָא

This vowel pattern is affected by guttural letters, such as ח, ע, and ר, particularly when they come at the end of the root. Thus אָמַר and יָדַע are participles, derived from the theoretical forms אָמֵר and יָדֵעַ. (Do not confuse these with the Hebrew 3d person masculine singular perfect, which looks identical.)

Aramaic also has a passive participle. As in Hebrew, this form is characterized by its theme vowel. In Hebrew that is $\bar{u}$ (e.g., בָּרוּךְ, כָּתוּב); in Aramaic, it is $\bar{\imath}$:

		Masculine	*Feminine*
singular	absolute	כְּתִיב	כְּתִיבָה
	construct	כְּתִיב	כְּתִיבַת
	determined	כְּתִיבָא	כְּתִיבְתָא
plural	absolute	כְּתִיבִין	כְּתִיבָן
	construct	כְּתִיבֵי	כְּתִיבָת
	determined	כְּתִיבַיָּא	כְּתִיבָתָא

If you have studied the text of the Hebrew Bible, you may recognize the term כְּתִיב, which was used by the Masoretes to indicate places where the "written" text (כְּתִיב) differs from what is to be "read" (קְרִי). In such passages, many editions of the Bible print the consonants of the כְּתִיב and the vowels of the קְרִי. For example, the name Jerusalem is often printed יְרוּשָׁלַם, with an extra vowel between the last two consonants. The name was apparently pronounced יְרוּשָׁלֵם when these texts were written (כְּתִיב), just as it is in the Aramaic sections of the Bible (compare the English "Jerusalem"); however, by the time the vowels were added, the final *segol* had shifted to the diphthong *a-i*, yielding the reading (קְרִי) יְרוּשָׁלַיִם.

VOCABULARY

To Be Learned		*Reference*	
there is	אִיתַי	foundations	אֻשִּׁין
search	בקר	build	בנה
D perfect 3 m pl	בַּקַּרוּ	*G infinitive*	לְמִבְנֵה
Dt (passive) imf 3 ms	יִתְבַּקַּר	*Gt (pass.) participle*	מִתְבְּנֵה
treasure	גְּנַז	*Gt (pass.) imf 3 ms*	יִתְבְּנֵא
gold	דְּהַב	give	יהב
if	הֵן	*Gt imf 3 fs*	תִּתְיְהִב
good	טָב	scroll	מְגִלָּה
silver	כְּסַף	expenses	נִפְקְתָא
from	מִן	wish (noun)	רְעוּ
we/our	־נָא	give *(G pass. participle)*	שִׂים
there	תַּמָּה	find	שכח
		be found	הִשְׁתְּכַח
		finished	שְׁלִם
		return	תוב
		H (trans. imf 3 mpl)	יַהֲתִיבוּן

FROM THE BIBLE (Ezra 5:16–6:5)

אֱדַיִן שֵׁשְׁבַּצַּר אֲתָא יְהַב אֻשַּׁיָּא דִּי בֵית אֱלָהָא דִּי בִירוּשְׁלֶם וּמִן אֱדַיִן וְעַד כְּעַן מִתְבְּנֵא
וְלָא שְׁלִם. וּכְעַן הֵן עַל מַלְכָּא טָב יִתְבַּקַּר בְּבֵית גִּנְזַיָּא דִּי מַלְכָּא תַּמָּה דִּי בְּבָבֶל הֵן
אִיתַי דִּי מִן כּוֹרֶשׁ מַלְכָּא שִׂים טְעֵם לְמִבְנֵא בֵית אֱלָהָא בִירוּשְׁלֶם וּרְעוּת מַלְכָּא עַל
דְּנָה יִשְׁלַח עֲלֶינָא. בֵּאדַיִן דָּרְיָוֶשׁ מַלְכָּא שָׂם טְעֵם וּבַקַּרוּ תַּמָּה בְּבָבֶל וְהִשְׁתְּכַח מְגִלָּה
חֲדָה וְכֵן כְּתִיב בְּגַוַּהּ: בִּשְׁנַת חֲדָה לְכוֹרֶשׁ מַלְכָּא כּוֹרֶשׁ מַלְכָּא שָׂם טְעֵם בֵּית אֱלָהָא
בִירוּשְׁלֶם יִתְבְּנֵא וְנִפְקְתָא מִן בֵּית מַלְכָּא תִּתְיְהִב וּמָאנֵי בֵית אֱלָהָא דִּי דַהֲבָה וְכַסְפָּא
דִּי נְבוּכַדְנֶצַּר הַנְפֵּק מִן הֵיכְלָא דִּי בִירוּשְׁלֶם יַהֲתִיבוּן.

EXERCISES

List the participle forms of the following verbs:

Active		יְהַב	נְטַל	יְדַע	שְׁאֵל
Sg. masc.	absolute				
	construct				
	determined				
Sg. fem.	absolute				
	construct				
	determined				
Pl. masc.	absolute				
	construct				
	determined				
Pl. fem.	absolute				
	construct				
	determined				

Passive		יהב	נטל	ידע	שאל
Sg. masc.	absolute				
	construct				
	determined				
Sg. fem.	absolute				
	construct				
	determined				
Pl. masc.	absolute				
	construct				
	determined				
Pl. fem.	absolute				
	construct				
	determined				

Translate the following sentences into English:

(1) נְבוּכַדְנֶצַּר אָמַר דִּי קִרְיְתָא תִּתְיְהִב לִיהוּדָאִין.

(2) מְגִלָּה רַבָּה שְׁלִיחָה לְפֶחָה.

(3) מַלְכָּא יְדַע דִּי עֲבִידָה בְּטֵלָה.

(4) אֲנַחְנָה יָדְעִין לְמִבְנֵה בַּיִת.

(5) אִיתַי דְּהַב בִּגְנַז תַּמָּה בְּבָבֶל.

(6) גֻּבְרַיָּא בַּקַּרוּ הֵן כְּסַף טָב יְהִיב לְסָפְרָא.

Translate into Aramaic:

(1) The men rose up against them.

(2) Who sent the silver and the gold from Trans-Euphrates?

(3) There is a governor inside Jerusalem.

(4) We gave a house to them.

(5) The scribe went to the city.

Chapter 10

VOCABULARY

Although it is helpful to know Hebrew when learning Aramaic, their similarities can also be a trap for the unwary Hebraist engaged in the study of an Aramaic text. For the two languages are not the same, and one must avoid unintentionally reading an Aramaic passage as if it were Hebrew when they actually diverge. An example of this is the forms אֲמַר and יָדַע, which would be G (*qal*) perfect verbs in Hebrew, but are participles in Aramaic.

Likewise, the languages' vocabulary, though often similar, are not identical. This was demonstrated in chapter 3 by the Gospel accounts of Jesus' words on the cross, which are taken from the beginning of Psalm 22. Although the Gospel versions are virtually identical with the original, the Hebrew word עזב (abandon) has been rendered with its Aramaic equivalent—שׁבק.

Vocabulary differences are evident in the very first Aramaic words in the Bible, which occur in the story of Jacob's flight from his father-in-law (Genesis 31:47). After Laban caught up with Jacob, they made an agreement, and Jacob erected a pile of stones, which he called גַּלְעֵד but which Laban identified as יְגַר שָׂהֲדוּתָא. Although both phrases mean "pile-witness" —Jacob's in Hebrew and Laban's in Aramaic—they, too, bear no resemblance whatsoever.

An especially common idea that is expressed differently in the two languages is "son," which is בַּר in Aramaic but בֵּן in Hebrew. Interestingly, this is not the only case where Hebrew and Aramaic words with the same meaning differ only in the latter's having a ר where Hebrew has a נ. The Aramaic word for "two" (תְּרֵין) correlates with the Hebrew שְׁנָיִם (remember that Aramaic ת can correspond to Hebrew שׁ).

On the other hand, the two languages sometimes use altogether different roots. Several of these are very common words having to do with motion:

	Hebrew	*Aramaic*
"come"	בוא	אתא
"go"	הלך	אזל
"go up"	עלה	סלק
"go down"	ירד	נחת
"go in"	בוא	עלל
"go out"	יצא	נפק

Complicating matters are words (or roots) which exist in both languages but are used differently. For example, רַב can mean either "many" or "great" in Hebrew, but in Aramaic it always means "great"—a concept which Hebrew usually expresses with גָּדוֹל. How, then, does Aramaic say "many"? With a totally different word—שַׂגִּיא.

	Hebrew	*Aramaic*
"big"	גָּדוֹל	רַב
"many"	רַב	שַׂגִּיא

Similarly, the verb עבד occurs in both languages; however, it means "to serve" or "work" in Hebrew, but "to make" or "do" in Aramaic. Thus it has the same meaning in Aramaic that עשׂה has in Hebrew. As if to compensate, Aramaic also uses another verb—פלח, which means "to serve."

	Hebrew	*Aramaic*
"do, make"	עשׂה	עבד
"work, serve, worship"	עבד	פלח

Translating Aramaic עבד as if it were Hebrew could, therefore, lead to serious misunderstanding.

The very common Hebrew verbs נתן and שׂים also occur in Aramaic, where שׂים has a far broader semantic range than its Hebrew cognate, which means "put" in Aramaic. It can mean "issue (a decree)," "appoint," or "give (a name)"; it also occurs in several idioms, including "have regard for" (שִׂים טְעֵם עַל) and "set the mind on" (שִׂים בָּל לְ).

In biblical Aramaic נתן appears only in the imperfect and infinitive; perfect and participle forms of "give" are expressed with the more characteristically Aramaic verb יהב. This root also occurs in Hebrew parts of the Bible, where its imperative (הָבָה and הָבוּ) is used both literally ("give") and with the connotation "let us." Thus Rachel implores Jacob הָבָה לִי בָנִים ("Give me sons," Genesis 30:1), whereas the inhabitants of Babel say: הָבָה נִבְנֶה לָּנוּ עִיר ("Let's build a city for ourselves," Genesis 11:4).

VOCABULARY

To Be Learned		*Reference*	
I	אֲנָה	build	בנה
man	אֱנָשׁ	*G inf*	מִבְנֵא
destroy (D)	חבל	be	הוה
infinitive	חַבָּלָה	*G impv 3 mpl*	הֱווֹ
all	כֹּל	*G imf 3 ms*	לֶהֱוֵא
what	מָה	*G imf 3 fs*	תֶּהֱוֵא
dunghill	נְוָלוּ	*G imf 3 mpl*	לֶהֱוֹן
message, word	פִּתְגָם	life	חַיִּין
pray (D)	צלה	need	חַשַׁח
participle m pl	מְצַלִּין	hand	יַד
distant	רַחִיק	give	יהב
leave (alone)	שבק	*Gt (passive) participle*	
G imv m pl	שְׁבֻקוּ	*m s*	מִתְיְהֵב
		f pl	מִתְיַהֲבָא
		overthrow (D)	מגר
		D imf 3 m s	יְמַגַּר
		property	נְכַס
		expenses	נִפְקָה
		do	עבד
		Gt (passive) imf 3 ms	יִתְעֲבֵד
		people	עַם
		sacrifice (H)	קרב
		H participle m pl	מְהַקְרְבִין
		change (D, H)	שנה
		H (trans) imf 3 ms	יְהַשְׁנֵא

FROM THE BIBLE (Ezra 6:6–12)

כְּעַן תַּתְּנַי פַּחַת עֲבַר־נַהֲרָה שְׁתַר־בּוֹזְנַי וּכְנָוָתְהוֹן רַחִיקִין הֲווֹ מִן תַּמָּה.

שְׁבֻקוּ לַעֲבִידַת בֵּית אֱלָהָא וּמִנִּי שִׂים טְעֵם לִיהוּדָיֵא לְמִבְנֵא בֵּית אֱלָהָא וּמִנִּכְסֵי

מַלְכָּא נִפְקְתָא תֶּהֱוֵא מִתְיַהֲבָא לְגֻבְרַיָּא אִלֵּךְ דִּי לָא לְבַטָּלָא. וּמָה חַשְׁחָן לֶאֱלָהּ

שְׁמַיָּא לֶהֱוֵא מִתְיְהֵב לְהֹם דִּי לֶהֱוֹן מְהַקְרְבִין לֶאֱלָהּ שְׁמַיָּא וּמְצַלַּיִן לְחַיֵּי מַלְכָּא.

וּמִנִּי שִׂים טְעֵם דִּי כָל אֱנָשׁ דִּי יְהַשְׁנֵא פִּתְגָמָא דְנָה וּבַיְתֵהּ נְוָלוּ יִתְעֲבֵד עַל דְּנָה.

וֵאלָהָא יְמַגַּר כָּל מֶלֶךְ וְעַם דִּי יִשְׁלַח יְדֵהּ לְהַשְׁנָיָה לְחַבָּלָה בֵּית אֱלָהָא דִּי בִירוּשְׁלֶם.

אֲנָה דָרְיָוֶשׁ שָׂמֵת טְעֵם.

The phrase דִּי לָא לְבַטָּלָא (v. 8) literally means "in order not to stop (the work),"
i.e., "not to stop."

EXERCISES

Find the Hebrew and English words that mean the same as each of the following Aramaic
words. (Be careful—not all the Hebrew-Aramaic pairs are cognates.)

English translations: arm, big, come, do, document, dwell, give, go, god, go down,
gold, go out, go up, heaven, it will be, known, land, lie (*noun*), many, memo-
randum, one, ox, peace, return, sacrifice, scribe, six, snow, son, summer, there
is, this, to them, three, tree, two, weigh, we, work

Hebrew equivalents: אֶחָד, אֱלֹהִים, אֲנַחְנוּ, אֶרֶץ, בּוֹא, בֵּן, גָּדוֹל, הָלַךְ, הַסּוֹפֵר, זֶבַח, זֶה,
זָהָב, זִכָּרוֹן, זְרוֹעַ, יָדוּעַ, יִהְיֶה, יָצָא, יָרַד, יֵשׁ, יָשַׁב, כָּזָב, לָהֶם, נָתַן, סֵפֶר, עָבַד, עָלָה,
עֵץ, עָשָׂה, קַיִץ, רַב, שׁוּב, שׁוֹר, שֶׁלֶג, שָׁלוֹם, שָׁלוֹשׁ, שָׁמַיִם, שְׁנַיִם, שֶׁקֶל, שֵׁשׁ

	Hebrew equivalent	English translation
אֶדְרָע		
אֲזַל		
אִיתַי		
אֱלָהַיָּא		

	Hebrew equivalent	English translation
אֲנַחְנָה		
אָע		
אַרְעָא		
אתה		
בַּר		
דְּבַח		
דְּהַב		
דָּכְרָן		
דְּנָה		
חַד		
יְדִיעַ		
יהב		
יתב		
כִּדְבָה		
לֶהֱוֵא		
לְהֹם		
נחת		
נפק		
סלק		
סְפַר		
סָפְרָא		

	Hebrew equivalent	English translation
עֲבַר		
פְּלַח		
קַיִט		
רַב		
שַׂגִּיא		
שְׁלָם		
שְׁמַיָּא		
שֵׁת		
תּוּב		
תּוֹר		
תְּלַג		
תְּלָת		
תְּקַל		
תְּרֵי		

Translate into Aramaic:

(1) The treasures are far from the dunghill.

(2) I wrote a letter to the scribes.

(3) He sent God's message to the city.

(4) The head of the province is a man.

(5) Leave everything there!

(6) They are praying to God to destroy the earth.

Chapter 11

INDEPENDENT PRONOUNS, אִיתַי

In the Semitic languages, pronouns exist in several different forms. Some of these stand alone, while others are suffixes which can be attached to the end of words, including verbs, where they serve as direct objects, nouns, indicating possession, or prepositions, of which they are the object.

Aramaic's pronominal suffixes will be described in chapter 13. The independent forms look very much like their Hebrew equivalents, especially if one allows for the sound changes already described as characteristic of each language.

		Singular	*Plural*
1		אֲנָה	אֲנַחְנָה
2	masculine	אַנְתְּ (or אַנְתָּה)*	אַנְתּוּן (or אַנְתֹּם)
	feminine	אַנְתִּי	אַנְתֵּן
3	masculine	הוּא	הִמּוֹ (or אִנּוּן or הִמּוֹן)
	feminine	הִיא	אִנִּין

Although 2d person Hebrew pronouns do not have a נ where their Aramaic equivalents do, the *dagesh* in the ת indicates that there was once a נ which has now assimilated to the ת. (The *dagesh* in the Aramaic forms is *lene*, since these letters follow a now closed syllable.) Although the 2d person feminine singular pronoun (אַנְתִּי) may appear unfamiliar, its Hebrew equivalent (אַתִּי) can be found several places in the Hebrew Bible, albeit only as the כְּתִיב.** The ִי- ending is also used to mark feminine forms of the Hebrew imperfect (תִּכְתְּבִי) and imperative (כְּתְבִי).

One of the differences between Hebrew and Aramaic has to do with the verb "to be." Although the root היה exists in both languages, neither one uses it in the present tense. For that, Hebrew uses noun sentences, in which there simply is no verb:

---

* Most Bibles show a mixed form אַנְתָּה, which has the consonants (כְּתִיב) for אַנְתָּה and the vowels (קְרִי) for אַנְתְּ.

** Cf. Judges 17:2, 1 Kings 14:2, 2 Kings 4:16,23, 8:1, Jeremiah 4:30, and Ezekiel 36:13.

54

דָּוִד מֶלֶךְ.   David is king.

דָּוִד הַמֶּלֶךְ.   David is the king.

Aramaic accomplishes this differently—by using the 3d person pronouns as a copula:

כּוֹרֶשׁ הוּא מֶלֶךְ.   Cyrus is king.

כּוֹרֶשׁ הוּא מַלְכָּא.   Cyrus is the king.

The subject of such sentences need not be in the 3d person:

אֲנַחְנָא הִמּוֹ עַבְדוֹהִי.   We are his servants. (Ezra 5:11)

אַנְתְּ הוּא רֵאשָׁה דִּי דַהֲבָא.   You are the head of gold. (Daniel 2:38)

This same construction also occurs in biblical Hebrew; for example:

אַתָּה הוּא מַלְכִּי.   You are my king. (Psalm 44:5)

Sometimes Aramaic uses the particle אִיתַי to express the present tense of "to be." Like the Hebrew word יֵשׁ, to which it may be related,* אִיתַי normally means "there is":

אִיתַי אֱלָהּ בִּשְׁמַיָּא.   There is a god in heaven. (Daniel 2:28)

לָא אִיתַי אֱלָהּ אָחֳרָן.   There is no other god. (Daniel 3:29)

Also like יֵשׁ, אִיתַי is used with the preposition -לְ to indicate possession:

חֲלָק בַּעֲבַר־נַהֲרָא לָא אִיתַי לָךְ.
You (will) have no portion in Trans-Euphrates. (Ezra 4:16)

Notice that Aramaic uses לָא (= Hebrew לֹא) to negate אִיתַי, whereas in Hebrew an entirely separate word (אַיִן) functions as the negative of יֵשׁ. Centuries after the Bible was written, לָא and אִיתַי merged into a single word— לֵית. Thus Targum Onkelos, an Aramaic translation of the Pentateuch, renders the Hebrew phrase וְלֶחֶם אֵין בְּכָל הָאָרֶץ (Genesis 47:13) as וְלַחְמָא לֵית בְּכָל אַרְעָא. The Masoretes used this same word, abbreviated as ל, to identify forms which occur only once in the Hebrew Bible. Examples can be seen in the marginal notes on almost any page of the *Biblia Hebraica* or in many editions of the rabbinic Bible (מִקְרָאוֹת גְּדוֹלוֹת).

---

* Note 2 Samuel 14:19 and Micah 6:10, where the word אַשׁ may have the same meaning (and perhaps אִישׁ in Proverbs 18:24).

In addition to those functions, אִיתַי can also serve as a copula (present tense of "to be," i.e. "am, are, is"). This is clearest in those passages where it has a pronominal suffix (see chapter 13) and cannot, therefore, easily be rendered "there is/are":*

לֵאלָהָיִךְ לָא אִיתַנָא פָלְחִין.   We do not worship your god. (Daniel 3:18)

VOCABULARY

To Be Learned		*Reference*	
exactly	אָסְפַּרְנָא	*plural construct of* בַּר	בְּנֵי
priest	כָּהֵן	exile	גָּלוּ
thus	כְּנֵמָא	joy	חֶדְוָה
writing	כְּתָב	dedication	חֲנֻכָּה
reign	מַלְכוּ	day	יוֹם
book	סְפַר	month	יְרַח
just as	קֳבֵל (לְ)	prophecy	נְבוּאָה
rest	שְׁאָר	succeed (H)	צלח
they completed	שַׁכְלִלוּ	*H participle m pl*	מַצְלְחִין
six	שֵׁת	establish (H)	קוּם
		H pf 3 m pl	הֲקִימוּ
		he finished	שֵׁיצִיא

FROM THE BIBLE (Ezra 6:13–18)

אֱדַיִן תַּתְּנַי פַּחַת עֲבַר־נַהֲרָה שְׁתַר־בּוֹזְנַי וּכְנָוָתְהוֹן לָקֳבֵל דִּי שְׁלַח דָּרְיָוֶשׁ מַלְכָּא כְּנֵמָא

אָסְפַּרְנָא עֲבַדוּ. וְיהוּדָיֵא בָּנַיִן וּמַצְלְחִין בִּנְבוּאַת חַגַּי וּזְכַרְיָה בַּר עִדּוֹא וּשְׁכְלִלוּ מִן

טַעַם אֱלָהּ יִשְׂרָאֵל וּמִטְּעֵם כּוֹרֶשׁ וְדָרְיָוֶשׁ וְאַרְתַּחְשַׁשְׂתְּא מֶלֶךְ פָּרָס וְשֵׁיצִיא בַּיְתָה דְנָה

עַד יוֹם תְּלָתָה לִירַח אֲדָר דִּי הִיא שְׁנַת שֵׁת לְמַלְכוּת דָּרְיָוֶשׁ מַלְכָּא. וַעֲבַדוּ בְנֵי

יִשְׂרָאֵל כָּהֲנַיָּא וְלֵוָיֵא וּשְׁאָר בְּנֵי גָלוּתָא חֲנֻכַּת בֵּית אֱלָהָא דְנָה בְּחֶדְוָה. וַהֲקִימוּ

כָהֲנַיָּא וְלֵוָיֵא עַל עֲבִידַת אֱלָהָא דִּי בִירוּשְׁלֶם כִּכְתָב סְפַר מֹשֶׁה.

---

* Compare the Hebrew אִם יֶשְׁךָ מוֹשִׁיעַ — "if you will save" (Judges 6:36; cf. Genesis 24:42 and 49).

Proper Names

אֲדָר — Last month of the Hebrew calendar (late winter).

לֵוָיֵא — Ritual officials whose ancestry was traced back to Jacob's son Levi.

פָּרַס — Sixth-century empire founded by Cyrus II when he conquered Media, Lydia, and Babylon.

EXERCISES

Fill in the correct pronoun and translate into English:

(1) _____ דְּבַחְתְּ תּוֹר לֵאלָהָא.

(2) _____ יְדַע דִּי שָׁבַיָּא בִּמְדִינָתָא.

(3) _____ יְהַבְתֶּן סִפְרָא לְפֶחָה.

(4) _____ כְּתַבְתּוּן אִגַּרְתָה.

(5) _____ נְפַלוּ לְאַרְעָא.

(6) _____ נְפְקְנָא מִבַּיְתָא.

(7) _____ פְּלַחַת בִּירוּשְׁלֶם.

(8) _____ שָׂם טְעֵם.

(9) _____ שְׁלַחְתִּי פִּתְגָם לְבָבֶל.

(10) _____ יְדְעֵת לְמִבְנֵא בַּיִת.

(11) _____ סְלִקוּ לִשְׁמַיָּא.

(12) _____ שְׁלַחְנָא מְגִלָּה לְבֵית גִּנְזַיָּא.

Translate the following sentences into English:

(1) אִיתַי הֵיכַל בְּקִרְיְתָא רַבְּתָא.

(2) אַנְתּוּן הִמּוֹ כָהֲנֵי אֱלָהָא דִּי שְׁמַיָּא.

(3) בֵּית אֱלָהָא אִיתַי בִּירוּשְׁלֶם.

(4) לְגַבְרָא לָא אִיתַי רֵאשׁ.

(5) זְרוּבָּבֶל הוּא פֶּחָה דִּי יְהוּדָיֵא.

(6) כְּנֵמָא כְּתִיב בִּסְפַר דָּרְיָוֶשׁ: אֲנַחְנָא מְצַלִּין לְאַרְעָא.

(7) אַנְתְּ הוּא מֶלֶךְ שְׁלָם.

(8) אֱדַיִן שַׁכְלִלוּ עֲבִידַת בֵּית תַּקִּיף.

Translate into Aramaic:

(1) The six men did exactly as the king said.

(2) We gave the rest of the kingdom to Darius.

(3) The decree is in writing.

(4) There is no palace in Judah.

(5) She is sending a book to the priest there.

Chapter 12

PREPOSITIONS

Some Aramaic prepositions are prefixed to an object; others can stand on their own:

Prefixed		*Independent*	
in	בְּ-	after	אַחֲרֵי
like, as	כְּ-	between	בֵּין
to, for	לְ-	from	מִן
from	מִ-	until	עַד
		on, concerning, to, against	עַל
		with	עִם
		under	תְּחוֹת

Prefixed prepositions are vocalized according to the same patterns that are used in Hebrew. -בְּ, -כְּ, and לְ- normally have a silent *sh'va*, which shifts to a *ḥiriq* (e.g., -בִּ) when the next consonant has a silent *sh'va*.

לְהֵיכְלָא.	to the palace
לִמְדִינְתָּא.	to the province

When מִן is attached to its object, the נ assimilates, where possible, to the first consonant of the following noun (e.g., מִטַּעַם).

Several other prepositions are unique to Aramaic. Some of these obviously originated from nouns (compare the Hebrew לִפְנֵי and בְּתוֹךְ):

בָּאתַר — From the noun אֲתַר ("place"), the preposition means "after" (i.e. "in place of"). Because the א has no vowel, it can drop out, leaving בָּתַר (e.g., Daniel 2:39 on p. 87; for a later development of this form, see p. 153).

גּו — (When standing alone, it is spelled גּוֹא)—"midst"; can be combined with other prepositions, such as -בְּ and -לְ to mean "inside (i.e. in the midst) of" or "into."

לָקֳבֵל — (Notice the composite *sh'va* under the ק, as explained on p. 19)—"opposite, corresponding to"; this preposition often occurs in the expanded form -כָּל קֳבֵל דְּ ("because").

קֳדָם — "In front of"; though literally spatial, it can also be used temporally (e.g., קַדְמָה, "former time"; cf. Hebrew לִפְנֵי, "to the face of").

Aramaic has a direct object marker just like the Hebrew אֵת. Its form is יָת. (The Phoenician equivalent is spelled אית.) Although it is common in later texts (see the synagogue inscription on p. 173 and the Targum Pseudo-Jonathan to Genesis 22:1–2 on pp. 198–200) as well as in Syriac and Nabatean, it occurs only once in the Bible (Daniel 3:12), where direct objects are more often indicated by the preposition -לְ:

e.g., הַרְגִּזוּ אֲבָהֳתַנָא לֶאֱלָהּ שְׁמַיָּא

Our ancestors angered the God of heaven. (Ezra 5:12)*

VOCABULARY

To Be Learned		*Reference*	
judgment	דִּין	tax	בְּלוֹ
judge	דַּיָּן	search	בקר
law	דָּת	*D inf*	בַּקָּרָה
be	הוא	ram	דְּכַר
G imperfect 3 ms	לֶהֱוֵא	him/his	הֵ-
go	הלך	*1s sf*	יַ-
G infinitive	מְהָךְ	bring	יבל
G imperfect 3 ms	יְהָךְ	*H inf*	הֵיבָלָה

---

* This same usage occurs occasionally in biblical Hebrew, e.g., זְכֹר לְאַבְרָהָם וּלְיִצְחָק וּלְיִשְׂרָאֵל ("Remember Abraham, Isaac, and Israel"—Exodus 32:13).

To Be Learned		Reference	
know	יְדַע	give	יְהַב
H (inform) ptc m pl	מְהוֹדְעִין	*Gt ptc pl m pl*	מִתְיַהֲבִין
H imf 2 m pl	תְּהוֹדְעוּן	be pleasing	יְטַב
be willing (D)	נדב	*G imf 3 ms*	יֵיטַב
Dt ptc ms	מִתְנַדַּב	you	־ךָ
people	עַם	appoint (D)	מנה
ask	שׁאל	*imperative*	מֶנִּי
G imf 3ms + 2mpl	יִשְׁאֶלֶנְכוֹן	do	עבד
authorized	שַׁלִּיט	*G inf*	מֶעְבַּד
		Gt imf 3 ms	יִתְעֲבֵד
		G imf 2 mpl	תַּעַבְדוּן
		buy	קנה
		G imf 2 ms	תִּקְנֵה
		sacrifice (D)	קרב
		D imf 2 ms	תְּקָרֵב
		impose (lit. throw)	רמה
		G inf	לְמִרְמֵא
		wish	רְעוּ
		deliver (H)	שׁלם
		imperative	הַשְׁלֵם

FROM THE BIBLE (Ezra 7:12–26)

Ezra 6:19–7:11 is in Hebrew. After describing the celebration of the Passover by those who had returned from the exile and those "who had separated themselves from the impurity of the nations of the land," it announces the return of more exiles. Among them was Ezra, a priest and "scribe, expert in the Teaching of Moses," who presented a letter he had received from Artaxerxes, the text of which is given in Aramaic:

אַרְתַּחְשַׁסְתְּא מֶלֶךְ מַלְכַיָּא לְעֶזְרָא כָהֲנָא סָפַר דָּתָא דִּי אֱלָהּ שְׁמַיָּא: מְנִי שִׂים טְעֵם דִּי
כָל מִתְנַדַּב בְּמַלְכוּתִי מִן עַמָּא יִשְׂרָאֵל וְכָהֲנוֹהִי וְלֵוָיֵא לִמְהָךְ לִירוּשְׁלֵם עִמָּךְ יְהָךְ.
מִן קֳדָם מַלְכָּא שְׁלִיחַ לְבַקָּרָה עַל יְהוּד וְלִירוּשְׁלֵם בְּדָת אֱלָהָךְ וּלְהֵיבָלָה כְּסַף וּדְהַב
דִּי מַלְכָּא לֶאֱלָהּ יִשְׂרָאֵל דִּי בִירוּשְׁלֵם וְכֹל כְּסַף וּדְהַב בְּכֹל מְדִינַת בָּבֶל
לְבֵית אֱלָהֲהֹם דִּי בִירוּשְׁלֵם. אָסְפַּרְנָא תִקְנֵא בְּכַסְפָּא דְנָה דִּכְרִין וְתִקְרֵב הִמּוֹ
בִּירוּשְׁלֵם. וּמָה דִּי עֲלָךְ יִיטַב בִּשְׁאַר כַּסְפָּא וְדַהֲבָה לְמֶעְבַּד כִּרְעוּת אֱלָהֲכֹם
תַּעַבְדוּן. וּמָאנַיָּא דִּי מִתְיַהֲבִין לָךְ לְבֵית אֱלָהָךְ הַשְׁלֵם קֳדָם אֱלָהּ יְרוּשְׁלֵם. וּמִנִּי אֲנָה
אַרְתַּחְשַׁסְתְּא מַלְכָּא שִׂים טְעֵם דִּי כָל דִּי יִשְׁאֲלֶנְכוֹן עֶזְרָא כָהֲנָא סָפַר דָּתָא דִּי אֱלָהּ
שְׁמַיָּא אָסְפַּרְנָא יִתְעֲבֵד. כָּל דִּי מִן טַעַם אֱלָהּ שְׁמַיָּא יִתְעֲבֵד לְבֵית אֱלָהּ
שְׁמַיָּא. וּלְכֹם מְהוֹדְעִין דִּי כָל כָּהֲנַיָּא וְלֵוָיֵא בְּלוֹ לָא שַׁלִּיט לְמִרְמֵא עֲלֵיהֹם.
וְאַנְתְּ עֶזְרָא כְּחָכְמַת אֱלָהָךְ מְנִי דַיָּנִין לְכָל עַמָּא דִּי בַּעֲבַר-נַהֲרָה לְכָל יָדְעֵי דָּתֵי
אֱלָהָךְ וְדִי לָא יָדַע תְּהוֹדְעוּן. וְכָל דִּי לָא לֶהֱוֵא עָבֵד דָּתָא דִּי אֱלָהָךְ וְדָתָא
דִּי מַלְכָּא אָסְפַּרְנָא דִינָה לֶהֱוֵא מִתְעֲבֵד מִנֵּהּ.

This concludes the Aramaic section of Ezra. You may wish to read the rest of the book either in Hebrew or in English translation.

EXERCISES

Translate the following sentences into English:

(1) הוּא שְׁאֵל עַל דַּת מַלְכָּא.

(2) עַמָּא דְנָה שַׁלִּיט לְהֵיבָלָא מָאנַיָּא מִן הֵיכְלָא.

(3) נְבוּכַדְנֶצַּר הֲוָה מֶלֶךְ בָּבֶל מִן עָלְמָא.

(4) מַן מִתְנַדַּב לְמֶעְבַּד נְוָלוּ עַל אַרְעָא.

(5) אַנְתּוּן תְּהוֹדְעוּן לְדַיָּנָא דִּי לֶהֱוֵא מְרַד בִּמְדִינְתָּא.

Translate into Aramaic:

(1) We will go to Jerusalem with Ezra.

(2) The city will be built after they give tax to the king.

(3) The judgment was between the king and the people.

(4) They said: Leave the book in Babylon.

(5) The head was in the sky.

Chapter 13

PRONOMINAL SUFFIXES

Besides independent pronouns, Aramaic also has pronominal suffixes, which can be attached to verbs (direct object), to nouns (possession), and to prepositions (object). Although the actual suffixes can vary, depending on the nature of the word to which they are attached, the various possibilities are all similar to each other and to the independent forms of the pronouns.

singular	1 common	אֲנָה	־ִי (on verbs ־ַנִי)
	2 masculine	אַנְתְּ	־ָךְ
	2 feminine	אַנְתִּי	־ִכִי
	3 masculine	הוּא	־ֵהּ (־ֵהִי, ־וֹהִי־)
	3 feminine	הִיא	־ַהּ
plural	1 common	אֲנַחְנָה	־ָנָא
	2 masculine	(אַנְתֹּם) אַנְתּוּן	־כֹם (־כֹון)
	2 feminine	אַנְתֵּן	־כֵן
	3 masculine	(אִנּוּן) הִמּוֹ	־הֹם (־הֹון)
	3 feminine	אִנִּין	־הֵן

Notice the resemblance between these suffixes and their Hebrew counterparts, which extends to the use of ת as a base for the 2d person independent pronouns while the suffixes have a כ (thus Hebrew אַתָּה and ־ךָ). The exact form of the suffixes depends on the number and gender of the noun to which they are attached.

66

SUFFIX	SINGULAR NOUNS		PLURAL NOUNS	
	Masculine	*Feminine*	*Masculine*	*Feminine*
1 singular	פִּשְׁרִי	מַלְכוּתִי	פִּשְׁרַי	מַלְכְוָתִי
2 m s	פִּשְׁרָךְ	מַלְכוּתָךְ	* פִּשְׁרָיךְ	מַלְכְוָתָךְ
f s	פִּשְׁרֵכִי	מַלְכוּתֵכִי	פִּשְׁרַיְכִי	מַלְכְוָתֵכִי
3 m s	פִּשְׁרֵהּ	מַלְכוּתֵהּ	פִּשְׁרוֹהִי	מַלְכְוָתֵהּ
3 f s	פִּשְׁרַהּ	מַלְכוּתַהּ	* פִּשְׁרַיהּ	מַלְכְוָתַהּ
1 plural	פִּשְׁרַנָא	מַלְכוּתַנָא	* פִּשְׁרַינָא	מַלְכְוָתַנָא
2 m p	פִּשְׁרְכֹם (כֹון-)	מַלְכוּתְכֹם (כֹון-)	פִּשְׁרֵיכֹם (כֹון-)	מַלְכְוָתְכֹם (כֹון-)
f p	פִּשְׁרְכֵן	מַלְכוּתְכֵן	פִּשְׁרֵיכֵן	מַלְכְוָתְכֵן
3 m p	פִּשְׁרְהֹם (הֹון-)	מַלְכוּתְהֹם (הֹון-)	פִּשְׁרֵיהֹם (הֹון-)	מַלְכְוָתְהֹם (הֹון-)
3 f p	פִּשְׁרְהֵן	מַלְכוּתְהֵן	פִּשְׁרֵיהֵן	מַלְכְוָתֵן

As in Hebrew, these suffixes are attached to a shortened form of the noun, such as פִּשְׁר- (which is the same base as that used for the determined suffix— פִּשְׁרָא), rather than the absolute פְּשַׁר. Sometimes, however, they are added to irregular forms of the words. This happens most often with words that refer to family members, such as אַב (אֲבוּהִי, אֲבָהָתָא), אַח (אֲחָיךְ), and בַּר (בְּרֵהּ).

When these suffixes are attached to nouns, they express possession:

> e.g.,   בֵּיתִי   my house
>   אֱלָהֵהּ   his god
>   חַבְרְתַהּ   her companion

This can help explain an Aramaic phrase which is preserved in the New Testament:

μαραναθα =   מָרַנָא תָה   "Our master, come!" (1 Corinthians 16:22)**

Pronominal suffixes can also appear on prepositions and on verbs. The prepositions -לְ, מִן, עִם, -בְּנִי, לְוָת, and לְקָבֵל take the pronominal endings that go on singular nouns; others, such as עַל, אַחֲרֵי, בֵּין, קֳדָם, and תְּחוֹת, take those for plural nouns.

---

     * These are really mixed forms. The ' (which is not pronounced) belongs to the כְּתִיב, where it would have been part of a diphthong (e.g., פִּשְׁרָיךְ); cf. the 3rd person masculine singular suffix Hebrew uses for plural nouns, such as אֱלָהָיו.
     ** Cf. Revelation 22:20.

singular	1	לִי	עֲלַי
	2 masculine	לָךְ	עֲלָיךְ
	2 feminine	* לְכִי	* עֲלֵיכִי
	3 masculine	לֵה	עֲלוֹהִי
	3 feminine	לַהּ	עֲלֵיהּ
plural	1	לַנָא	עֲלֵינָא
	2 masculine	(לְכוֹן) לְכֹם	* עֲלֵיכֹם
	2 feminine	* לְכֵן	* עֲלֵיכֵן
	3 masculine	(לְהוֹן) לְהֹם	(עֲלֵיהוֹן) עֲלֵיהֹם
	3 feminine	* לְהֵן	* עֲלֵיהֵן

The suffixes for plural nouns are also used with the particle of existence (אִיתַי) and are then translated as the subject of a copula (see chapter 11):

לֵאלָהָיךְ לָא אִיתַינָא פָלְחִין We do not worship your god. (Daniel 3:18)

הַאִיתָיךְ כָּהֵל לְהוֹדָעֻתַנִי Are you able to inform me? (Daniel 2:26)

Pronominal suffixes commonly appear as direct objects of a verb. (This same structure occurs in Hebrew, although its pronominal suffixes can also be attached to אֵת in forms like אוֹתוֹ.) Because the exact form of the suffix (and the verbal base onto which it is attached) varies, it is not practical to try to memorize all possibilities. Here are some examples to demonstrate what such forms look like on one verb:

		Perfect	*Imperfect*
singular	1	הוֹדְעֻתַּנִי	** יְהוֹדְעִנַּנִי
	2 masculine	הוֹדְעָךְ	————
	3 masculine	————	אֲהוֹדְעִנֵּהּ
plural	1	הוֹדְעֻתֶּנָא	————

---

* These are hypothetical forms, which do not actually occur in the Bible.

** Note that the נ is doubled before the pronominal suffix.

When a noun is emphasized by being placed at the beginning of a sentence or clause, its place in the sentence proper is taken by a subsequent (resumptive) pronoun. This usage is called "casus pendens" (lit. "the hanging case") because the noun is technically neither the subject nor the object of the sentence.

e.g., בַּיְתָא דְנָה סַתְרֵהּ This house—he destroyed it. (Ezra 5:12)

VOCABULARY

To Be Learned		*Reference*	
another	אָחֳרָן	kill (H)	אבד
tell (D, H)	חוא	*H infinitive*	הוֹבָדָא
D imperfect 1 pl	נְחַוֵּא	say	אמר
D imf 3 ms + 3 fs	יְחַוִּנַּהּ	*G imf 3 ms*	יֵאמַר
H imf 1 pl	נְהַחֲוֵה	*G imperative*	אֱמַר
H imf 2 mpl	תְּהַחֲוֹן	limb	הַדָּם
H imv mpl + 1 s	הַחֲוֹנִי	buy	זבן
H inf	לְהַחֲוָיָא	inform (H)	ידע
wise	חַכִּים	*H imf 2 mpl*	תְּהוֹדְעֻנַּנִי
dream	חֵלֶם	be able	יכל
except	לָהֵן	difficult	יַקִּיר
word, thing	מִלָּה	glory	יְקָר
time	עִדָּן	receive	קבל
answer	ענה	*D imf 2 mpl*	תְּקַבְּלוּן
G pf 3 mpl	עֲנוֹ	be angry	קצף
interpretation	פְּשַׁר	issue	שׂים
change	שׁנה	*Gt (passive) imperfect*	
Dt (passive) imperfect		*3 mpl*	יִתְּשָׂמוּן
3 ms	יִשְׁתַּנֵּה		

FROM THE BIBLE (Daniel 2:4–13)

The opening section of Daniel (1:1–2:4) is written in Hebrew. Read it in the original or in translation before beginning the Aramaic selection for this chapter.

מַלְכָּא אֲמַר חֶלְמָא לְעַבְדַּיְךְ וּפִשְׁרָא נְחַוֵּא. עָנֵה מַלְכָּא וְאָמַר לְכַשְׂדָּיֵא: הֵן לָא.

תְהוֹדְעוּנַּנִי חֶלְמָא וּפִשְׁרֵהּ הַדָּמִין תִּתְעַבְדוּן וּבָתֵּיכוֹן נְוָלִי יִתְּשָׂמוּן וְהֵן חֶלְמָא וּפִשְׁרֵהּ

תְּהַחֲוֹן יְקָר שַׂגִּיא תְּקַבְּלוּן מִן קָדָמָי. לָהֵן חֶלְמָא וּפִשְׁרֵהּ הַחֲוֹנִי. עֲנוֹ וְאָמְרִין:

מַלְכָּא חֶלְמָא יֵאמַר לְעַבְדוֹהִי וּפִשְׁרָה נְהַחֲוֵה. עָנֵה מַלְכָּא וְאָמַר: יַדַּע אֲנָה דִּי עִדָּנָא

אַנְתּוּן זָבְנִין עַד דִּי עִדָּנָא יִשְׁתַּנֵּא. עֲנוֹ כַשְׂדָּיֵא קָדָם מַלְכָּא וְאָמְרִין: לָא אִיתַי אֱנָשׁ

דִּי מִלַּת מַלְכָּא יוּכַל לְהַחֲוָיָה. כָּל מֶלֶךְ רַב מִלָּה כִדְנָה לָא שְׁאֵל לְכָל כַּשְׂדָּי וּמִלְתָא

דִּי מַלְכָּה שָׁאֵל יַקִּירָה. וְאָחֳרָן לָא אִיתַי דִּי יְחַוִּנַּהּ קָדָם מַלְכָּא לָהֵן אֱלָהִין.

מַלְכָּא קְצַף שַׂגִּיא וַאֲמַר לְהוֹבָדָה לְכָל חַכִּימֵי בָבֶל.

Proper Names

כַּשְׂדָּי — This term, which originally designated the inhabitants of a geographic region, came to mean "magician"; it is used with both meanings in the book of Daniel (cf. 5:11 and 30 on pp. 126 and 137). Although it is spelled with a שׂ here and throughout the book of Daniel, it occurs with ס (כַּסְדָּי) in Ezra 5:12 (see p. 38). Over time, שׂ tended to be replaced by ס, even in words where the former was historically correct. A similar process took place in post-biblical Hebrew; however, it is only beginnng to occur in the Bible (cf. Artaxerxes' name, which is spelled with a ס in Ezra 7:21; see p. 64).

Although the forms אֲמַר and יַדַּע look like Hebrew perfects, they are participles in Aramaic (compare the syntactically parallel עָנֵה); the perfect would be אֲמַר and יְדַע. אֱמַר is imperative.

EXERCISES

Translate:

אֲבוּךְ	כָּהֲנוֹהִי
אַחֲרֵיהוֹן	עַבְדָּיךְ
אִיתַיכוֹן	עֲלַי
אִיתוֹהִי	עֲלָיִךְ
אֱלָהִי	עִמֵּהּ
אֱלָהֵהּ	לְקָבְלָךְ
בָּתְרָךְ	קָדְמוֹהִי
בֵּינֵיהוֹן	רֵאשְׁהוֹן
בֵּיתֵהּ	שְׁמֵהּ
בְּרֵהּ	שְׁמָהָתְהֹם
בְּגַוֵּהּ	תְּחוֹתוֹהִי
הֵיכְלִי	תְּלָתְהוֹן
יָתְהוֹן	

Translate into Aramaic:

(1) The king will be a servant in another time.

(2) The wise men answered the head of the province.

(3) The interpretation will change if the scribe goes out from the city.

(4) There is a word in my dream that I did not know.

(5) We will tell everything except the name of our god.

(6) His house is on a dunghill.

Chapter 14

DEMONSTRATIVE, RELATIVE, AND INTERROGATIVE PRONOUNS

Besides the personal pronouns, there are demonstratives ("this, that," etc.), relatives (which, that), and interrogatives (who, what). In Hebrew, the singular forms of the demonstrative pronouns are built around the letter ז (זֶה, זֹאת); Aramaic uses ד:

		Singular	*Plural*
Near (this, these)	masculine	דְּנָה	אֱלֵין (also אֵל and אֵלֶּה)
	feminine	דָּא	
Far (that, those)	masculine	דֵּךְ	אִלֵּךְ
	feminine	דָּךְ	
	masculine and feminine	דִּכֵּן	

Third person pronouns can also be used as demonstratives:

הוּא צַלְמָא רֵאשֵׁהּ דִּי דְהַב

That statue—its head was of gold. (Daniel 2:32)

וּבְיוֹמֵיהוֹן דִּי מַלְכַיָּא אִנּוּן

And in the days of those kings   (Daniel 2:44)

As in Hebrew, the demonstratives can function either as nouns, which stand on their own, or act like adjectives, in which case they usually follow the noun they modify (which must be determined):

בַּיְתָא דְנָה	this house (Ezra 5:3, 12, 6:15)
כֹּל דְּנָה יְדַעְתָּ	you know all of this (Daniel 5:22)
כִּדְנָה תֵּאמְרוּן לְהוֹם	thus ("like this") shall you say to them (Jeremiah 10:11)

We have already encountered the Aramaic relative pronoun דִּי ("which, that"). It is especially common after verbs of perception and communication, such as יְדַע, אֲמַר, and שְׁמַע, and frequently introduces direct quotations. It can also express purpose or cause.

הֵיכְלָא דִּי בִירוּשְׁלֶם   the temple which is in Jerusalem (Ezra 5:14)

יָדַע אֲנָה דִּי עִדָּנָא אַנְתּוּן זָבְנִין   I know that you are buying time. (Daniel 2:8)

עָנֵה מַלְכָּא וְאָמַר לְחַכִּימֵי בָבֶל דִּי כָל אֱנָשׁ דִּי יִקְרֵה כְּתָבָה דְנָה
וּפִשְׁרֵהּ יְחַוִּנַּנִי אַרְגְּוָנָא יִלְבַּשׁ

> The king answers and says to the wise men of Babylon: "Any man who will read this writing and tell me its interpretation will wear purple." (Daniel 5:7)

אַנְתְּ כָּהֵל דִּי רוּחַ אֱלָהִין קַדִּישִׁין בָּךְ

> You are able because the spirit of the holy gods is in you. (Daniel 4:15)

שְׁמָהָתְהֹן שְׁאֵלְנָא . . . דִּי נִכְתֻּב שֻׁם גֻּבְרַיָּא דִּי בְרָאשֵׁהֹם

> We asked their names so that we can write the names of the men who are at their head. (Ezra 5:10)

In addition to standing on its own, דִּי is often attached to various prepositions to form a relative phrase:

כְּדִי	when
מִן דִּי	after, because
כָּל קֳבֵל דִּי	inasmuch as, because
עַד דִּי	until

The interrogative pronouns are מַן ("who") and מָה ("what"). They can also be joined with the relative דִּי to form indefinite pronouns:

מַן דִּי	whoever
מָה דִּי	whatever

VOCABULARY

To Be Learned		*Reference*	
father	אַב	bless	בְּרַךְ
plural	אֲבָהָת	*D pass. participle*	מְבָרַךְ
destroy (H)	אבד	power	גְּבוּרָה
H imf 3 mpl	יְהוֹבְדוּן	companion	חֲבַר
H imf 2 ms	תְּהוֹבֵד	tell (D, H)	חוה
H infinitive	לְהוֹבָדָה	*D imf 1 s*	אַחֲוֵא
seek	בעה	*H infinitive*	לְהַחֲוָיָה
G infinitive	לְמִבְעֵה	inform (H)	ידע
reveal	גלה	*H perfect 3 ms*	הוֹדַע
passive perfect 3 ms	גְּלִי	thus	כֵּן
time	זְמָן	appoint (D)	מנה
wisdom	חָכְמָה	*G perfect 3 ms*	מַנִּי
enter	עלל	deep	עַמִּיק
G perfect 3 ms	עַל	establish, raise up (H)	קוּם
H imv 3 ms	הַעֵל	*H participle ms*	מְהָקֵים
thereupon	כָּל קֳבֵל דְּנָה	compassion	רַחֲמִין
secret	רָז	change (H—transitive)	שנה
praise (D)	שבח	*H participle ms*	מְהַשְׁנֵא
D participle ms	מְשַׁבַּח		

FROM THE BIBLE (Daniel 2:14–24)

בֵּאדַיִן דָּנִיֵּאל בְּעָה מִן מַלְכָּא דִּי זְמָן יִנְתֶּן לֵהּ וּפִשְׁרָא לְהַחֲוָיָה לְמַלְכָּא. אֱדַיִן דָּנִיֵּאל

לְבַיְתֵהּ אֲזַל וְלַחֲנַנְיָה מִישָׁאֵל וַעֲזַרְיָה חַבְרוֹהִי מִלְּתָא הוֹדַע וְרַחֲמִין לְמִבְעֵא מִן קֳדָם

אֱלָהּ שְׁמַיָּא עַל רָזָה דְּנָה דִּי לָא יְהוֹבְדוּן דָּנִיֵּאל וְחַבְרוֹהִי עִם חַכִּימֵי בָבֶל.

אֱדַיִן לְדָנִיֵּאל רָזָה גֱלִי. אֱדַיִן דָּנִיֵּאל בָּרִךְ לֶאֱלָהּ שְׁמַיָּא. עָנֵה דָנִיֵּאל וְאָמַר.

לֶהֱוֵא שְׁמֵהּ דִּי אֱלָהָא מְבָרַךְ מִן עָלְמָא וְעַד עָלְמָא דִּי חָכְמְתָא וּגְבוּרְתָא דִּי לֵהּ הִיא

וְהוּא מְהַשְׁנֵא עִדָּנַיָּא וְזִמְנַיָּא. מְהָקֵים מַלְכִין יָהֵב חָכְמְתָא לְחַכִּימִין. הוּא גָּלֵא

עַמִּיקָתָא. לָךְ אֱלָהּ אֲבָהָתִי מְשַׁבַּח אֲנָה דִּי חָכְמְתָא וּגְבוּרְתָא יְהַבְתְּ לִי וּכְעַן הוֹדַעְתַּנִי

דִּי בְעֵינָא מִנָּךְ דִּי מִלַּת מַלְכָּא הוֹדַעְתֶּנָא. כָּל קֳבֵל דְּנָה דָּנִיֵּאל עַל עַל אַרְיוֹךְ דִּי מַנִּי

מַלְכָּא לְהוֹבָדָה לְחַכִּימֵי בָבֶל. אֲזַל וְכֵן אֲמַר לֵהּ. לְחַכִּימֵי בָבֶל אַל תְּהוֹבֵד. הַעֵלְנִי

קֳדָם מַלְכָּא וּפִשְׁרָא לְמַלְכָּא אֲחַוֵּא.

Proper Nouns

אַרְיוֹךְ — the captain of Nebuchadnezzar's guard

דָּנִיֵּאל — a Jew who was taken to Babylon, where he served in the royal court, interpreting dreams and surviving great danger.

עֲזַרְיָה, מִישָׁאֵל, חֲנַנְיָה — young Judean exiles trained in the Babylonian court

EXERCISES

Translate into English:

(1) יָדַעְנָא רָזַיָּא אֵלֵּין.

(2) מַן בְּנָה הֵיכְלָא דֵךְ?

(3) סָפְרָא כְּתַב דִּי חָכְמָה אֲבָדָה מִבָּבֶל בְּזְמַן נְבוּכַדְנֶצַּר.

(4) דָּנֵיֵּאל עַל לִשְׁמַיָּא.

(5) כָּל קֳבֵל דְּנָה גֶּלִי דִּי מְהָקֵים מַלְכָּא רֵאשׁ פֶּחָה עַל קִרְיְתָא דָא.

(6) אִיתַי אֱנָשׁ דִּי בָּעֵה רַחֲמִין.

Translate into Aramaic:

(1) This father praises the law of God.

(2) I am authorized to seek that book in the treasure house.

(3) These provinces are under a strong king.

(4) They left that letter there.

(5) We are giving many vessels in the midst of the earth.

Chapter 15

G IMPERFECT

The verbal system of most Northwest Semitic languages has two major tenses (or aspects)—one formed by adding suffixes to the root (the perfect), while the other (the imperfect) adds prefixes, with suffixes used to indicate plurals. (By contrast, Akkadian, which is an East Semitic language, has two distinct prefix tenses—one for the past, and the other for future action.)

Having already examined Aramaic's perfect conjugation, we can now consider the imperfect. Although the vowels are somewhat different, the basic structure is the same as in Hebrew:

G Imperfect

	Singular	*Plural*
1st person	אֶכְתֻּב	נִכְתֻּב
2d masculine	תִּכְתֻּב	תִּכְתְּבוּן
feminine	תִּכְתְּבִין	תִּכְתְּבָן
3d masculine	יִכְתֻּב	יִכְתְּבוּן
feminine	תִּכְתֻּב	יִכְתְּבָן

As in Hebrew, the theme vowel (the one under the second root letter) is not fixed, but can vary from root to root. Although *u* is the most common theme vowel (as in the case of כתב above), it is not universal:

e.g., יִפֵּל (root נפל) he will fall
    * יִנְתֵּן (root נתן) he will give
    יִשְׁלַט (root שלט) he will rule
    יִלְבַּשׁ (root לבש) he will wear

---

* Notice that the initial נ does not assimilate in this form as it does in the Hebrew equivalent (יִתֵּן) and, indeed, in the form יִפֵּל given above.

A very important exception to this pattern involves the verb הוה (to be), in which several third person forms begin with ־ל:

לֶהֱוֵא	he will be
לֶהֱוֹן	they (masc.) will be
לֶהֱוְיָן	they (fem.) will be

Thus:

אֱלָהּ רַב הוֹדַע לְמַלְכָּא מָה דִּי לֶהֱוֵא אַחֲרֵי דְנָה

The great God informed the king what will be after this. (Daniel 4:45)

The jussive appears to be the same as the imperfect, although final ן may fall off of some plural forms.

VOCABULARY

To Be Learned			*Reference*	
stone	אֶבֶן		but	בְּרַם
break off	גזר		exile	גָּלוּ
is broken off	הִתְגְּזֶרֶת		arm	דְּרָע
be crushed	דקק		breast	חֲדֵה
H perfect 3 ms	הַדֵּק		tell	חוא
see	חזה		*H infinitive*	לְהַחֲוָיָה
clay	חֲסַף		inform (H)	ידע
mountain	טוּר		*H perfect 3 ms*	הוֹדַע
copper	נְחָשׁ		*H imperfect 3 mpl*	יְהוֹדְעוּן
iron	פַּרְזֶל		be able	יכל
statue	צְלֵם		thigh	יַרְכָה
foot	רְגַל		be able	כהל
			hit	מחא
			belly	מְעֵה
			enter	עלל
			H perfect 3 ms	הַנְעֵל
			find	שכח
			H perfect 1 s	הַשְׁכַּחַת
			leg	שָׁק

FROM THE BIBLE (Daniel 2:25–36)

אֱדַיִן אַרְיוֹךְ הַנְעֵל לְדָנִיֵּאל קֳדָם מַלְכָּא וְכֵן אֲמַר לֵהּ: הַשְׁכַּחַת גְּבַר מִן בְּנֵי גָלוּתָא

דִּי יְהוּד דִּי פִשְׁרָא לְמַלְכָּא יְהוֹדַע. עָנֵה מַלְכָּא וְאָמַר לְדָנִיֵּאל דִּי שְׁמֵהּ בֵּלְטְשַׁאצַּר:

הַאִיתָיךְ כָּהֵל לְהוֹדָעֻתַנִי חֶלְמָא דִּי חֲזֵית וּפִשְׁרֵהּ? עָנֵה דָנִיֵּאל קֳדָם מַלְכָּא וְאָמַר:

רָזָה דִּי מַלְכָּא שָׁאֵל לָא חַכִּימִין יָכְלִין לְהַחֲוָיָה לְמַלְכָּא בְּרַם אִיתַי אֱלָהּ בִּשְׁמַיָּא

גָּלֵא רָזִין וְהוֹדַע לְמַלְכָּא נְבוּכַדְנֶצַּר מָה דִּי לֶהֱוֵא. וַאֲנָה לָא בְחָכְמָה דִּי אִיתַי בִּי

רָזָא דְנָה גְּלִי לִי לָהֵן דִּי פִשְׁרָא לְמַלְכָּא יְהוֹדְעוּן. אַנְתְּ מַלְכָּא חָזֵה הֲוַיְתָ צֶלֶם

חַד שַׂגִּיא. צַלְמָא דִּכֵּן רַב. הוּא צַלְמָא — רֵאשֵׁהּ דִּי דְהַב טָב חֲדוֹהִי וּדְרָעוֹהִי

דִּי כְסַף מְעוֹהִי וְיַרְכָתֵהּ דִּי נְחָשׁ שָׁקוֹהִי דִּי פַרְזֶל רַגְלוֹהִי מִנְּהֵן דִּי פַרְזֶל וּמִנְּהֵן

דִּי חֲסַף. חָזֵה הֲוַיְתָ עַד דִּי הִתְגְּזֶרֶת אֶבֶן דִּי לָא בִידַיִן וּמְחָת לְצַלְמָא עַל רַגְלוֹהִי

דִּי פַרְזְלָא וְחַסְפָּא וְהַדֵּקֶת הִמּוֹן. בֵּאדַיִן דָּקוּ כַחֲדָה פַּרְזְלָא חַסְפָּא נְחָשָׁא כַּסְפָּא

וְדַהֲבָא וַהֲווֹ כְּעוּר מִן אִדְּרֵי קַיִט וּנְשָׂא הִמּוֹן רוּחָא וְכָל אֲתַר לָא הִשְׁתֲּכַח לְהוֹן

וְאַבְנָא דִּי מְחָת לְצַלְמָא הֲוָת לְטוּר רַב. דְּנָה חֶלְמָא וּפִשְׁרֵהּ נֵאמַר

קֳדָם מַלְכָּא.

EXERCISES

Conjugate the following verbs in the G imperfect:

		פרק	שלט
singular	1		
	2 m		
	2 f		
	3 m		
	3 f		
plural	1		
	2 m		
	2 f		
	3 m		
	3 f		

		דבח	נתן
singular	1		
	2 m		
	2 f		
	3 m		
	3 f		
plural	1		
	2 m		
	2 f		
	3 m		
	3 f		

Identify the form of the following imperfect verbs:

	Root	Person	Gender	Number
תֵּאכַל				
נֵאמַר				
אֶבְעֵא				
תֶּהֱוֵא				
לֶהֱוֹן				
נִכְתֻּב				
תַּעַבְדוּן				
יִפְלְחוּן				
אֶקְרֵא				

Translate into Aramaic:

(1) I will write a letter on the stone from the mountain.

(2) She will send a message to the scribe.

(3) He broke the foot and the head off of the statue.

(4) That man sees vessels of clay which Daniel smashed.

(5) There is iron under the earth.

(6) We will ask to build a palace there.

(7) The Judeans left copper in Babylon.

Chapter 16

ADJECTIVES AND GENITIVE CONSTRUCTIONS (דִּי)

Aramaic adjectives behave very much like nouns—they have number and gender, and can be determined or undetermined. Moreover, their endings are exactly the same as those for nouns.

		Masculine	*Feminine*
singular	absolute	רַחִיק	רַחִיקָה
	determined	רַחִיקָא	רַחִיקְתָּא
plural	absolute	רַחִיקִין	רַחִיקָן
	determined	* רַחִיקַיָּא	רַחִיקָתָא

In general, adjectives must agree with the noun that they modify in number, gender, and determination; however, predicate adjectives are always undetermined.

Another way in which Aramaic expresses description is with nouns. This is done by using genitival constructions, such as construct phrases in which two nouns are joined together:

שֵׁם אֱלָהָא the name of God

As in Hebrew, these word pairs are treated as if they were one word. Therefore, the first word loses its accent, with a resulting shift in vowels.

Another way of expressing genitival relationships is with the conjunction דִּי ("which, of"):

שֵׁם דִּי אֱלָהָא the name of God

---

* The ending for plural determined gentilics is יַ-ָ.

84

Later on, Aramaic inserted a pronominal suffix (see chapter 13), which anticipates the genitive word, into this construction:

שְׁמֵהּ דִּי אֱלָהָא   His name, the one of God

i.e., the name of God

This construction eventually became almost normative in both Hebrew and Aramaic. However, it was still relatively uncommon in the biblical period, although it does sometimes occur (e.g., הִנֵּה מִטָּתוֹ שֶׁלִּשְׁלֹמֹה — "Behold, the bed of Solomon," Song of Songs 3:7).

Genitival constructions are not limited to possession. They can also indicate the composition of an object or what it is attached to:

שְׁבִיבִין דִּי נוּר   flames of fire (Daniel 7:9)

צְלֵם דִּי דְהַב   statue of gold (Daniel 3:1)

אֶצְבְּעָן דִּי יַד אֱנָשׁ   fingers of a human hand,

i.e., human fingers (Daniel 5:5)

VOCABULARY

To Be Learned		*Reference*	
another	אָחֳרִי	after	אַחֲרֵי
field	בַּר	face (pl.)	אֲנַף
dwell	דּוּר	finger	אֶצְבַּע
G participle m pl	דָּאְרִין	after (lit. "in place of")	בָּתַר
animal	חֵיוָה	reveal	גלה
be able	יכל	*G infinitive*	לְמִגְלֵא
fall	נפל	smash (H)	דקק
bow down	סגד	*H participle m s*	מְהַדֵּק
fourth	רְבִיעָי	destroy (D)	חבל
rule	שלט	*Dt (passive) imf 3 fs*	תִּתְחַבַּל
third	תְּלִיתָי	inform (H)	ידע
		H imf 3 ms	הוֹדַע
		day	יוֹם
		bird	עוֹף
		divided	פְּלִיגָה
		rise	קוּם
		H imf 3 ms	יְקִים
		foot	רְגַל
		leave, abandon	שבק
		Gt (passive) imf 2 fs	תִּשְׁתְּבִק
		breakable	תְּבִיר

FROM THE BIBLE (Daniel 2:37–49)

אַנְתְּ מַלְכָּא מֶלֶךְ מַלְכַיָּא דִּי אֱלָהּ שְׁמַיָּא מַלְכוּתָא יְהַב לָךְ וּבְכָל דִּי דָארִין בְּנֵי אֲנָשָׁא חֵיוַת בָּרָא וְעוֹף שְׁמַיָּא יְהַב בִּידָךְ וְהַשְׁלְטָךְ בְּכָלְּהוֹן. אַנְתְּ הוּא רֵאשָׁה דִּי דַהֲבָא. וּבָתְרָךְ תְּקוּם מַלְכוּ אָחֳרִי אֲרַעָא מִנָּךְ וּמַלְכוּ תְלִיתָיָא אָחֳרִי דִּי נְחָשָׁא דִּי תִשְׁלַט בְּכָל אַרְעָא. וּמַלְכוּ רְבִיעָיָה תֶּהֱוֵא תַקִּיפָה כְּפַרְזְלָא מְהַדֵּק כֹּלָּא. וְדִי חֲזַיְתָה רַגְלַיָּא וְאֶצְבְּעָתָא מִנְּהֵן חֲסַף וּמִנְּהֵן פַּרְזֶל מַלְכוּ פְלִיגָה תֶּהֱוֵה וְאֶצְבְּעָת רַגְלַיָּא מִנְּהֵן פַּרְזֶל וּמִנְּהֵן חֲסַף מִן מַלְכוּתָא תֶּהֱוֵה תַקִּיפָה וּמִנַּהּ תֶּהֱוֵה תְבִירָה. וּבְיוֹמֵיהוֹן דִּי מַלְכַיָּא אִנּוּן יְקִים אֱלָהּ שְׁמַיָּא מַלְכוּ דִּי לְעָלְמִין לָא תִתְחַבַּל וּמַלְכוּתָה לְעַם אָחֳרָן לָא תִשְׁתְּבִק וְהִיא תְּקוּם לְעָלְמַיָּא. כָּל קֳבֵל דִּי חֲזַיְתָ דִּי מִטּוּרָא אִתְגְּזֶרֶת אֶבֶן דִּי לָא בִידַיִן וְהַדֵּקֶת פַּרְזְלָא נְחָשָׁא חַסְפָּא כַּסְפָּא וְדַהֲבָא. אֱלָהּ רַב הוֹדַע לְמַלְכָּא מָה דִּי לֶהֱוֵא אַחֲרֵי דְנָה. בֵּאדַיִן מַלְכָּא נְבוּכַדְנֶצַּר נְפַל עַל אַנְפּוֹהִי וּלְדָנִיֵּאל סְגִד. עֲנֵה מַלְכָּא לְדָנִיֵּאל וְאָמַר. אֱלָהֲכוֹן הוּא אֱלָהּ אֱלָהִין וְגָלֵה רָזִין דִּי יְכֵלְתָּ לְמִגְלֵא רָזָה דְנָה. אֱדַיִן מַלְכָּא הַשְׁלְטֵהּ עַל כָּל מְדִינַת בָּבֶל וְעַל כָּל חַכִּימֵי בָּבֶל.

EXERCISES

Translate into English:

(1) אֲנַחְנָא דָאֲרִין בְּבֵית דִּי דְהַב.

(2) יִשְׁלַט מַלְכָּא עַל מְדִינַת עֲבַר־נַהֲרָא.

(3) חַגֵּי הַדֵּק חֵיוָה תַקִּיפָה.

(4) אֱנָשׁ רְבִיעִי אֲזַל.

(5) הִמּוֹ יִסְגְּדוּן לְרֵאשֵׁהּ דִּי צַלְמָא.

(6) אִיתַי אֶצְבְּעָן שַׂגִּיאָן עַל יַד דָּרְיָוֶשׁ.

Translate into Aramaic:

(1) The interpretation of the fourth decree is written in the temple.

(2) They fall from their feet and they pray to God.

(3) We went out to the distant field.

(4) The wise scribe came with a third message.

(5) We were able to build another house.

Chapter 17

Numbers

We have already encountered several Aramaic numerals which are etymologically related to their Hebrew equivalents. Thus "1" is חַד, which is only lacking the initial א of its Hebrew cognate אֶחָד. "3" and "6" are תְּלָת and שֵׁת, reflecting the Aramaic realization of Semitic *th* as ת, where Hebrew uses שׁ (hence שָׁלוֹשׁ and שֵׁשׁ).

As in Hebrew, Aramaic numerals, which can appear either before or after the nouns to which they refer, have both masculine and feminine forms.

	Masculine	*Feminine*
1	חַד	חֲדָה
2	תְּרֵין (תְּרֵי)	תַּרְתֵּין (תַּרְתֵּי)
3	תְּלָתָה	תְּלָת
4	אַרְבְּעָה	אַרְבַּע
5	חַמְשָׁא	חֲמֵשׁ
6	שִׁתָּה	שֵׁת
7	שִׁבְעָה	שְׁבַע
8	תְּמָנְיָה	תְּמָנֶה
9	תִּשְׁעָה	תְּשַׁע
10	עֲשָׂרָה	עֲשַׂר

As in Hebrew, except for "1," the simpler form is used with feminine nouns, whereas the form ending with הָ‎ is used with masculine nouns:

e.g.,   גֻּבְרִין אַרְבְּעָא   4 men (Daniel 3:25)

                       אַמִּין שֵׁת   6 cubits (Daniel 3:1)

The number "2" has a construct form (תְּרֵי‎), which is used in the phrase for "12" (תְּרֵי־עֲשַׂר‎).

The decades between ten and one hundred are based on plural forms of the digits; thus twenty is עֶשְׂרִין‎, thirty is תְּלָתִין‎, and so on. Larger numbers include מְאָה‎ (100), אֲלַף‎ (1,000) and רִבּוֹ‎ (10,000). (Recall that 200 is מָאתַיִן‎, as noted on p. 27.)

As the determined state became the "normal" form for nouns in later Aramaic, the language had to develop another way to indicate whether a word was determined or not. To do this, the numeral "one" (חַד‎) was used as a marker of *in*determinacy. Intimations of this practice can be found in the Bible:

צְלֵם חַד   an image (Daniel 2:31)

מְגִלָּה חֲדָה   a scroll (Ezra 6:2)

חַד‎ is also used to indicate multiples:

חַד שִׁבְעָה   seven times more than. . . . (Daniel 3:19)

Ordinal numbers (except for "2") end with יִ‎:

first	קַדְמָי
second	* תִּנְיָן
third	תְּלִיתָי
fourth	רְבִיעִי

---

*This form is much closer to the Hebrew שֵׁנִי‎ than is the cardinal form תְּרֵין‎.

VOCABULARY

To Be Learned		*Reference*	
furnace	אַתּוּן	live (G)	חיה
music	זְמָר	strength	חַיִל
kind	זַן	dedication	חֲנֻכָּה
burn	יקד	when	כְּדִי
fire	נוּר	gather	כנש
worship	פלח	*G infinitive*	לְמִכְנַשׁ
sound	קָל	*Dt participle m pl*	מִתְכַּנְּשִׁין
horn	קֶרֶן	herald	כָּרוֹז
throw	רמה	prefect	סְגַן
Gt imf 3 ms	יִתְרְמֵא	rise	קוּם
hear	שמע	*G participle m pl*	קָאְמִין
		H perfect 3 ms	הֲקֵים
		call	קרא
		approach	קרב
		pay attention	שִׂים טְעֵם

FROM THE BIBLE (Daniel 3:1–12)

נְבוּכַדְנֶצַּר מַלְכָּא עֲבַד צְלֵם דִּי דְהַב וּשְׁלַח לְמִכְנַשׁ לְסִגְנַיָּא וּפַחֲוָתָא לַחֲנֻכַּת צַלְמָא דִּי

הֲקֵים נְבוּכַדְנֶצַּר מַלְכָּא. בֵּאדַיִן מִתְכַּנְּשִׁין סִגְנַיָּא וּפַחֲוָתָא לַחֲנֻכַּת צַלְמָא דִּי הֲקֵים

נְבוּכַדְנֶצַּר מַלְכָּא וְקָאֲמִין לָקֳבֵל צַלְמָא דִּי הֲקֵים נְבוּכַדְנֶצַּר וְכָרוֹזָא קָרֵא בְחָיִל:

לְכוֹן אָמְרִין עַמְמַיָּא: בְּעִדָּנָא דִּי תִשְׁמְעוּן קָל קַרְנָא וְכֹל זְנֵי זְמָרָא תִּפְּלוּן וְתִסְגְּדוּן

לְצֶלֶם דַּהֲבָא דִּי הֲקֵים נְבוּכַדְנֶצַּר מַלְכָּא וּמַן דִּי לָא יִפֵּל וְיִסְגֻּד יִתְרְמֵא לְגוֹא אַתּוּן

נוּרָא יָקִדְתָּא. כָּל קֳבֵל דְּנָה בֵּהּ זִמְנָא כְּדִי שָׁמְעִין כָּל עַמְמַיָּא קָל קַרְנָא וְכֹל זְנֵי

זְמָרָא נָפְלִין כָּל עַמְמַיָּא סָגְדִין לְצֶלֶם דַּהֲבָא דִּי הֲקֵים נְבוּכַדְנֶצַּר מַלְכָּא. כָּל קֳבֵל

דְּנָה בֵּהּ זִמְנָא קְרִבוּ גֻּבְרִין כַּשְׂדָּאִין. עֲנוֹ וְאָמְרִין לִנְבוּכַדְנֶצַּר מַלְכָּא: מַלְכָּא לְעָלְמִין

חֱיִי. אַנְתְּ מַלְכָּא שָׂמְתָּ טְעֵם דִּי כָל אֱנָשׁ דִּי יִשְׁמַע קָל קַרְנָא וְכֹל זְנֵי זְמָרָא יִפֵּל וְיִסְגֻּד

לְצֶלֶם דַּהֲבָא וּמַן דִּי לָא יִפֵּל וְיִסְגֻּד יִתְרְמֵא לְגוֹא אַתּוּן נוּרָא יָקִדְתָּא. אִיתַי גֻּבְרִין

יְהוּדָאִין שַׁדְרַךְ מֵישַׁךְ וַעֲבֵד־נְגוֹ. גֻּבְרַיָּא אִלֵּךְ לָא שָׂמוּ עֲלָיךְ מַלְכָּא טְעֵם. לֵאלָהָיךְ

לָא פָלְחִין וּלְצֶלֶם דַּהֲבָא דִּי הֲקֵימְתָּ לָא סָגְדִין.

Proper Nouns

שַׁדְרַךְ, מֵישַׁךְ, עֲבֵד־נְגוֹ—Names given to Hananiah, Mishael, and Azariah by Babylonian officials

EXERCISES

How many different pairs of numbers can you list that add up to 10?

_____ + _____   _____ + _____

_____ + _____   _____ + _____

_____ + _____

Fill in the blank with the correct Aramaic numbers:

4 + 5 = _____ 10^3 = _____

7 - _____ = 6   2 + _____ = 5

8 ÷ 4 = _____   20 × 10 = _____

20 ÷ _____ = 2   4 + 2 = _____

8 - 3 = _____ 3^2 = _____

1 + 2 = _____   56 ÷ 8 = _____

2 × 3 = _____   10 - 2 = _____

8 ÷ 2 = _____   60 + 40 = _____

_____ + 1 = 6   17 ÷ 17 = _____

11 - 9 = _____   24 - _____ = 16

7 + 0 = _____   19,286 + _____ = 29,286

_____ - 4 = 2   10 × 2 = _____

17 - _____ = 13   6 + 6 _____

Translate into Aramaic:

(1) The first man is the head of the province.

(2) We pray to the God of heaven.

(3) Five secrets were in the dream.

(4) The sound went out from Babylon like a fire.

(5) They will worship a statue of iron.

(6) There are 10,000 books burning in the palace.

(7) One horn is thrown into the furnace.

(8) They heard four kinds of music.

Chapter 18

G-IMPERATIVE AND INFINITIVE

As in Hebrew, Aramaic imperatives are based on the corresponding imperfect forms, from which the (pronominal) prefix has been removed and some necessary adjustments made for shifting vowels. The resulting forms are:

	Singular	*Plural*
masculine	כְּתֻב	כְּתֻבוּ
feminine	כְּתֻבִי	כְּתֻבָה

Technically, the forms derive from the jussive, which is very much like the imperfect except without the final ן on plural forms. It is, therefore, understandable, that negative commands are expressed with the full jussive along with אַל:

חֶלְמָא וּפִשְׁרֵא אַל יְבַהֲלָךְ

> Don't let the dream and interpretation frighten you. (Daniel 4:16)

That leaves only one G form which has not yet been described—the infinitive. It is characterized by a prefixed -מִ:

מִכְתַּב

The infinitive frequently appears with the preposition -לְ and sometimes with the negative לָא to express a prohibition (see the inscription on p. 171).

Interestingly, the infinitive of the verb בנה ("build") occurs with both a prefixed -לְ (לִבְנֵא in Ezra 5:3, 13) and, sometimes, an additional מ (לְמִבְנֵא in Ezra 5:2, 6:8). This form is expanded still further in one passage by the addition of a feminine (or perhaps determinative) ending: לְמִבְנְיָה (Ezra 5:9).

95

VOCABULARY

To Be Learned		*Reference*	
heat	אֲזָה	see	חֲזָה
G infinitive	לְמֵזֵא	*G pass. part.* ("proper")	חֲזֵה
pass. part.	אֲזֵה	urgent	מַחְצְפָה
come	אֲתָא	because	מִן דִּי
H (bring) passive		go up	סְלֵק
perfect 3 mpl	הֵיתָיוּ	*H perf. 3mpl* (sacrifice)	הַסִּקוּ
H infinitive	לְהַיְתָיָה	true	צְדָא
need	חַשַׁח	rise	קוּם
hand	יַד	*H perfect 1 sg*	הֲקֵימֶת
very	יַתִּיר	anger	רְגַז
bind (D)	כְּפַת	throw	רְמָה
D infinitive	לְכַפָּתָה	*Gt imperfect 2 mpl*	תִּתְרְמוֹן
D pass. part. mpl	מְכַפְּתִין	seven	שִׁבְעָה
ready	עֲתִיד	seven times	חַד שִׁבְעָה
kill (D)	קְטַל	reply (H)	תּוּב
he saves	יְשֵׁיזִב	*H infinitive + 2 ms*	לַהֲתָבוּתָךְ
imperf. 3ms + 2 mpl	יְשֵׁיזְבִנְכוֹן		
infinitive + 1pl	לְשֵׁיזָבוּתַנָא		
hour	שָׁעָה		

FROM THE BIBLE (Daniel 3:13–23)

בֵּאדַיִן נְבוּכַדְנֶצַּר בִּרְגַז אֲמַר לְהַיְתָיָה לְשַׁדְרַךְ מֵישַׁךְ וַעֲבֵד־נְגוֹ. בֵּאדַיִן גֻּבְרַיָּא אִלֵּךְ

הֵיתָיוּ קֳדָם מַלְכָּא. עָנֵה נְבוּכַדְנֶצַּר וְאָמַר לְהוֹן: הַצְדָּא שַׁדְרַךְ מֵישַׁךְ וַעֲבֵד נְגוֹ

לֵאלָהַי לָא אִיתֵיכוֹן פָּלְחִין וּלְצֶלֶם דַּהֲבָא דִּי הֲקֵימֶת לָא סָגְדִין? כְּעַן הֵן אִיתֵיכוֹן

עֲתִידִין דִּי בְעִדָּנָא דִּי תִשְׁמְעוּן קָל קַרְנָא וְכֹל זְנֵי זְמָרָא תִּפְּלוּן וְתִסְגְּדוּן לְצַלְמָא דִּי

עַבְדֵת וְהֵן לָא תִסְגְּדוּן בַּהּ שַׁעֲתָה תִּתְרְמוֹן לְגוֹא אַתּוּן נוּרָא יָקִדְתָּא. וּמַן הוּא אֱלָהּ דִּי

יְשֵׁיזְבִנְכוֹן מִן יְדָי. עֲנוֹ שַׁדְרַךְ מֵישַׁךְ וַעֲבֵד־נְגוֹ וְאָמְרִין לְמַלְכָּא: נְבוּכַדְנֶצַּר לָא

הַשְׁחִין אֲנַחְנָא עַל דְּנָה פִּתְגָם לַהֲתָבוּתָךְ. הֵן אִיתַי אֱלָהַנָא דִּי אֲנַחְנָא פָלְחִין יָכִל

לְשֵׁיזָבוּתַנָא מִן אַתּוּן נוּרָא יָקִדְתָּא וּמִן יְדָךְ מַלְכָּא יְשֵׁיזִב וְהֵן לָא יְדִיעַ לֶהֱוֵא לָךְ

מַלְכָּא דִּי לֵאלָהָיךְ לָא אִיתַנָא פָלְחִין וּלְצֶלֶם דַּהֲבָא דִּי הֲקֵימְתָּ לָא נִסְגֻּד. בֵּאדַיִן

נְבוּכַדְנֶצַּר עֲנֵה וְאָמַר לְמֵזֵא לְאַתּוּנָא חַד שִׁבְעָה עַל דִּי חֲזֵה לְמֵזְיֵהּ וּלְכַפָּתָה לְשַׁדְרַךְ

מֵישַׁךְ וַעֲבֵד־נְגוֹ לְמִרְמֵא לְאַתּוּן נוּרָא יָקִדְתָּא. כָּל קֳבֵל דְּנָה מִן דִּי מִלַּת מַלְכָּא

מַחְצְפָה וְאַתּוּנָא אֵזֵה יַתִּירָא אֵזֵה יַתִּירָא גֻּבְרַיָּא אִלֵּךְ דִּי הַסִּקוּ לְשַׁדְרַךְ מֵישַׁךְ וַעֲבֵד־נְגוֹ קַטִּל הִמּוֹן

נוּרָא. וְגֻבְרַיָּא אִלֵּךְ תְּלָתֵּהוֹן שַׁדְרַךְ מֵישַׁךְ וַעֲבֵד־נְגוֹ נְפַלוּ לְגוֹא־אַתּוּן נוּרָא־יָקִדְתָּא

מְכַפְּתִין.

NOTE that 3d person plural verbs are often used indefinitely ("they . . ."); in such cases, they are often best translated into English with passive verbs. For example, גֻּבְרַיָּא אִלֵּךְ הֵיתָיו literally means "they [indefinite] brought those men," but is better rendered, "these men were brought."

EXERCISES

Fill in the complete conjugation of the verb כתב:

		Perfect	*Imperfect*	*Participles*		*Imperative*
				Active	*Passive*	
sing.	1 cs					
	2ms			ms		
	2fs			fs		
	3ms					
	3fs			mp		
	fp			fp		
pl.	1cp					
	2mp					
	2fp				*Infinitive:*	
	3mp					
	3fp					

What form are the following verbs?

	Root	Form	Person	Gender	Number	Meaning
מֶעְבַּד						
שְׁבַקוּ						
מֶחֱזֵא						
אָכְלִי						
מִגְלֵא						
אֲמַר						
מִבְנֵא						
מִכְנַשׁ						
מִבְעֵא						
מִקְרֵא						
מְפַשַּׁר						

Translate into Aramaic:

(1) Do not kill these strong men.

(2) God is ready to make a place in the heavens.

(3) The hand will write a very good letter.

(4) The king needs to burn this city with fire.

(5) Hear the sound of music in the distant field.

(6) They brought the bound scribe to a dunghill.

(7) The people will save many treasures.

Chapter 19

D CONJUGATION

The second major conjugation in Aramaic is called D because the middle letter of the root is *doubled.* (It is also known as *paᶜᶜel.*) As in the Hebrew *piᶜel,* a *dagesh* is used to indicate the doubled letter. Also as in Hebrew, the first root letter of Aramaic verbs in the D conjugation always has a vowel. (This is not true of G forms, such as כְּתַבוּ.) These two features are related: since the first of the two letters indicated by the *dagesh* always has a *sh'va,* it must be preceded by a vowel.

In other regards, the prefixes and suffixes are the same in the D as in the G conjugation:

		Perfect	Imperfect
Singular	1	קַבְּלֵת	אֲקַבֵּל
	2 masculine	קַבֵּלְתְּ	תְּקַבֵּל
	2 feminine	קַבֵּלְתִּי	תְּקַבְּלִין
	3 masculine	קַבֵּל	יְקַבֵּל
	3 feminine	קַבְּלַת	תְּקַבֵּל
Plural	1	קַבֵּלְנָא	נְקַבֵּל
	2 masculine	קַבֵּלְתּוּן	תְּקַבְּלוּן
	2 feminine	קַבֵּלְתֵּן	תְּקַבְּלָן
	3 masculine	קַבִּלוּ	יְקַבְּלוּן
	3 feminine	קַבְּלָה	יְקַבְּלָן

If the second consonant is a guttural and cannot, therefore, be doubled (i.e. take a *dagesh*), the preceding vowel is usually lengthened:

e.g., בָּרְכֵת perfect, 1 singular

בָּרֵךְ perfect, 3 masculine singular

100

As one would expect, imperative forms correspond to those for the second person imperfect, without the prefixed -תְּ:

D Imperative

	Masculine	*Feminine*
Singular	קַבֵּל	קַבְּלִי
Plural	קַבְּלוּ	קַבֵּלָה

Finally, the participle and infinitive forms follow patterns which, as we shall see, are typical of all the derived (non-G) conjugations: participles begin with מ- and infinitives end with the suffix הָ-:

D Participle

	Masculine	*Feminine*
Singular	מְקַבֵּל	מְקַבְּלָה
Plural	מְקַבְּלִין	מְקַבְּלָן

D Infinitive   קַבָּלָה

VOCABULARY

To Be Learned		*Reference*	
four	אַרְבַּע	sign	אָת
body	גְּשֵׁם	bless (D)	ברך
generation	דָּר	resemble	דמה
damage	חֲבָל	behold	הָא
surely	יַצִּיב	is it not (interrogative)	הֲלָא
how	כְּמָה	scorch	חרך
grow great (G)	שׂגא	*Dt (passive) pf 3 ms*	הִתְחָרַךְ

	To Be Learned			*Reference*	
hair	. . . .	שְׂעַר	angel	. . . .	מַלְאַךְ
dominion	. . . .	שָׁלְטָן	make, do	. . . .	עבד
loosen	. . . .	שׁרה		*Gt (pass.) imperfect*	
	pass. participle mpl . . .	שָׁרַיִן		*3ms*	יִתְעֲבֵד
			go out	. . . .	נפק
				imperative mpl	פֻּקוּ
			cause to prosper (H)	. . . . .	צלח
			negligence (?)	. . . .	שָׁלָה
			three	. . . .	תְּלָת

FROM THE BIBLE (Daniel 3:24–33)

אֱדַיִן נְבוּכַדְנֶצַּר מַלְכָּא קָם עָנֵה וְאָמַר: הֲלָא גֻבְרִין תְּלָתָא רְמֵינָא לְגוֹא נוּרָא מְכַפְּתִין?

עָנַיִן וְאָמְרִין לְמַלְכָּא: יַצִּיבָא מַלְכָּא. עָנֵה וְאָמַר: הָא אֲנָה חָזֵה גֻּבְרִין אַרְבְּעָה שְׁרַיִן

מַהְלְכִין בְּגוֹא נוּרָא וַחֲבָל לָא אִיתַי בְּהוֹן וְרֵוֵהּ דִּי רְבִיעָיָא דָּמֵה לְבַר אֱלָהִין. בֵּאדַיִן קְרֵב

נְבוּכַדְנֶצַּר לִתְרַע אַתּוּן נוּרָא יָקִדְתָּא עָנֵה וְאָמַר: שַׁדְרַךְ מֵישַׁךְ וַעֲבֵד־נְגוֹ עַבְדוֹהִי דִּי אֱלָהָא

עִלָּאָה פֻּקוּ וֶאֱתוֹ. בֵּאדַיִן נָפְקִין שַׁדְרַךְ מֵישַׁךְ וַעֲבֵד־נְגוֹ מִן גּוֹא נוּרָא. לָא שְׁלֵט נוּרָא

בְּגֶשְׁמְהוֹן וּשְׂעַר רֵאשְׁהוֹן לָא הִתְחָרַךְ. עָנֵה נְבוּכַדְנֶצַּר וְאָמַר: בְּרִיךְ אֱלָהֲהוֹן דִּי

שַׁדְרַךְ מֵישַׁךְ וַעֲבֵד־נְגוֹ דִּי שְׁלַח מַלְאֲכֵהּ וְשֵׁיזִב לְעַבְדוֹהִי דִּי יְהַבוּ גֶשְׁמְהוֹן דִּי לָא

יִפְלְחוּן וְלָא יִסְגְּדוּן לְכָל אֱלָהּ לָהֵן לֵאלָהֲהוֹן. וּמִנִּי שִׂים טְעֵם דִּי כָל עַם דִּי יֵאמַר

שָׁלָה עַל אֱלָהֲהוֹן דִּי שַׁדְרַךְ מֵישַׁךְ וַעֲבֵד־נְגוֹ הַדָּמִין יִתְעֲבֵד וּבַיְתֵהּ נְוָלִי יִתְעֲבֵד כָּל קֳבֵל דִּי לָא אִיתַי

אֱלָהּ אָחֳרָן דִּי יִכֻּל לְהַצָּלָה כִּדְנָה. בֵּאדַיִן מַלְכָּא הַצְלַח לְשַׁדְרַךְ מֵישַׁךְ וַעֲבֵד־נְגוֹ בִּמְדִינַת בָּבֶל.

נְבוּכַדְנֶצַּר מַלְכָּא לְכָל עַמְמַיָּא דִּי דָאֲרִין בְּכָל אַרְעָא: שְׁלָמְכוֹן יִשְׂגֵּא. אָתַיָּא דִּי

עֲבַד עִמִּי אֱלָהָא עִלָּאָה שְׁפַר קֳדָמַי לְהַחֲוָיָה. אָתוֹהִי כְּמָה רַבְרְבִין וְתִמְהוֹהִי כְּמָה תַקִּיפִין. מַלְכוּתֵהּ מַלְכוּת עָלַם וְשָׁלְטָנֵהּ עִם דָּר וְדָר.

EXERCISES

Identify the form of the following verbs which appear in the Bible in the D conjugation:

	Root	Tense	Person	Gender	Number
מְמַלֵּל					
בִּטְּלוּ					
יְטַעֲמוּן					
שַׁבְּחֵת					
מְהַדַּר					
חַבְּלוּ					
לְנַסָּכָה					
הַדְּרֵת					
חַבָּלָה					
יְבַקַּר					
מְמַלְלָא					
מְהַלֵּךְ					
מַנִּיתָ					
מְפַשַּׁר					
תְּקַבְּלוּן					
קַטֵּל					

	Root	Tense	Person	Gender	Number
יְשַׁמְּשׁוּן					
שַׁבַּחְתָּ					
מְצַבְּעִין					
לְקַטָּלָה					
יְמַלֵּל					
מְשָׁרֵא					
יְבַהֲלוּ					
בַּדַּרוּ					
מְשַׁבַּח					

Fill in the full conjugation of the verb חבל ("damage") in the D:

	Perfect	Imperfect	Participles	Imperative
sing. 1 cs				
2ms			ms	
2fs			fs	
3ms				
3fs			mp	
fp			fp	
pl. 1cp				
2mp				
2fp			*Infinitive:*	
3mp				
3fp				

Translate into Aramaic:

(1) They bound his body from head to foot.

(2) Surely, we will destroy four provinces.

(3) The king gave dominion to his son for eternity.

(4) How wise you are to leave the rebellious city in peace.

(5) She is praising the judge, who grew great in this generation.

(6) I searched in the treasure house, and there was damage there.

(7) Tell us the interpretation of your dream.

(8) The wise men said to loosen the hair from my head.

Chapter 20

H CONJUGATION

Semitic languages have four basic verbal conjugations, which are generally identified by the letters G, D, H, and N on the basis of their form. (The Hebrew terms *pi'el, hif'il,* and *nif'al* correspond to the vocalization of the 3d person masculine singular perfect of each conjugation; according to this system, the *qal,* which literally means "simple," would be called *pa'al.*) We have already considered the Aramaic G (chapters 8, 9, 15, and 18) and D (chapter 19) conjugations. Since biblical Aramaic has no N (*nif'al*) conjugation, that leaves only the H.

Its general pattern is the same as that of the other conjugations, except for the obvious presence of the prefixed ה-. Since that usually has an "*a*" vowel, the conjugation is sometimes called the <u>haf</u>'el in contrast to the <u>hif</u>'il. However, unlike Hebrew, the initial ה is usually retained in Aramaic participles and imperfects. (It typically elides in Hebrew so that מְהַשְׁלִיךְ becomes מַשְׁלִיךְ and תְּהַשְׁלִיךְ becomes תַּשְׁלִיךְ).

			Perfect	*Imperfect*
Singular	1		הַשְׁלֵטֶת	אֲהַשְׁלֵט
	2	masculine	הַשְׁלֵטְתְּ	תְּהַשְׁלֵט
	2	feminine	הַשְׁלֵטְתִּי	תְּהַשְׁלְטִין
	3	masculine	הַשְׁלֵט	יְהַשְׁלֵט
	3	feminine	הַשְׁלֵטַת	תְּהַשְׁלֵט
Plural	1		הַשְׁלֵטְנָא	נְהַשְׁלֵט
	2	masculine	הַשְׁלֵטְתּוּן	תְּהַשְׁלְטוּן
	2	feminine	הַשְׁלֵטְתֵּן	תְּהַשְׁלְטָן
	3	masculine	הַשְׁלֵטוּ	יְהַשְׁלְטוּן
	3	feminine	הַשְׁלֵטָה	יְהַשְׁלְטָן

Having said this, we should add that the הַ- does sometimes elide in biblical Aramaic, precisely as in Hebrew. (This may be due to Hebrew influence.)

106

As was true with the G and D conjugations, in Aramaic as in Hebrew, the imperative forms are based on the imperfect, without the pronominal prefixes:

H Imperative

	Masculine	*Feminine*
Singular	הַשְׁלֵט	הַשְׁלְטִי
Plural	הַשְׁלְטוּ	הַשְׁלְטָה

The prefixed הַ-, which is characteristic of this conjugation, is also retained in the participles:

H Participle

	Masculine	*Feminine*
Singular	מְהַשְׁלֵט	מְהַשְׁלְטָה
Plural	מְהַשְׁלְטִין	מְהַשְׁלְטָן

Finally, the H infinitive is, like the D, characterized by the ending הָ-ָ:

הַשְׁלָטָה

VOCABULARY

To Be Learned		*Reference*	
tree	אִילָן	last	אָחֳרֵין
behold	אֲלוּ	trouble	אֲנַס
disturb (D)	בהל	vision	חֱזוּ
fear (D—scare)	דחל	seek shade (H)	טלל
magician	חַרְטֹם	food	מָזוֹן
foliage	עֳפִי	reach	מטא

To Be Learned

holy . . . . קַדִּישׁ

grow . . . . רבה

wind . . . . רוּחַ

under . . . . תְּחוֹת

Reference

enter . . . . עלל

G participle ms . . . . . . עַל

G participle mpl . . . . עָלִּין

H infinitive . . . . . . לְהַנְעָלָה

branch . . . . עֲנַף

bird . . . . צִפַּר

height . . . . רוּם

beautiful . . . . שַׁפִּיר

FROM THE BIBLE (Daniel 4:1–9)

אֲנָה נְבוּכַדְנֶצַּר הֲוֵית בְּבֵיתִי. חֵלֶם חֲזֵית וִידַחֲלִנַּנִי. וְחֶזְוֵי רֵאשִׁי יְבַהֲלֻנַּנִי וּמִנִּי שִׂים
טְעֵם לְהַנְעָלָה קֳדָמַי לְכֹל חַכִּימֵי בָבֶל דִּי פְשַׁר חֶלְמָא יְהוֹדְעֻנַּנִי. בֵּאדַיִן עָלְלִין
חַרְטֻמַיָּא וְכַשְׂדָּיֵא וְחֶלְמָא אָמַר אֲנָה קֳדָמֵיהוֹן וּפִשְׁרֵהּ לָא מְהוֹדְעִין לִי. וְעַד אָחֳרֵין
עַל קָדָמַי דָּנִיֵּאל דִּי שְׁמֵהּ בֵּלְטְשַׁאצַּר כְּשֻׁם אֱלָהִי וְדִי רוּח אֱלָהִין קַדִּישִׁין בֵּהּ וְחֶלְמָא
קֳדָמוֹהִי אַמְרֵת: בֵּלְטְשַׁאצַּר רַב חַרְטֻמַיָּא דִּי אֲנָה יִדְעֵת דִּי רוּחַ אֱלָהִין קַדִּישִׁין בָּךְ
וְכָל רָז לָא אָנֵס לָךְ. חֶזְוֵי חֶלְמִי דִי חֲזֵית וּפִשְׁרֵהּ אֱמַר. וְחֶזְוֵי רֵאשִׁי חָזֵה הֲוֵית
וַאֲלוּ אִילָן בְּגוֹא אַרְעָא וְרוּמֵהּ שַׂגִּיא. רְבָה אִילָנָא וְרוּמֵהּ יִמְטֵא לִשְׁמַיָּא. עָפְיֵהּ
שַׁפִּיר וּמָזוֹן לְכֹלָּא בֵהּ. תְּחֹתוֹהִי תַּטְלֵל חֵיוַת בָּרָא וּבְעַנְפוֹהִי יְדֻרָן צִפֲּרֵי שְׁמַיָּא.

Proper Names

בֵּלְטְשַׁאצַּר — The Babylonian name given to Daniel (see Daniel 1:7), which means "May he protect his life" in Akkadian.

EXERCISES

Identify the form of the following H verbs:

	Root	Tense	Person	Gender	Number
מַהְלְכִין					
לְהַחֲוָיָה					
נְהַחֲוֵה					
הֻשְׁפָּלָה					
הֶחֱסְנוּ					
לְהַשְׁנָיָה					
הוֹדַעְנָא					
מְהוֹדְעִין					
מְהַנְזְקַת					
תְּהַנְזִק					
הַצְלַח					
מְהַחְצְפָה					
יְהֻשְׁפַּל					
הַרְגִּזוּ					
הַרְגִּשׁוּ					
הַשְׁכַּחַת					
לְהַשְׁכָּחָה					
מְהַשְׁנֵא					

Fill in the full conjugation of the verb קְרַב in the H:

		Perfect	*Imperfect*	*Participles*	*Imperative*
sing.	1 cs				
	2ms		ms		
	2fs		fs		
	3ms				
	3fs		mp		
	fp		fp		
pl.	1cp				
	2mp				
	2fp			*Infinitive:*	
	3mp				
	3fp				

Translate into Aramaic:

(1) The sound of the horn reaches the heavens.

(2) Behold, the wind is smashing the vessels under the palace.

(3) The hair grew like foliage.

(4) The bird brought gold out of the tree.

(5) The word of the king frightened the holy men of Babylon.

(6) The magicians fear that God will make Daniel ruler over them.

(7) The scribes said to bring the message before God.

Chapter 21

WEAK VERBS

Weak verbs contain letters that cause phonological problems when they occur in certain situations. For example, some letters cannot take certain vowels, while others tend to assimilate with adjoining consonants. Because the "weaknesses" which cause problems for these roots typically have to do with the pronunciation of specific consonants, many irregularities are common to Hebrew and Aramaic.

Some letters encounter problems when they occur at the beginning of a root. For example, when the letter נ is preceded by a vowel but has none of its own (i.e. when it has a silent *sh'va*), it often assimilates to the following letter. Thus, the imperfect of the root נפל (*fall*) includes forms like יִפֵּל (compare the Hebrew יִפֹּל). Since the imperative is based on this form (without the pronominal prefix), it frequently has no נ at all (e.g., שָׂא from נשא and פֻּק from נפק). However, Aramaic is not as consistent in this as is Hebrew. Thus, the נ remains in several forms of the verb נתן, such as תִּנְתֵּן and יִנְתֵּן (the *dagesh* in the ת is *lene*) and frequently in H forms (תְּהַנְזִק, הַנְפֵּק, etc.). Alternatively, it is possible that these forms are actually secondary developments. In other words, rather than having been retained, the נ may have initially assimilated and then later returned through a process of nasalized dissimilation. This process can be seen in other Aramaic verbs; for example, the H infinitives הַנְסָקָה and הַנְעָלָה are derived from the roots סלק and עלל respectively (see chapter 22). If a similar process was at work with נתן, the imperfect would have developed in something like the following stages:

$$יִנְתֵּן \;\rightarrow\; יִתֵּן \text{ (assimilation) } \;\rightarrow\; יִנְתֵּן \text{ (dissimilation/nasalization)}$$

A similar development takes place with the root ידע. Its imperfect, 2 masculine singular form should have been תִּידַע, but that apparently became תִּדְּדַע, with the י assimilating to the ד), and then תִּנְדַּע, as the first ד dissimilated, becoming a (nasal) נ. This process also lies behind the name of the Mandeans, which comes from the root ידע and is used for a gnostic group that claims special religious knowledge (cf. מַנְדַּע, "knowledge," in Daniel 4:31 and 33 on p. 120).

The verb יְדַע demonstrates another characteristic of the Northwest Semitic languages, namely the shift of initial ו to י. (The root was originally ודע.) Sometimes the initial י is lost altogether, as in the infinitive and imperative (e.g., הַב; see p. 49 above). However, under other circumstances, the shift to י never takes place at all. Hebrew examples include *hifʿil* and *nifʿal* forms such as הוֹלִיד and נוֹלַד, both of which come from the root ילד. Analogously, Aramaic has H forms such as הוֹתֵב and לְהוֹדָעָה from the roots יתב and ידע.

Gutturals often cause nearby vowels to shift to an *ah* sound (i.e. a *pataḥ* or *qameṣ*). We have already seen examples of this in the G active participle (אָמַר). The same phenomenon is responsible for D participles such as מְשַׁבַּח, G perfect forms like עַבְדֵת ("I made"), and G imperfects such as תַּעַבְדוּן.

"Hollow" verbs have a long vowel—either *î* or *û*—instead of a middle consonant. Because their roots do not have three consonants, these verbs inevitably encounter problems fitting into "regular" conjugations. (This clearly does not apply to verbs such as חוה, "tell," in which the middle ו or י is consonantal.) Hollow roots have no middle letter at all in the G perfect (e.g., שָׂמֶת, "I ordered"). However, the G participle often developed an א in the middle position, apparently in an effort to make the verb more clearly triliteral—e.g., קָאֵם (he rises).* (In some verbs the *kĕtîv* has an א but the *qĕrê* a י, e.g., דָּאֲנִין/דָּאֲנִין in Ezra 7:25 and דָּאֲרִין/דָּיְרִין in Daniel 2:38.) The long middle vowel does appear in the imperfect, where the pronominal prefix takes a *sh'va* (e.g., יְקוּם; contrast Hebrew, where the pronominal prefix takes a *qameṣ*, reflecting how that language treats short vowels in syllables preceding the accent).

Final ה and א are not as distinct in Aramaic as they are in Hebrew. One of them may appear in forms attributed to roots derived from the other, such as מְשָׁרֵא from the root שרה and הִתְמְלִי from the root מלא. This blurring also occurs in the suffixes used for feminine and determined forms, which should be הָ- and אָ- respectively, but are not consistently distinguished. This ambiguity is compounded by the tendency of א to become quiescent and even fall away. This is evident in the root אתא, the H conjugation of which, as we have seen, has forms such as the infinitive לְהַיְתָיָה and the masculine singular third person perfect הַיְתִי, where there is a י instead of the expected א. As a consequence, the following forms are all derived from initial-א verbs:

---

* The same form occurs in the Hebrew passage Hosea 10:14.

תְּהוֹבֵד (Daniel 2:24)—from the root אבד in the H conjugation, with the א acting like a י, which then "becomes" a ו.

מְהֵימַן (Daniel 2:45, 6:5)—an H passive participle from the root אמן, where the א has become and remained a י (just like הֵיתִי).

מֵמַר (Ezra 5:11)—the א in this G infinitive has dropped (so too in the infinitives מֵחָא and מֵזָא); the same form occurs in Daniel 2:9 with the א intact (מֵאמַר).

Final ה verbs (which were originally final י) follow patterns familiar from Hebrew, except that the perfect, 3 plural suffix is ו- (e.g., בְּנוֹ, "they built"):

		Perfect	Imperfect		Participles		Imperative
					Active	Passive	
sing.	1 cs	בְּנֵית	אֶבְנֵא	ms	בָּנֵה	בְּנֵה	בְּנִי
	2ms	בְּנַיְתָ	תִּבְנֵא	fs	בָּנְיָה	בַּנְיָה	
	2fs	בְּנַיְתִי	תִּבְנֵין	mp	בָּנַיִן	בְּנַיִן	בְּנוֹ
	3ms	בְּנָה	יִבְנֵא	fp	בָּנְיָן	בְּנַיָן	
	3fs	בְּנָת	תִּבְנֵה				
pl.	1cp	בְּנֵינָא	נִבְנֵא	Infinitive	מִבְנֵא		
	2mp	בְּנֵיתוּן	תִּבְנוֹן				
	2fp	בְּנֵיתֵן	תִּבְנְיָן				
	3mp	בְּנוֹ	יִבְנוֹן				
	3fp	בְּנָה	יִבְנְיָן				

Geminate verbs (those in which the second and third root consonants are the same) are handled in a variety of ways:

(1) Sometimes these roots behave as if they were perfectly regular (e.g., קַצִּצוּ ,יְמַלִּל, מְרָעַע ,שַׁכְלִלוּ ,תַּטְלִל).

(2) Often, the repeated consonant appears only once, sometimes without any indication that it is doubled. In those cases, the vowel pattern may shift (e.g., גֹּדּוּ ,תְּרַע, מְחָן ,נַדַּת).

(3) In certain cases, the doubling (gemination) one would have expected in the final letter of the root shifts to the first letter (this is most common in H forms of the root דקק, such תַּדֵּק, מְהַדֵּק, and הַדִּקוּ).

VOCABULARY

To Be Learned		*Reference*	
cut down	גדד	but	בְּרַם
dew	טַל	in order that	(עַד) דִּבְרָה
be able	כהל	living	חַי
heart	לְבַב	give	יהב
reach	מטא	*Gt imperf 3 ms*	יִתְיְהִב
descend	נחת	food	מָזוֹן
Most High	עֶלִי	flee	נוד
want	צבה	enemy	עָר
be wet	צבע	call	קרא
Dt	יִצְטַבַּע	greatness	רְבוּ
		be appalled	שמם
		ʾitpolel perf.	אֶשְׁתּוֹמַם
		root	שְׁרַשׁ

FROM THE BIBLE (Daniel 4:10–20)

חָזֵה הֲוֵית בְּחֶזְוֵי רֵאשִׁי וַאֲלוּ קַדִּישׁ מִן שְׁמַיָּא נָחִת. קָרֵא וְכֵן אָמַר: גֹּדּוּ אִילָנָא תְּנֻד

חֵיוְתָא מִן תַּחְתּוֹהִי בְּרַם שָׁרְשׁוֹהִי בְּאַרְעָא שְׁבֻקוּ וּבְטַל שְׁמַיָּא יִצְטַבַּע. לִבְבֵהּ מִן

אֲנָשָׁא יְשַׁנּוֹן וּלְבַב חֵיוָה יִתְיְהִב לֵהּ עַד דִּי יִנְדְּעוּן חַיַּיָּא דִּי שַׁלִּיט עֶלָּיָא

בְּמַלְכוּת אֲנָשָׁא וּלְמַן דִּי יִצְבֵּא יִתְּנִנַּהּ. דְּנָה חֶלְמָא חֲזֵית אֲנָה מַלְכָּא נְבוּכַדְנֶצַּר וְאַנְתְּ

בֵּלְטְשַׁאצַּר פִּשְׁרֵא אֱמַר כָּל קֳבֵל דִּי כָּל חַכִּימֵי מַלְכוּתִי לָא יָכְלִין פִּשְׁרָא לְהוֹדָעֻתַנִי

וְאַנְתְּ כָּהֵל דִּי רוּחַ אֱלָהִין קַדִּישִׁין בָּךְ. אֱדַיִן דָּנִיֵּאל דִּי שְׁמֵהּ בֵּלְטְשַׁאצַּר אֶשְׁתּוֹמַם

כְּשָׁעָה חֲדָה. עָנֵה מַלְכָּא וְאָמַר. בֵּלְטְשַׁאצַּר חֶלְמָא וּפִשְׁרֵא אַל יְבַהֲלָךְ.

עָנֵה בֵלְטְשַׁאצַּר וְאָמַר. חֶלְמָא וּפִשְׁרֵהּ לְעָרָיךְ. אִילָנָא דִּי חֲזַיְתָ דִּי רְבָה וּתְקִף וְיִמְטֵא

לִשְׁמַיָּא וּמְזוֹן לְכֹלָּא בֵהּ, תְּחֹתוֹהִי תְּדוּר חֵיוַת בָּרָא—אַנְתְּ הוּא מַלְכָּא דִּי רְבַית

וּרְבוּתָךְ רְבָת וּמְטָת לִשְׁמַיָּא. וְדִי חֲזָה מַלְכָּא קַדִּישׁ נָחִת מִן שְׁמַיָּא וְאָמַר גֹּדּוּ אִילָנָא

וְחַבְּלוּהִי בְּרַם שָׁרְשׁוֹהִי בְּאַרְעָא שְׁבֻקוּ וּבְטַל שְׁמַיָּא יִצְטַבַּע.

EXERCISES

Identify the form of the following verbs:

	Root	Conjugation	Tense	Person	Gender	Number
טָאֵב						
דַּע						
מִנְתַּן						
יִקְרוֹן						
יְהוֹבְדוּן						
יָדַע						
יַחְלְפוּן						
תִּפְּלוּן						
הַדֶּקֶת						

	Root	Conjugation	Tense	Person	Gender	Number
הוֹתֵב						
שָׂם						
מְהָקֵים						
אֶבְעֵא						
פֻּקוּ						
אֲתוֹ						
הֵיבֵל						
נֵאמַר						
הוֹבְדָה						
יִנְדְּעוּן						
יִפֵּל						

Translate into Aramaic:

(1) Then the magicians knew that the king heard the dream.

(2) I am able to bind the body on top of the mountain.

(3) Wisdom is like a burning fire.

(4) The interpretation damaged all who heard it.

(5) One man builds a house, and another man smashes it.

(6) My hair is wet with dew.

(7) The interpretation of the dream changed the king's heart.

(8) A holy one came down when he heard the word of the Most High.

(9) They cut down the tree that reached into the heavens.

(10) We went to praise them.

Chapter 22

UNUSUAL VERBS

There are several common verbs with idiosyncratic forms. Some of these have already been described.

הוה (to be)—As noted in chapter 15, imperfect 3d person forms often use a prefixed ־ל (thus לֶהֱוֵא, לֶהֱוֹן, לֶהֱוֵין). Although in biblical Aramaic this involves only the verb הוה, the prefix is more extensively attested in later dialects, including rabbinic Aramaic, Syriac, and Mandaic.

הלך (go)—Participles are conjugated in the D and H (מְהַלֵּךְ and מְהַלְכִין). Imperfect and infinitive forms are kept in the G conjugation, where they act as if they were derived from a hollow root (הוך) with no middle consonant nor any evidence of assimilation—thus, יְהָךְ (he will go) and לִמְהָךְ (to go).

יכל (be able) has several different forms. The imperfect follows the pattern יִכַּל, תִּכַּל, although some Aramaic passages have the same (יוּכַל) as is known from Hebrew. Participles can be based on either יכל (יָכֵל, יָכְלָה, יָכְלִין, יָכְלָן) or כהל (כָּהֵל, כָּהֲלָה, כָּהֲלִין, כָּהֲלָן).

סלק (go up)—Whenever the initial ס has a silent *sh'va*, the ל assimilates to it. This happens in several H forms, such as הַסִּקוּ (lift up!) and הֻסַּק (be lifted up). In the H infinitive, the double ס then *dissimilates*, resulting in the form הַנְסָקָה through a process of nasalization:

$$(\text{i.e., } \text{הַסְלָקָה} \rightarrow \text{הַסָּקָה} \rightarrow \text{הַנְסָקָה})$$

עלל (enter)—The G participle of this geminate root has two forms, with the *kĕtîv* showing both ל's (עֲלֲלַת and עָלְלִין), but the *qĕrê* only one (עַלַת and עָלִין). Nasalization sometimes occurs in the H forms of this verb, yielding the perfect, 3d person masculine singular form הַנְעֵל and the infinitive הַנְעָלָה, which exists alongside of הֶעָלָה.

119

VOCABULARY

To Be Learned		*Reference*	
bless (D)	בְּרַך	living	חַי
strength	חַיִל	pass by	חֲלַף
drive out	טְרַד	month	יְרַח
day	יוֹם	because	מִן דִּי
dwelling	מְדוֹר	understanding	מַנְדַּע
lift	נְטַל	eye	עַיִן
pass away (G)	עֲדָה	enduring	קַיָּם
mouth	פֻּם	seven	שִׁבְעָה
end	קְצָת	root	שֹׁרֶשׁ
return	תּוּב	restore (H)	תְּקַן
		H passive	הָתְקְנַת
		twelve	תְּרֵי עֲשַׂר

FROM THE BIBLE (Daniel 4:21–34)

דְּנָה פִשְׁרָא דִי מְטָת עַל מַלְכָּא: לָךְ טָרְדִין מִן אֲנָשָׁא וְעִם חֵיוַת בָּרָא לֶהֱוֵה מְדֹרָךְ

וּמִטַּל שְׁמַיָּא לָךְ מְצַבְּעִין וְשִׁבְעָה עִדָּנִין יַחְלְפוּן עֲלָיךְ עַד דִּי תִנְדַּע דִּי שַׁלִּיט עִלָּיָא

בְּמַלְכוּת אֲנָשָׁא וּלְמַן דִּי יִצְבֵּא יִתְּנִנַּהּ. וְדִי אֲמַרוּ לְמִשְׁבַּק שָׁרְשׁוֹהִי דִּי אִילָנָא —

מַלְכוּתָךְ לָךְ קַיָּמָה מִן דִּי תִנְדַּע דִּי שַׁלִּטִן שְׁמַיָּא. כֹּלָּא מְטָא עַל נְבוּכַדְנֶצַּר מַלְכָּא.

לִקְצָת יַרְחִין תְּרֵי־עֲשַׂר עַל הֵיכַל מַלְכוּתָא דִּי בָבֶל מְהַלֵּךְ הֲוָה. עָנֵה מַלְכָּא וְאָמַר:

הֲלָא דָא הִיא בָּבֶל רַבְּתָא דִּי אֲנָה בֱנַיְתַהּ לְבֵית מַלְכוּ? מִלְּתָא בְּפֻם מַלְכָּא וְקָל מִן

שְׁמַיָּא נְפַל. לָךְ אָמְרִין נְבוּכַדְנֶצַּר מַלְכָּא: מַלְכוּתָה עֲדָת מִנָּךְ וּמִן אֲנָשָׁא לָךְ טָרְדִין

וְעִם חֵיוַת בָּרָא מְדֹרָךְ וְשִׁבְעָה עִדָּנִין יַחְלְפוּן עֲלָיךְ עַד דִּי תִנְדַּע דִּי שַׁלִּיט עִלָּיָא

בְּמַלְכוּת אֲנָשָׁא וּלְמַן דִּי יִצְבֵּא יִתְּנִנַּהּ. בַּהּ שַׁעֲתָא מִן אֲנָשָׁא טְרִיד וּמִטַּל שְׁמַיָּא גִּשְׁמֵהּ

יִצְטַבַּע. וְלִקְצָת יוֹמַיָּה אֲנָה נְבוּכַדְנֶצַּר עַיְנַי לִשְׁמַיָּא נִטְלֵת וּמַנְדְּעִי עֲלַי יְתוּב וּלְעִלָּיָא

בָּרְכֵת וּלְחַי עָלְמָא שַׁבְּחֵת דִּי שָׁלְטָנֵהּ שָׁלְטָן עָלַם וּמַלְכוּתֵהּ עִם דָּר וְדָר וּכְמִצְבְּיֵהּ

עָבֵד בְּחֵיל שְׁמַיָּא וְדָאֲרֵי אַרְעָא וְלָא אִיתַי דִּי יְמַחֵא לֵהּ: מָה עֲבַדְתְּ? בֵּהּ זִמְנָא מַנְדְּעִי

יְתוּב עֲלַי וְעַל מַלְכוּתִי הָתְקְנַת וְרִבוּ יַתִּירָה הוּסְפַת לִי.

EXERCISES

Identify the form of the following verbs:

	Root	Conjugation	Tense	Person	Gender	Number
הַנְעֵל						
הֶעֱל						
לְהֶוֵה						
הֲוֹו						
הַסִּקוּ						
הֻנְסָקָה						
מְהַלְכִין						
מְהַלֵּךְ						
יְהָךְ						
יְכֵלְתָּ						
יָכֹל						
תֻּכַל						
יוּכַל						
כָּהֲלִין						

Translate into Aramaic:

(1) The priests drove the governor from the city.

(2) The animal's dwelling is in a tree.

(3) At the end of the day his strength passed away.

(4) The magician lifted his hands and blessed the silver statue.

(5) I returned to bring the letter up to the top of the mountain.

Chapter 23

SYNTAX

Aramaic syntax differs from that of biblical Hebrew in some important ways. For example, we have already pointed out that Aramaic's definite object marker (יָת), which is cognate to the Hebrew אֵת, occurs only once in the Bible (Daniel 3:12; see p. 62). More often, definite direct objects are marked with the preposition -לְ:

אֱדַיִן אַרְיוֹךְ . . . הַנְעֵל לְדָנִיֵּאל קֳדָם מַלְכָּא

Then Arioch . . . brought Daniel before the king. (Daniel 2:25)

Many times, however, definite direct objects stand alone, without any indicator at all:

כָּל אֱנָשׁ דִּי יְהַשְׁנֵא פִּתְגָמָא דְנָה . . .

Anyone who will change this message. . . . (Ezra 6:11)

On the other hand, the relationship between nouns and adjectives is very much like that in Hebrew. Adjectives follow the nouns they modify and must agree not only with respect to number and gender, but determination as well (just as in Hebrew both must have or lack the definite article). However, as in Hebrew, this applies only if the adjective is attributive, that is, if it describes the noun; when it is predicative, they need agree only with respect to number and gender:

מַלְכָּא רַבָּא   the great king

מַלְכָּא רַב   the king is great

Similar rules apply to demonstratives. When they function as adjectives, they normally follow the noun they modify, which *must* be definite (i.e. determined). However, demonstrative pronouns need not be directly adjacent to the noun to which they refer, and the noun may or may not be determined:

גֻּבְרַיָּא אִלֵּין   these men
אִלֵּין גֻּבְרִין   these are men
אִלֵּין גֻּבְרַיָּא   these are the men

Aramaic sentence structure is, overall, far looser than Hebrew's. To be sure, there are numerous cases of the familiar verb-subject-object word order:

מְהוֹדְעִין אֲנַחְנָה לְמַלְכָּא   We inform the king. (Ezra 4:16)

However, it is more common for the object to come first:

וְשִׁמְשַׁי . . . רְחוּם עַל מַלְכָּא שְׁלַח פִּתְגָמָא   The king sent a message to Rehum and Shimshai. (Ezra 4:17)

Frequently, it is reiterated by a resumptive pronoun:

גֻּבְרַיָּא אִלֵּךְ . . . קַטִּל הִמּוֹן שְׁבִיבָא דִּי נוּרָא   Those men—the flame of fire killed them. (Daniel 3:22)

Sometimes, the subject comes at the very beginning of a sentence:

רְחוּם . . . וְשִׁמְשַׁי . . . כְּתַבוּ אִגְּרָה חֲדָה עַל יְרוּשְׁלֶם לְאַרְתַּחְשַׁשְׁתְּא מַלְכָּא   Rehum and Shimshai wrote a letter concerning Jerusalem to Artaxerxes, the king. (Ezra 4:8)

Finally, both the particle אִיתַי (functioning as a copula) and the verb הוה are often used with Aramaic participles. Although in such situations the participles are technically predicate nouns or adjectives, the resulting verb phrases come very close to comprising compound tenses:

e.g.,   לֵאלָהָיךְ לָא אִיתַנָא פָלְחִין   We *do not worship* your god. (Daniel 3:18)

אַנְתְּ מַלְכָּא חָזֵה הֲוַיְתָ   Oh king, you *were seeing.* (Daniel 2:31)

VOCABULARY

To Be Learned		*Reference*	

finger	אֶצְבַּע	wood	אָע
splendor	זִיו	purple	אַרְגְּוָן
wine	חֲמַר	disturb (D)	בהל
wear	לבש	*Dt (pass.) part. ms*	מִתְבָּהַל
meal	לְחֶם	taste	טְעֵם
interpret	פשר	understanding	מַנְדַּע
read, call	קרא/קרה	wall	כְּתַל
Gt (pass.) imperf. 3ms	יִתְקְרֵי	banquet	מִשְׁתְּא
thought	רַעְיוֹן	illumination	נַהִירוּ
find	שכח	palm	פַּס
Gt (pass.) perf. 3fs	הִשְׁתְּכַחַת	change (G)	שנה
drink	שתה	*Dt (pass.) imperf. 3p*	יִשְׁתַּנּוֹ
		ruler (over 1/3 kingdom)	תַּלְתִּי

FROM THE BIBLE (Daniel 5:1–12)

בֵּלְשַׁאצַּר מַלְכָּא עֲבַד לְחֶם רַב וְחַמְרָא שָׁתֵה. בֵּלְשַׁאצַּר אֲמַר בִּטְעֵם חַמְרָא לְהַיְתָיָה

לְמָאנֵי דַּהֲבָא וְכַסְפָּא דִּי הַנְפֵּק נְבוּכַדְנֶצַּר אֲבוּהִי מִן הֵיכְלָא דִּי בִירוּשְׁלֵם וְיִשְׁתּוֹן

בְּהוֹן. בֵּאדַיִן הַיְתִיו מָאנֵי דַהֲבָא דִּי הַנְפִּקוּ מִן הֵיכְלָא דִּי בֵית אֱלָהָא דִּי בִירוּשְׁלֵם

וְשַׁבַּחוּ לֵאלָהֵי דַּהֲבָא וְכַסְפָּא נְחָשָׁא פַרְזְלָא אָעָא וְאַבְנָא. בַּהּ שַׁעֲתָה נְפַקָה אֶצְבְּעָן

דִּי יַד אֱנָשׁ וְכָתְבָן עַל כְּתַל הֵיכְלָא דִּי מַלְכָּא וּמַלְכָּא חָזֵה פַּס יְדָה דִּי כָתְבָה.

אֱדַיִן מַלְכָּא זִיוֹהִי שְׁנוֹהִי וְרַעְיֹנֹהִי יְבַהֲלוּנֵּהּ. קָרֵא מַלְכָּא בְּחַיִל לְהֶעָלָה כַּשְׂדָּיֵא.

עָנֵה מַלְכָּא וְאָמַר לְחַכִּימֵי בָבֶל דִּי כָל אֱנָשׁ דִּי יִקְרֵה כְּתָבָה דְנָה וּפִשְׁרֵהּ יְחַוִּנַּנִי

אַרְגְּוָנָא יִלְבַּשׁ וְתַלְתִּי בְמַלְכוּתָא יִשְׁלַט. אֱדַיִן עָלֲלִין כֹּל חַכִּימֵי מַלְכָּא וְלָא כָהֲלִין

כְּתָבָא לְמִקְרֵא וּפִשְׁרָא לְהוֹדָעָה לְמַלְכָּא. אֱדַיִן מַלְכָּא בֵּלְשַׁאצַּר שַׂגִּיא מִתְבָּהַל

וְזִיוֹהִי שָׁנַיִן עֲלוֹהִי. מַלְכְּתָא לָקֳבֵל מִלֵּי מַלְכָּא לְבֵית מִשְׁתְּיָא עַלַּת.

עֲנָת מַלְכְּתָא וַאֲמֶרֶת: מַלְכָּא לְעָלְמִין חֱיִי אַל יְבַהֲלוּךְ רַעְיוֹנָךְ וְזִיוָיךְ אַל יִשְׁתַּנּוֹ.

אִיתַי גְּבַר בְּמַלְכוּתָךְ דִּי רוּחַ אֱלָהִין קַדִּישִׁין בֵּהּ וּבְיוֹמֵי אֲבוּךְ נַהִירוּ וְחָכְמָה כְּחָכְמַת

אֱלָהִין הִשְׁתְּכַחַת בֵּהּ וּמַלְכָּא נְבֻכַדְנֶצַּר אֲבוּךְ רַב חַרְטֻמִּין וְכַשְׂדָּאִין הֲקִימֵהּ אֲבוּךְ

מַלְכָּא. כָּל קֳבֵל דִּי רוּחַ יַתִּירָה וּמַנְדַּע מְפַשַּׁר חֶלְמִין הִשְׁתְּכַחַת בֵּהּ בְּדָנִיֵּאל דִּי מַלְכָּא

שָׂם שְׁמֵהּ בֵּלְטְשַׁאצַּר. כְּעַן דָּנִיֵּאל יִתְקְרִי וּפִשְׁרָה יְהַחֲוֵה.

EXERCISES

Rewrite the following sentences twice, expressing the direct object differently each time:

(1) מַלְכָּא כְּפַת חַרְטֻמַיָּא.

(a)

(b)

(2) יַת חֶלְמָא פְּשַׁר דָּנִיֵּאל.

(a)

(b)

(3) קְטַלוּ גֻּבְרַיָּא לְכָהֲנַיָּא.

(a)

(b)

Now rearrange each of the original sentences above twice, beginning with a different word each time.

(1a)

(1b)

(2a)

(2b)

(3a)

(3b)

Translate each sentence into English:

(1)

(2)

(3)

Translate into Aramaic:

(1) They drank wine with the meal.

(2) The big finger wrote a message.

(3) The golden vessels were found in the temple.

(4) The priest called the people to pray.

(5) The queen wore gold on her head.

(6) The strong thoughts frightened me.

(7) The wall of the house is wood.

(8) The splendor of his wisdom went out to the whole land.

Chapter 24

PASSIVE CONJUGATIONS

The G passive participle (e.g., כְּתִיב), which was described in chapter 9, is only a small part of a far more elaborate system, one which is significantly more developed in Aramaic than in biblical Hebrew. There one finds a *qal* (G) passive participle (e.g., בָּרוּךְ) as well as two passive conjugations—the *puʿal* and the *hofʿal*. These latter two really belong to the *piʿel* (D) and the *hifʿil* (H), as is evident from the fact that they share the characteristic features of those conjugations—the doubled middle root letter of the *piʿel* and the prefixed ה of the *hifʿil*. Where they differ from the active forms is in their vowel pattern, for which both use *u-a*. These conjugations are, therefore, called *internal* passives of the *piʿel* and *hifʿil*.

Although biblical Hebrew's *qal* has only a passive participle, some anomalous forms have led scholars to suspect that at one time it too must have had a full internal passive. Whatever the facts about that, there are internal passives for all the major conjugations in biblical Aramaic.

The G passive is characterized by the theme vowel *î*, which is found in both the participle and perfect forms. (There are no imperfect forms for any of the internal passive conjugations in the Bible.)

G PASSIVE		*Perfect*				*Participle*	
		Singular	*Plural*				
1		כְּתִיבֵת	כְּתִיבְנָא	singular	masculine		כְּתִיב
2	masculine	כְּתִיבְתָּ	כְּתִיבְתּוּן		feminine		כְּתִיבָה
	feminine	כְּתִיבְתִּי	כְּתִיבְתֵּן				
3	masculine	כְּתִיב	כְּתִיבוּ	plural	masculine		כְּתִיבִין
	feminine	כְּתִיבַת	כְּתִיבָה		feminine		כְּתִיבָן

The D passive resembles the Hebrew *puᶜal*, except that the participle has a *pataḥ (a)* theme vowel instead of *u*. Since Aramaic rules of pronunciation call for this vowel to be reduced to a *sh'va* in all forms of the passive participle except the masculine singular, that is the only participial form in which the active and the passive differ.

D PASSIVE

		Perfect		Participle		
		Singular	*Plural*			
1		קֻבְּלֵת	קֻבַּלְנָא	singular	masculine	מְקַבַּל
2	masculine	קֻבַּלְתָּ	קֻבַּלְתּוּן		feminine	מְקַבְּלָה
	feminine	קֻבַּלְתִּי	קֻבַּלְתֶּן			
3	masculine	קֻבַּל	קֻבַּלוּ	plural	masculine	מְקַבְּלִין
	feminine	קֻבְּלַת	קֻבַּלָה		feminine	מְקַבְּלָן

The H internal passive follows the same pattern in the perfect as the Hebrew *hofᶜal*, while the passive participle is identical with its active counterpart, except that the theme vowel shifts from *ṣere* to *pataḥ* (when it shows), precisely as occurs in the D passive.

H PASSIVE

		Perfect		Participle		
		Singular	*Plural*			
1		הֻשְׁלְטֵת	הֻשְׁלַטְנָא	singular	masculine	מְהֻשְׁלַט
2	masculine	הֻשְׁלַטְתָּ	הֻשְׁלַטְתּוּן		feminine	מְהֻשְׁלְטָה
	feminine	הֻשְׁלַטְתִּי	הֻשְׁלַטְתֶּן			
3	masculine	הֻשְׁלַט	הֻשְׁלַטוּ	plural	masculine	מְהֻשְׁלְטִין
	feminine	הֻשְׁלְטַת	הֻשְׁלַטָה		feminine	מְהֻשְׁלְטָן

As in Hebrew, the initial vowel in the perfect may be either a short *ŏ* (הָ) or *ŭ* (הֻ).

VOCABULARY

To Be Learned		Reference	
glory	יְקָר	purple	אַרְגְּוָן
throne	כָּרְסֵא	lacking	חַסִּיר
master	מָרֵא	proclaim (H)	כרז
greatness	רְבוּ	count (G)	מנה
rise	רום	remove (H)	עדה
G pass. part. ms	רִים	divide	פרס
H (causative) part. ms	מְרִים	kill	קטל
Hitpolʿel (reflexive)		chiefs	רַבְרְבָנִין
perf. 2 ms	הִתְרוֹמַמְתָּ	weigh	תקל
write	רשם		
be like	שוה		
be finished	שלם		
be low (*H causative*)	שפל		
rule (over 1/3 of kingdom)	תַּלְתָּא		

FROM THE BIBLE (Daniel 5:13–29)

בֵּאדַיִן דָּנִיֵּאל הֻעַל קֳדָם מַלְכָּא. עָנֵה מַלְכָּא וְאָמַר לְדָנִיֵּאל: אַנְתְּ הוּא דָנִיֵּאל דִּי מִן

בְּנֵי יְהוּד דִּי הַיְתִי מַלְכָּא אַבִי מִן יְהוּד. וְשִׁמְעֵת עֲלָיִךְ דִּי רוּחַ אֱלָהִין בָּךְ וְחָכְמָה

יַתִּירָה הִשְׁתְּכַחַת בָּךְ. וּכְעַן הֻעַלּוּ קָדָמַי חַכִּימַיָּא דִּי כְתָבָה דְנָה יִקְרוֹן וּפִשְׁרֵהּ

לְהוֹדָעֻתַנִי וְלָא כָהֲלִין פְּשַׁר מִלְּתָא לְהַחֲוָיָה. וַאֲנָה שִׁמְעֵת עֲלָיִךְ דִּי תִכּל פִּשְׁרִין

לְמִפְשַׁר. כְּעַן הֵן תִּכּל כְּתָבָא לְמִקְרֵא וּפִשְׁרֵהּ לְהוֹדָעֻתַנִי אַרְגְּוָנָא תִלְבַּשׁ וְתַלְתָּא

בְּמַלְכוּתָא תִשְׁלַט. בֵּאדַיִן עָנֵה דָנִיֵּאל וְאָמַר קֳדָם מַלְכָּא: כְּתָבָא אֶקְרֵא לְמַלְכָּא

וּפִשְׁרָא אֲהוֹדְעִנֵּהּ. אַנְתְּ מַלְכָּא אֱלָהָא עִלָּיָא מַלְכוּתָא וּרְבוּתָא וִיקָרָא יְהַב לִנְבֻכַדְנֶצַּר

אֲבוּךְ. וּמִן רְבוּתָא דִּי יְהַב לֵהּ כֹּל עַמְמַיָּא הֲווֹ דָחֲלִין מִן קֳדָמוֹהִי. דִּי הֲוָה צָבֵא

הֲוָא קָטֵל וְדִי הֲוָה צָבֵא הֲוָה מָרִים וְדִי הֲוָה צָבֵא הֲוָה מַשְׁפִּיל. וּכְדִי רִם לִבְבֵהּ

וְרוּחֵהּ הֲנָחַת מִן כָּרְסֵא מַלְכוּתֵהּ וִיקָרָה הֶעְדִּיו מִנֵּהּ. וּמִן בְּנֵי אֲנָשָׁא טְרִיד וְלִבְבֵהּ עִם חֵיוְתָא שַׁוִּי וּמְטַל שְׁמַיָּא גִּשְׁמֵהּ יִצְטַבַּע עַד דִּי יְדַע דִּי שַׁלִּיט אֱלָהָא עִלָּאָ בְּמַלְכוּת אֲנָשָׁא וּלְמַן דִּי יִצְבֵּה יְהָקֵים עֲלַיהּ. וְאַנְתְּ בְּרֵהּ בֵּלְשַׁאצַּר לָא הַשְׁפֵּלְתְּ לִבְבָךְ כָּל קֳבֵל דִּי כָל דְּנָה יְדַעְתָּ. וְעַל מָרֵא שְׁמַיָּא הִתְרוֹמַמְתָּ וּלְמָאנַיָּא דִי בַיְתֵהּ הַיְתִיו קֳדָמָיךְ וְאַנְתְּ וְרַבְרְבָנָיךְ שֵׁגְלָתָךְ וּלְחֵנָתָךְ חַמְרָא שָׁתַיִן בְּהוֹן וְלֵאלָהֵי כַסְפָּא וְדַהֲבָא נְחָשָׁא פַרְזְלָא אָעָא וְאַבְנָא דִּי לָא חָזַיִן וְלָא שָׁמְעִין וְלָא יָדְעִין שַׁבַּחְתָּ. בֵּאדַיִן מִן קֳדָמוֹהִי שְׁלִיחַ יְדָא וּכְתָבָא דְנָה רְשִׁים. וּדְנָה כְתָבָא דִּי רְשִׁים: מְנֵא מְנֵא תְּקֵל וּפַרְסִין. דְּנָה פְּשַׁר מִלְּתָא: מְנֵא—מְנָה אֱלָהָא מַלְכוּתָךְ וְהַשְׁלְמַהּ. תְּקֵל—תְּקִילְתָּה וְהִשְׁתְּכַחַתְּ חַסִּיר. פְּרֵס— פְּרִיסַת מַלְכוּתָךְ וִיהִיבַת לְמָדַי וּפָרָס. בֵּאדַיִן אֲמַר בֵּלְשַׁאצַּר וְהַלְבִּישׁוּ לְדָנִיֵּאל אַרְגְּוָנָא וְהַכְרִזוּ עֲלוֹהִי דִּי לֶהֱוֵא שַׁלִּיט תַּלְתָּא בְּמַלְכוּתָא.

Proper Names

מָדַי — Region in western Iran from which a powerful kingdom emerged in the seventh century, but was conquered by Cyrus of Persia in the sixth century.

EXERCISES

Identify the form of the following verbs:

	Root	Conjugation (G, D, H)	Tense	Person	Gender	Number
שְׁלִיחַ						
יְהִיב						
קְטִילַת						
מְפָרַשׁ						
עֲשִׂית						

Root	Conjugation (G, D, H)	Tense	Number	Gender	Person
מְעָרַב					
שִׂים					
הֻסְפַת					
יְהִיבַת					
חֲשִׁיבִין					
זְקִיף					
זְהִירִין					
שְׂמַת					
דְּחִיל					
גְּמִיר					
יְהִיבוּ					
פְּרִיסַת					
מְכַפְּתִין					
שְׁלַם					

Translate into Aramaic:

(1) The letter was written in Jerusalem.

(2) He is raising the palace on the mountain.

(3) The throne was lowered from the heavens.

(4) The master's dream was interpreted there.

(5) The great gods are praised on earth.

(6) They asked him to bring the silver to the big building.

(7) Daniel became ruler, and his glory was like a king.

(8) God gave greatness to the province and to its governor.

(9) The earth was finished in six days.

Chapter 25

REFLEXIVE CONJUGATIONS

Just as each major conjugation has an internal passive, so can each theoretically be made reflexive by adding the prefix הִתְ-. Hebrew normally does this only for the D (*pi^el*) conjugation (for other possibilities, see pp. 32–33). Aramaic, however, uses this prefix as a passive for both G and D.* We have already seen examples of verbs in both of these conjugations (e.g., הִתְבְּנֵה, הִתְיְהִב, הִתְבַּקַּר, הִתְעֲבֵד).

There are some clues that can help determine which conjugation is involved:

(a) Spelling—whether the middle root letter is doubled (D) or not (G)

(b) Etymology—whether the verbal root normally appears in the G or D

In any case, these conjugations follow the same general principles as other Aramaic conjugations and their Hebrew equivalents:

(1) Perfect forms use the standard suffixes.

(2) The prefixed -ה elides in the imperfect and the participle because of its location between a prefix (pronominal in the case of the imperfect; מ- for the participle) and the following ת.**

(3) Infinitives end with the suffix הָ-.

(4) Initial sibilants (שׁ, שׂ, צ, ס, ז) switch places (metathesize) with the ת of the prefix, which becomes ט (a sharpened dental) when the root begins with צ (a sharpened sibilant) and ד (a voiced dental) when the first root letter is ז (a voiced sibilant).

---

* The Bible may contain a trace of this for the H conjugation if the words מַלְכִים תְּהַנְזִק in Ezra 4:13 are redivided to read מַלְכִּי מִתְהַנְזִק ("my king is damaged"), as some have suggested.

** Compare the Hebrew definite article, which elides when it is preceded by a preposition (e.g., בַּבַּיִת→בְּהַבַּיִת) and the prefixed ה of the H conjugation both in Hebrew and sometimes in Aramaic (see p. 106). In talmudic Aramaic, the ת also elides.

The actual forms are exactly what one would expect:

			Gt	Dt
PERFECT				
Singular	1		הִתְקְטֵלֵת	הִתְחַבְּלֵת
	2	masculine	הִתְקְטֵלְתְּ	הִתְחַבַּלְתְּ
	2	feminine	הִתְקְטֵלְתִּי	הִתְחַבַּלְתִּי
	3	masculine	הִתְקְטֵל	הִתְחַבַּל
	3	feminine	הִתְקְטְלַת	הִתְחַבְּלַת
Plural	1		הִתְקְטֵלְנָא	הִתְחַבַּלְנָא
	2	masculine	הִתְקְטֵלְתּוּן	הִתְחַבַּלְתּוּן
	2	feminine	הִתְקְטֵלְתֵּן	הִתְחַבַּלְתֵּן
	3	masculine	הִתְקְטִלוּ	הִתְחַבַּלוּ
	3	feminine	הִתְקְטִלָה	הִתְחַבַּלָה
IMPERFECT				
Singular	1		אֶתְקְטֵל	אֶתְחַבַּל
	2	masculine	תִּתְקְטֵל	תִּתְחַבַּל
	2	feminine	תִּתְקַטְלִין	תִּתְחַבְּלִין
	3	masculine	יִתְקְטֵל	יִתְחַבַּל
	3	feminine	תִּתְקְטֵל	תִּתְחַבַּל
Plural	1		נִתְקְטֵל	נִתְחַבַּל
	2	masculine	תִּתְקַטְלוּן	תִּתְחַבְּלוּן
	2	feminine	תִּתְקַטְלָן	תִּתְחַבְּלָן
	3	masculine	יִתְקַטְלוּן	יִתְחַבְּלוּן
	3	feminine	יִתְקַטְלָן	יִתְחַבְּלָן
PARTICIPLES				
Singular	masculine		מִתְקְטֵל	מִתְחַבַּל
	feminine		מִתְקַטְלָה	מִתְחַבְּלָה
Plural	masculine		מִתְקַטְלִין	מִתְחַבְּלִין
	feminine		מִתְקַטְלָן	מִתְחַבְּלָן
INFINITIVE			הִתְקְטָלָה	הִתְחַבָּלָה

VOCABULARY

To Be Learned		*Reference*	
satrap	אֲחַשְׁדַּרְפַּן	petition	בָּעוּ
be faithful (H)	אמן	take counsel (Dt)	יעט
H pass. part.	מְהֵימַן	hundred	מְאָה
lion	אַרְיֵה	suffer damage	נזק
pit	גּוֹב	distinguish self (Dt)	נצח
night	לֵילֵי	chief	סָרֵךְ
pretext	עִלָּה	above	עֵלָּא
receive (D)	קבּל	twenty	עֶשְׂרִין
statute	קְיָם	intend	עשׁת
assemble (H)	רגשׁ	establish (D)	קום
please	שׁפר	*D infinitive*	לְקַיָּמָה
		negligence	שָׁלוּ

FROM THE BIBLE (Daniel 5:30–6:10)

בֵּהּ בְּלֵילְיָא קְטִיל בֵּלְאשַׁצַּר מַלְכָּא כַשְׂדָּיָא וְדָרְיָוֶשׁ מָדָיָא קַבֵּל מַלְכוּתָא כְּבַר שְׁנִין שִׁתִּין וְתַרְתֵּין. שְׁפַר קֳדָם דָּרְיָוֶשׁ וַהֲקִים עַל מַלְכוּתָא לַאֲחַשְׁדַּרְפְּנַיָּא מְאָה וְעֶשְׂרִין דִּי לֶהֱוֹן בְּכָל מַלְכוּתָא. וְעֵלָּא מִנְּהוֹן סָרְכִין תְּלָתָא דִּי דָנִיֵּאל חַד מִנְּהוֹן דִּי לֶהֱוֹן אֲחַשְׁדַּרְפְּנַיָּא אִלֵּין יָהֲבִין לְהוֹן טַעְמָא וּמַלְכָּא לָא לֶהֱוֵא נָזִק. אֱדַיִן דָּנִיֵּאל דְּנָה הֲוָא מִתְנַצַּח עַל סָרְכַיָּא וַאֲחַשְׁדַּרְפְּנַיָּא כָּל קֳבֵל דִּי רוּחַ יַתִּירָא בֵּהּ וּמַלְכָּא עֲשִׁית לַהֲקָמוּתֵהּ עַל כָּל מַלְכוּתָא. אֱדַיִן סָרְכַיָּא וַאֲחַשְׁדַּרְפְּנַיָּא הֲווֹ בָעַיִן עִלָּה לְהַשְׁכָּחָה לְדָנִיֵּאל וְכָל עִלָּה לָא יָכְלִין לְהַשְׁכָּחָה כָּל קֳבֵל דִּי מְהֵימַן הוּא וְכָל שָׁלוּ לָא הִשְׁתְּכַחַת עֲלוֹהִי. אֱדַיִן גֻּבְרַיָּא אִלֵּךְ אָמְרִין דִּי לָא נְהַשְׁכַּח לְדָנִיֵּאל כָּל עִלָּא לָהֵן הַשְׁכַּחְנָה עֲלוֹהִי בְּדָת אֱלָהֵהּ. אֱדַיִן סָרְכַיָּא וַאֲחַשְׁדַּרְפְּנַיָּא אִלֵּן הַרְגִּשׁוּ עַל מַלְכָּא וְכֵן אָמְרִין לֵהּ: דָּרְיָוֶשׁ מַלְכָּא לְעָלְמִין חֱיִי. אִתְיָעַטוּ כֹּל סָרְכֵי מַלְכוּתָא וַאֲחַשְׁדַּרְפְּנַיָּא וּפַחֲוָתָא לְקַיָּמָה קְיָם מַלְכָּא דִּי כָל דִּי יִבְעֵה בָעוּ מִן כָּל אֱלָהּ וֶאֱנָשׁ עַד יוֹמִין תְּלָתִין לָהֵן מִנָּךְ מַלְכָּא יִתְרְמֵא לְגֹב אַרְיָוָתָא. כְּעַן מַלְכָּא תְּרַשֵּׁם כְּתָבָא דִּי לָא לְהַשְׁנָיָה כְּדָת מָדַי וּפָרַס דִּי לָא תֶעְדֵּא. כָּל קֳבֵל דְּנָה מַלְכָּא דָּרְיָוֶשׁ רְשַׁם כְּתָבָא.

EXERCISES

Identify the base conjugation and form of the following Aramaic verbs:

	Root	Base Conjugation (G or D)	Tense	Person	Gender	Number
מִתְיְהֵב						
הִתְמְלִי						
יִצְטַבַּע						
הִתְחָרַךְ						
מִתְנַשְּׂאָה						
הִזְדַּמִנְתּוּן						
מִשְׁתַּכַּל						
יִתְקְרִי						
תִּשְׁתְּבִק						
תִּתְעַבְדוּן						
הִשְׁתְּכַחַת						
יִתְעֲבֵד						
יִשְׁתַּמְעוּן						
הִתְנַדַּבוּ						
יִתְבַּקַּר						

	Root	Base Conjugation (G or D)	Tense	Person	Gender	Number
מִתְכַּנְּשִׁין						
יִשְׁתַּנֵּא						
הִתְגְּזֶרֶת						
יִתְבְּנֵא						
תִּתְחַבַּל						
הִתְרְחִצוּ						

Translate into Aramaic:

(1) The wise father wrote a statute at night.

(2) The strong lion fell into the big pit.

(3) The satraps assembled before the throne.

(4) The message was received in the rebellious city.

(5) Surely, the faithful priest will be pleasing to the people.

(6) The governor sought a pretext to kill the men.

Chapter 26

OTHER CONJUGATIONS

Alongside the major conjugations (G, D, and H) and their passive variations (*peʿil, puʿal, hofʿal, hitpeʿel,* and *hitpaʿal*) are a host of others. Many of these are familiar from Hebrew. For example, since hollow roots cannot occur in the D inasmuch as they do not have a middle root letter to double, they often use the *poʿlel* conjugation, in which the final letter is doubled, as if to compensate for the lack of a middle letter:

e.g., מְרוֹמֵם (masc. sing. participle from the root רום), "raise up"

The related *ʾetpoʿlel* conjugation is used for the geminate root שמם:

אֶשְׁתּוֹמַם, "be disturbed"

This word illustrates another phenomenon, which became characteristic of later Aramaic through a process that is only beginning to be evident in the Bible. We can see it by looking closely at the biblical passage where אֶשְׁתּוֹמַם occurs:

אֱדַיִן דָּנִיֵּאל דִּי שְׁמֵהּ בֵּלְטְשַׁאצַּר אֶשְׁתּוֹמַם כְּשָׁעָה חֲדָה   (Daniel 4:16)

Since דָּנִיֵּאל is the subject of אֶשְׁתּוֹמַם, the verb must be 3 masculine singular perfect ("then Daniel . . . was disturbed"); however, one would have expected the first letter of a perfect verb to begin with ה (for *hit-poʿlel*) instead of א. A similar anomaly occurs in several other words:

אִתְגְּזֶרֶת	(Daniel 2:45)	Root גזר; perfect 3 feminine singular
אֶתְכְּרִיַּת	(Daniel 7:15)	Root כרה; perfect 3 feminine singular
אֶשְׁתַּנִּי	(Daniel 3:19)	Root שנה; perfect 3 masculine singular
אֲקִימֵהּ	(Daniel 3:1)	Root קום; perfect 3 masculine singular with 3 masculine singular pronominal suffix
אֵתַרוּ	(Daniel 4:11)	Root נתר; imperative masculine plural
אֲחֵת	(Ezra 5:15)	Root נחת; imperative masculine singular

141

All of these forms would have been expected to begin with ה. When they were written, the letter ה must have weakened to the point that it was not heard. This weakening may also account for the vacillation between ה and א in final weak roots as well as in the feminine and determined endings (see pp. 26 and 113). Over time, then, the H conjugation became an א conjugation (i.e., *ʾafˁel* rather than *hafˁel*); analogously, Gt became *ʾitpeˁel* rather than *hitpeˁel,* and Dt became *ʾitpaˁˁel* rather than *hitpaˁˁel.* To be sure, this process is only beginning in the Bible, where a handful of initial-א forms exist alongside others with initial -ה. (Thus the perfect 3 masculine singular is given as אֲקִימָה in Daniel 3:1, but הֲקִימָה in 5:11, and the perfect 3 feminine singular is אִתְגְּזֶרֶת in Daniel 2:45 but הִתְגְּזֶרֶת in 2:34.) However, it may be more widespread than we can tell, since other examples of these conjugations could be obscured by the elision of the א with the participle's prefixed -מ or with the imperfect pronominal prefixes, so that we cannot identify all the words which belong to initial -א conjugations with certainty.*

The form אֶשְׁתִּיו (Daniel 5:3–4) also has a prefixed א; however, it does not occur in place of a ה, since the word means "he drank," which is normally expressed with the G conjugation of שתה. That א must, therefore, be regarded as prosthetic (see p. 15), rather than signalling a different conjugation.

Several other peculiar forms suggest that biblical Aramaic may have had yet another conjugation. These verbs begin with שׁ, which appears to be a prefix attached to more familiar 3-letter roots:

שֵׁיזִיב	save (Daniel 3:28; cf. vv. 15, 17; 16:15, 17, 21, 28), root: עזב
שֵׁיצִיא	complete (Ezra 6:15), root: יצא
שַׁכְלֵל	complete (Ezra 4:12; 5:3, 9, 11; 6:14), root: כלל
מְסוֹבְלִין	laid (Ezra 6:3), root: יבל, passive

Both Akkadian and Ugaritic have causative conjugations that begin with שׁ rather than ה. It is, therefore, reasonable to connect these words with a distinct conjugation. However, there are several reasons to regard them as Akkadian loanwords rather than evidence that there was a functioning *shafˁel* in Aramaic:

(1) the paucity of such forms, which are limited to a mere handful of roots;

(2) the fact that the causative conjugation normally begins with a prefixed -ה in the Northwest Semitic group of languages, to which Aramaic belongs;

(3) the ample evidence of a *hafˁel* (and *ʾafˁel*) in Aramaic;

---

* אֶשְׁתּוֹלְלוּ (Ps 76:6) may demonstrate the same process in Hebrew

(4) the presence of ס in one of these words (מְסוֹבְלִין), where the others have a שׁ; this is especially striking given that the same root occurs several times in the *hafᶜel* (viz., הֵיבֵל in Ezra 5:14; 6:5, and לְהֵיבָלָה in Ezra 7:15);

(5) the י in שֵׁיזִב, which is etymologically derived from the Semitic root עזב. Akkadian is unique among Semitic languages in not representing ע (although its presence can often be inferred from the shift of nearby vowels to *e*, another mark of Akkadian influence), so this form must have been taken over from Akkadian rather than generated within Aramaic.

For all these reasons, biblical Aramaic appears to have borrowed these verbs directly from Akkadian. They are, therefore, best regarded as loanwords from Akkadian *shafᶜel* forms rather than evidence of an Aramaic *shafᶜel*.

As a result of these separate processes, we can identify three distinct prefixes that can be added to roots in biblical Aramaic in order to make them causal and thus list three separate, if related, causal conjugations:

ה	*hafᶜel*
א	*ʾafᶜel*
שׁ	*shafᶜel*

VOCABULARY

To Be Learned		*Reference*	
prohibition	אֱסָר	also	אַף
exile	גָּלוּ	bottom	אַרְעִית
living	חַי	sign	אָת
when	כְּדִי	be evil	באשׁ
speak (D)	מלל	is it not *(interrogative)*	הֲלָא
close	סגר	innocence	זָכוּ
go up	סלק	angel	מַלְאַךְ
succeed (H)	צלח	flee	נדד
former time	קַדְמָה	women	נְשִׁין
approach	קרב	piece	קְרַץ
		accuse	אכל קרץ
		pay attention	שִׂים טְעֵם
		sleep	שְׁנָה

FROM THE BIBLE (Daniel 6:11–29)

וְדָנִיֵּאל כְּדִי יְדַע דִּי רְשִׁים כְּתָבָא עַל לְבַיְתֵהּ וְכַוִּין פְּתִיחָן לֵהּ בְּעִלִּיתֵהּ נֶגֶד יְרוּשְׁלֶם וְזִמְנִין תְּלָתָה בְּיוֹמָא הוּא בָּרֵךְ מְצַלֵּא

קֳדָם אֱלָהֵהּ כָּל קֳבֵל דִּי הֲוָא עָבֵד מִן קַדְמַת דְּנָה. אֱדַיִן גֻּבְרַיָּא אִלֵּךְ הַרְגִּשׁוּ וְהַשְׁכַּחוּ

לְדָנִיֵּאל בָּעֵא קֳדָם אֱלָהֵהּ. בֵּאדַיִן קְרִיבוּ וְאָמְרִין קֳדָם מַלְכָּא עַל אֱסָר מַלְכָּא:

הֲלָא אֱסָר רְשַׁמְתָּ דִּי כָל אֱנָשׁ דִּי יִבְעֵה מִן כָּל אֱלָהּ וֶאֱנָשׁ עַד יוֹמִין תְּלָתִין לָהֵן מִנָּךְ

מַלְכָּא יִתְרְמֵא לְגֹב אַרְיָוָתָא? עָנֵה מַלְכָּא וְאָמַר: יַצִּיבָא מִלְּתָא כְּדָת מָדַי וּפָרַס דִּי

לָא תֶעְדֵּא. בֵּאדַיִן עֲנוֹ וְאָמְרִין קֳדָם מַלְכָּא דִּי: דָּנִיֵּאל דִּי מִן בְּנֵי גָלוּתָא דִּי יְהוּד

לָא שָׂם עֲלָיִךְ מַלְכָּא טְעֵם וְעַל אֱסָרָא דִּי רְשַׁמְתָּ וְזִמְנִין תְּלָתָה בְּיוֹמָא בָּעֵא. אֱדַיִן

מַלְכָּא כְּדִי מִלְּתָא שְׁמַע שַׂגִּיא בְּאֵשׁ עֲלוֹהִי. בֵּאדַיִן גֻּבְרַיָּא אִלֵּךְ הַרְגִּשׁוּ עַל מַלְכָּא

וְאָמְרִין לְמַלְכָּא דַּע מַלְכָּא דִּי דָת לְמָדַי וּפָרַס דִּי כָל אֱסָר וּקְיָם דִּי מַלְכָּא יְהָקֵים

לָא לְהַשְׁנָיָה. בֵּאדַיִן מַלְכָּא אֲמַר וְהַיְתִיו לְדָנִיֵּאל וּרְמוֹ לְגֻבָּא דִּי אַרְיָוָתָא.

עָנֵה מַלְכָּא וְאָמַר לְדָנִיֵּאל: אֱלָהָךְ דִּי אַנְתְּ פָּלַח לֵהּ הוּא יְשֵׁיזְבִנָּךְ. וְהֵיתָיִת אֶבֶן

חֲדָה וְשֻׂמַת עַל פֻּם גֻּבָּא. אֱדַיִן אֲזַל מַלְכָּא לְהֵיכְלֵהּ וּבָת טְוָת וְשַׁנְתֵּהּ נַדַּת עֲלוֹהִי.

בֵּאדַיִן מַלְכָּא בִּשְׁפַּרְפָּרָא יְקוּם בְּנָגְהָא וּבְהִתְבְּהָלָה לְגֻבָּא דִּי אַרְיָוָתָא אֲזַל וּכְמִקְרְבֵהּ לְגֻבָּא לְדָנִיֵּאל עָנֵה

מַלְכָּא וְאָמַר לְדָנִיֵּאל: דָּנִיֵּאל עֲבֵד אֱלָהָא חַיָּא אֱלָהָךְ דִּי אַנְתְּ פָּלַח לֵהּ הַיְכִל

לְשֵׁיזָבוּתָךְ מִן אַרְיָוָתָא. אֱדַיִן דָּנִיֵּאל עִם מַלְכָּא מַלִּל: מַלְכָּא לְעָלְמִין חֱיִי.

אֱלָהִי שְׁלַח מַלְאֲכֵהּ וּסֲגַר פֻּם אַרְיָוָתָא וְלָא חַבְּלוּנִי כָּל קֳבֵל דִּי קֳדָמוֹהִי זָכוּ הִשְׁתְּכַחַת

לִי וְאַף קָדָמָיִךְ מַלְכָּא חֲבוּלָה לָא עַבְדֵת. בֵּאדַיִן מַלְכָּא שַׂגִּיא טְאֵב עֲלוֹהִי וּלְדָנִיֵּאל

אֲמַר לְהַנְסָקָה מִן גֻּבָּא. וְהֻסַּק דָּנִיֵּאל מִן גֻּבָּא וְכָל חֲבָל לָא הִשְׁתְּכַח בֵּהּ דִּי הֵימִן

בֵּאלָהֵהּ. וַאֲמַר מַלְכָּא וְהַיְתִיו גֻּבְרַיָּא אִלֵּךְ דִּי אֲכַלוּ קַרְצוֹהִי דִּי דָנִיֵּאל וּלְגֹב אַרְיָוָתָא

רְמוֹ אִנּוּן בְּנֵיהוֹן וּנְשֵׁיהוֹן וְלָא מְטוֹ לְאַרְעִית גֻּבָּא עַד דִּי שְׁלִטוּ בְהוֹן אַרְיָוָתָא.

בֵּאדַיִן דָּרְיָוֶשׁ מַלְכָּא כְּתַב לְכָל עַמְמַיָּא דִּי דָאֲרִין בְּכָל אַרְעָא שְׁלָמְכוֹן יִשְׂגֵּא.

מִן קֳדָמַי שִׂים טְעֵם דִּי בְּכָל שָׁלְטָן מַלְכוּתִי לֶהֱוֹן זָאעִין וְדָחֲלִין מִן קֳדָם אֱלָהֵהּ דִּי דָנִיֵּאל

דִּי הוּא אֱלָהָא חַיָּא וְקַיָּם לְעָלְמִין וּמַלְכוּתֵהּ דִּי לָא תִתְחַבַּל וְשָׁלְטָנֵהּ עַד סוֹפָא. מְשֵׁיזִב וּמַצִּל וְעָבֵד אָתִין

בִּשְׁמַיָּא וּבְאַרְעָא דִּי שֵׁיזִב לְדָנִיֵּאל מִן יַד אַרְיָוָתָא. וְדָנִיֵּאל דְּנָה הַצְלַח בְּמַלְכוּת

דָּרְיָוֶשׁ וּבְמַלְכוּת כּוֹרֶשׁ פָּרְסָיָא.

EXERCISES

Identify the root and conjugation of the following verbs:

נְפַקָה	הַב
הֵיבֵל	מְעַבֵּד
קָאֵם	תְּקַבְּלוּן
מְשֵׁיזֵב	הַסֵּק
יִפֵּל	דָּאֲנִין
יְדִיעַ	מְכַפְּתִין
אַחֲוָיָה	תּוּכַל
יִשְׁתַּנֵּא	מְנִית
הִתְחָרַךְ	פָּקוּ
הַנְעֵל	חֲזֵיתוּן
אִשְׁתַּנִּי	אֲקִימֵהּ
שֵׁיצִיא	מְבָרֵךְ
הֲוַת	יִשְׁתַּכְלְלוּן
פְּתִיחוּ	בְּעֵינָא
אַנְדַּע	הוֹתֵב
תְּהַשְׁכַּח	מֵמַר
תְּהוֹבַד	יְשֵׁיזֵב

לֶהֱוֺן	הֵיתִי
יִתְקְרֵי	מְהַקְרְבִין
יְהָקֵים	תְּרֹעַ
שָׂמֶת	יְהוֹדַע
תֶּעְדֵּא	עֱנוֹ
תִּתְבְּנֵא	הַדֵּקֶת
נְחֶוֵּא	יְהָךְ
יִשְׁנּוֹן	הִתְרוֹמַמְתָּ

Explain the *grammatical* difference between the following pairs of forms:

יְקִים (Daniel 2:44) and יְקוּם (Daniel 7:24)

לְהַנְעָלָה (Daniel 4:3) and לְהֶעָלָה (Daniel 5:7)

מִתְבָּהַל (Daniel 5:9) and הִתְבְּהָלָה (Daniel 2:25)

אֲמַר (Daniel 4:11) and אֲמַר (Ezra 5:15)

תִּתְיְהִב (Ezra 6:4) and תִּתְחַבַּל (Daniel 2:44)

מִתְנַשְּׂאָה (Ezra 4:19) and מִתְעֲבֵד (Ezra 5:8)

מִתְקַטְּלִין (Daniel 2:13) and לְהִתְקְטָלָה (Daniel 2:13)

הִתְגְּזֶרֶת (Daniel 2:34) and אִתְגְּזֶרֶת (Daniel 2:45)

Translate into Aramaic:

(1) The father saved the son from the wild animals (lit. "of the field").

(2) The scribe completed the work on the fourth kingdom.

(3) The king assembled the people to praise God at night.

(4) I sought to leave the city when the king issued that prohibition.

(5) I went up on the mountain when the lion approached.

(6) We are closing the statue's mouth.

(7) The Jews succeeded when they were driven out into exile.

(8) The living God spoke in former times.

Chapter 27

DANIEL 7

The biblical texts in the preceding chapters have all been changed from the original, if only to reduce the amount of new vocabulary they require to a reasonable level. In this chapter, we will read Daniel 7, the last Aramaic passage in the Bible, exactly as it appears. All the necessary vocabulary can be found in the glossary at the end of this book.

The chapter describes Daniel's vision of four animals, which symbolize a succession of four empires. The history of this theme is discussed in "The Theory of the Four Monarchies: Opposition History Under the Roman Empire" by J. W. Swain in *Classical Philology* 35 (1940) 1–21, "The Four Empires in the Fourth Sibyl and in the Book of Daniel" by David Flusser in *Israel Oriental Studies* 2 (1972) 148–75, and the commentaries by James Montgomery (International Critical Commentary; New York: Charles Scribner's Sons, 1927), Louis Hartman and Alexander Di Lella (Anchor Bible; Garden City, NY: Doubleday & Co., 1978), and John Collins (Hermeneia; Minneapolis: Fortress Press, 1993).

(1) בִּשְׁנַת חֲדָה לְבֵלְאשַׁצַּר מֶלֶךְ בָּבֶל דָּנִיֵּאל חֵלֶם חֲזָה וְחֶזְוֵי רֵאשֵׁהּ עַל מִשְׁכְּבֵהּ בֵּאדַיִן חֶלְמָא כְתַב רֵאשׁ מִלִּין אֲמַר.

Translate into English:

רֵאשׁ מִלִּין is understood by some scholars as meaning a "complete account"; others think it refers to the "essential contents." There is a similar Hebrew phrase in Psalm 119:160.

NOTICE the ל- prefixed to לְבֵלְאשַׁצַּר, which expresses possession, just like a construct phrase. The name itself is Babylonian (Bel-shar-uṣur) and means

"Bel guards the king." In Daniel 5 it occurs with the א following the שׁ (verses 1, 2, 9, 22, and 29); that kind of inconsistency is to be expected in the transliteration of a foreign name (compare our spellings Eileen and Ilene).

List all the verbs in this sentence and identify the form of each:

Verbal forms	Root	Conjugation	Tense	Person	Gender	Number

Translate each of the following words into Hebrew:

חֲדָה

רֵאשֵׁהּ

חֶלְמָא

מִלִּין

(2) עָנֵה דָנִיֵּאל וְאָמַר חָזֵה הֲוֵית בְּחֶזְוִי עִם לֵילְיָא וַאֲרוּ אַרְבַּע רוּחֵי שְׁמַיָּא מְגִיחָן לְיַמָּא רַבָּא. (3) וְאַרְבַּע חֵיוָן רַבְרְבָן סָלְקָן מִן יַמָּא שָׁנְיָן דָּא מִן דָּא.

Translate into English:

NOTICE: The meaning of עִם is apparently temporal ("at the time of") as in Daniel 3:33 and 4:31 (עִם דָּר וְדָר, see chapters 19 and 22).

"Wind" (רוּחַ) and "sea" (יַם) are common elements in ancient Near Eastern stories about primeval time, including the creation story in Genesis 1.

What form are the following verbs:

	Root	*Conjugation*	*Tense*	*Person*	*Gender*	*Number*
עֲנֵה						
חֲזֵה						
הֲוֵית						
סְלִקָן						
מְגִיחָן						

The subject of מְגִיחָן is _____; although that noun does not have a formal feminine ending (ה֯- or ת-), the verb's feminine ending makes its gender clear.

אֲמַר is equivalent to the Hebrew form _____.

The phrase חָזֵה הֲוֵית means _____.

(4) קַדְמָיְתָא כְאַרְיֵה וְגַפִּין דִּי נְשַׁר לַהּ חָזֵה הֲוֵית עַד דִּי מְרִיטוּ גַפֵּיהּ וּנְטִילַת מִן

אַרְעָא וְעַל רַגְלַיִן כֶּאֱנָשׁ הֳקִימַת וּלְבַב אֱנָשׁ יְהִיב לַהּ. (5) וַאֲרוּ חֵיוָה אָחֳרִי תִנְיָנָה

דָּמְיָה לְדֹב וְלִשְׂטַר חַד הֳקִמַת וּתְלָת עִלְעִין בְּפֻמַּהּ בֵּין שִׁנַּיהּ וְכֵן אָמְרִין לַהּ קוּמִי

אֱכֻלִי בְּשַׂר שַׂגִּיא. (6) בָּאתַר דְּנָה חָזֵה הֲוֵית וַאֲרוּ אָחֳרִי כִּנְמַר וְלַהּ גַּפִּין אַרְבַּע דִּי

עוֹף עַל גַּבַּיהּ וְאַרְבְּעָה רֵאשִׁין לְחֵיוְתָא וְשָׁלְטָן יְהִיב לַהּ.

Translate into English:

Translate the following words into Hebrew:

עִלְעִין

(The singular occurs in the Garden of Eden story.)

אָמְרִין

לְחֵיוְתָא

נְשַׁר

What form are the following verbs:

	Root	Conjugation	Tense	Person	Gender	Number
מְרִיטוּ						
נְטִילַת						
הֲקִימַת						
דָּמְיָה						
יְהִיב						

What is the subject of הֲקִימַת in verse 5? _____

This passage includes a series of ordinal numbers:

    "first"   קַדְמָיְתָא

    "second"   תִּנְיָנָה

    (for "third"   תְּלִיתָיָא, see Daniel 2:39 on p. 87.)

    "fourth"   רְבִיעָיָה   (see verse 7 below)

In post-biblical Aramaic, the ד in קַדְמָא ("first") assimilated to the מ, leaving the form קַמָּא; thus the three subdivisions of the talmudic tractate נְזִיקִין are called:

       בָּבָא בַתְרָא   בָּבָא מְצִיעָא   בָּבָא קַמָּא

בַּתְרָא is an adjectival form, which developed from בָּאתַר ("after," see verse 6 and p. 62), itself a composite of the preposition בְּ- ("in") and the noun אֲתַר ("place").

(7) בָּאתַר דְּנָה חָזֵה הֲוֵית בְּחֶזְוֵי לֵילְיָא וַאֲרוּ חֵיוָה רְבִיעָיָה דְּחִילָה וְאֵימְתָנִי וְתַקִּיפָא יַתִּירָא וְשִׁנַּיִן דִּי פַרְזֶל לַהּ רַבְרְבָן אָכְלָה וּמַדֱּקָה וּשְׁאָרָא בְּרַגְלַיהּ רָפְסָה וְהִיא מְשַׁנְּיָה מִן כָּל חֵיוָתָא דִּי קָדָמַיהּ וְקַרְנַיִן עֲשַׂר לַהּ. (8) מִשְׂתַּכַּל הֲוֵית בְּקַרְנַיָּא וַאֲלוּ קֶרֶן אָחֳרִי זְעֵירָה סִלְקָת בֵּינֵיהֵן וּתְלָת מִן קַרְנַיָּא קַדְמָיָתָא אֶתְעֲקַרָה מִן קֳדָמַיהּ וַאֲלוּ עַיְנִין כְּעַיְנֵי אֲנָשָׁא בְּקַרְנָא דָא וּפֻם מְמַלִּל רַבְרְבָן.

Translate into English:

NOTICE the suffix on יַתִּירָא (verse 7), which functions adverbially; it may be a remnant of an old accusative ending.

The adjectives אֵימְתָנִי (verse 7) and אָחֳרִי (verse 8) are both feminine singular.

What are the number and gender of:

		Number	*Gender*
רַבְרְבָן	(verses 7 and 8)		
חֵיוָתָא	(verse 7)		

What does the phrase מִשְׂתַּכַּל הֲוֵית (verse 8) mean?

What part of the sentence are the following words in verse 8?

פֻּם

מְמַלִּל

רַבְרְבָן

NOTICE the word order in the various clauses found in these sentences.

What form are the following verbs:

	Root	Conjugation	Tense	Person	Gender	Number
דְּחִילָה						
רָפְסָה						
מְשַׁנְּיָה						
מִשְׂתַּכַּל						
סִלְקָת						
אֶתְעֲקַרָה						

The subject of אֶתְעֲקַרָה (verse 8) is _____. Since this Gt verb is in the perfect, which normally begins with הִתְ, the prefixed א must have weakened from an original ה.

מַדֱּקָה and אָכְלָה (verse 7) are both the same form, albeit in different conjugations. To what conjugations do they belong?

אָכְלָה

מַדֱּקָה

What form are they? _____

NOTE that the root of מַדְקָה is דקק. The (doubling) *dagesh* would normally be expected in the ק rather than the ד; Hebrew has analogous forms (e.g., יִסֹּב, which comes from the root סבב).

קַרְנַיִן עֲשַׂר לַהּ expresses possession ("it had 10 horns"); this chapter of Daniel contains several other examples of this construction:

נַפִּין דִּי נְשַׁר לַהּ (verse 4) means _____.

לַהּ גַּפִּין אַרְבַּע דִּי עוֹף (verse 6) means _____.

שִׁנַּיִן דִּי פַרְזֶל לַהּ רַבְרְבָן (verse 7) means _____.

(9) חָזֵה הֲוֵית עַד דִּי כָרְסָוָן רְמִיו וְעַתִּיק יוֹמִין יְתִב לְבוּשֵׁהּ כִּתְלַג חִוָּר וּשְׂעַר רֵאשֵׁהּ כַּעֲמַר נְקֵא כָּרְסְיֵהּ שְׁבִיבִין דִּי נוּר גַּלְגִּלּוֹהִי נוּר דָּלִק. (10) נְהַר דִּי נוּר נָגֵד וְנָפֵק מִן קֳדָמוֹהִי אֶלֶף אַלְפִים יְשַׁמְּשׁוּנֵּהּ וְרִבּוֹ רִבְבָן קָדָמוֹהִי יְקוּמוּן דִּינָא יְתִב וְסִפְרִין פְּתִיחוּ.

Translate into English:

List all the passive verbs in this passage:

List all the active participles in this passage:

NOTICE that יְתִב is in the perfect; the *ḥireq* is the theme vowel. The phrase דִּינָא יְתִב means "sat in justice."

What other verbs can you find in this passage?

Verb	*Root*	*Conjugation*	*Tense*	*Person*	*Gender*	*Number*

Identify the suffixes on the following words:

כָּרְסָוָן (verse 9)

לְבוּשֵׁה (verse 9)

גַּלְגִּלּוֹהִי (verse 9)

שְׁבִיבִין (verse 10)

דִּינָא (verse 10)

This passage, which is widely regarded as a poem (note the parallelistic sentence structure), is one of several throne visions in the Bible (compare 1 Kings 22:19, Isaiah 6, and Ezekiel 1, 3:23–34 and 10:1, as well as 1 Enoch 14:18–23). "The ancient of days" (עַתִּיק יוֹמִין) is God.

(11) חָזֵה הֲוֵית בֵּאדַיִן מִן קָל מִלַּיָּא רַבְרְבָתָא דִּי קַרְנָא מְמַלְּלָה חָזֵה הֲוֵית עַד דִּי קְטִילַת חֵיוְתָא וְהוּבַד גִּשְׁמַהּ וִיהִיבַת לִיקֵדַת אֶשָּׁא. (12) וּשְׁאָר חֵיוָתָא הֶעְדִּיו שָׁלְטָנְהוֹן וְאַרְכָה בְחַיִּין יְהִיבַת לְהוֹן עַד זְמַן וְעִדָּן.

Translate into English:

קָל is equivalent to the Hebrew word _____.

קְטִילַת and הוּבַד are both passive forms; what are their roots and to what conjugations do they belong?

	Root	Conjugation
קְטִילַת		
הוּבַד		

What form are the following verbs:

	Root	Conjugation	Tense	Person	Gender	Number
מְמַלְּלָה						
הֶעְדִּיו						

Identify the suffixes on the following words:

מִלַּיָּא

אֶשָּׁא

גִּשְׁמֵהּ

רַבְרְבָתָא

What is the difference between חֵיוְתָא (verse 11) and חֵיוָתָא (verse 10)?

זְמַן and עִדָּן are synonyms; the phrase זְמַן וְעִדָּן should, therefore, probably be understood as a hendiadys, meaning "a time and a(nother) time," i.e., "two times."

(13) חָזֵה הֲוֵית בְּחֶזְוֵי לֵילְיָא וַאֲרוּ עִם עֲנָנֵי שְׁמַיָּא כְּבַר אֱנָשׁ אָתֵה הֲוָה וְעַד עַתִּיק יוֹמַיָּא מְטָה וּקְדָמוֹהִי הַקְרְבוּהִי. (14) וְלֵהּ יְהִיב שָׁלְטָן וִיקָר וּמַלְכוּ וְכֹל עַמְמַיָּא אֻמַיָּא וְלִשָּׁנַיָּא לֵהּ יִפְלְחוּן שָׁלְטָנֵהּ שָׁלְטָן עָלַם דִּי לָא יֶעְדֵּה וּמַלְכוּתֵהּ דִּי לָא תִתְחַבַּל.

Translate into English:

What is the function of the suffix on לֵילְיָא (verse 13)? The י corresponds to the final ה on the Hebrew form לַיְלָה, which cannot be a feminine ending since that invariably carries the accent; note the Hebrew form לֵיל, which occurs in Isaiah 16:3.

The phrase אָתֵה הֲוָה (verse 13) means _____ .

What is the relationship between מַלְכוּ and מַלְכוּתֵהּ (verse 14)?

What form are the following verbs:

	Root	Conjugation	Tense	Person	Gender	Number
אָתֵה						
מְטָה						
יֵעְדֵּה						
תִּתְחַבַּל						
יִפְלְחוּן						
הַקְרְבוּהִי						

What is the subject of:

הַקְרְבוּהִי   (verse 13)

יִפְלְחוּן   (verse 14)

The phrase כְּבַר אֱנָשׁ is famous, but problematic. בַּר is used in Aramaic, as בֶּן is in Hebrew, to indicate the possessor of a quality or the member of a class, in this case "human being" (אֱנָשׁ; cf. בֶּן אֱנוֹשׁ in Ps 144:3). The equivalent phrase (υἱὸς τοῦ ἀνθρώπου) occurs in the New Testament, where its meaning is widely debated. For further discussion, see "The Son of Man" by John Bowker in *Journal of Theological Studies* new series 28 (1977) pp. 19–48, and "The New Testament Title 'Son of Man' Philologically Considered" by Joseph A. Fitzmyer in *A Wandering Aramean: Collected Aramaic Essays* (Missoula, MT: Scholars Press, 1979) pp. 143–60.

(15) אֶתְכְּרִיַּת רוּחִי אֲנָה דָנִיֵּאל בְּגוֹא נִדְנֶה וְחֶזְוֵי רֵאשִׁי יְבַהֲלֻנַּנִי. (16) קִרְבֵת עַל

חַד מִן קָאֲמַיָּא וְיַצִּיבָא אֶבְעֵא מִנֵּהּ עַל כָּל דְּנָה וַאֲמַר לִי וּפְשַׁר מִלַּיָּא יְהוֹדְעִנַּנִי.

(17) אִלֵּין חֵיוָתָא רַבְרְבָתָא דִּי אִנִּין אַרְבַּע אַרְבְּעָה מַלְכִין יְקוּמוּן מִן אַרְעָא.

(18) וִיקַבְּלוּן מַלְכוּתָא קַדִּישֵׁי עֶלְיוֹנִין וְיַחְסְנוּן מַלְכוּתָא עַד עָלְמָא וְעַד עָלַם עָלְמַיָּא.

Translate into English:

NOTICE how the phrase אֲנָה דָנִיֵּאל functions as an appositive to the pronominal suffix of רוּחִי in verse 15, resulting in the meaning: "my spirit—me, Daniel. . . ."

The reference to Daniel's spirit as having a sheath (נִדְנֶה) suggests a distinction between the body and the mind, which emerged only late in the biblical period.

What form are the following verbs:

	Root	Conjugation	Tense	Person	Gender	Number
קִרְבֵת						
אֶבְעֵא						
יְהוֹדְעִנַּנִי						
יְקַבְּלוּן						
קָאֲמַיָּא						

NOTICE how the weak middle letter of the hollow root קוּם has been "strengthened" to an א.

Although אֶתְכְּרִיַּת (verse 15) clearly belongs to the Gt conjugation, the fact that it is perfect demonstrates that the א is not a pronominal prefix (the form is 3d person feminine singular), but softened from ה, making this an *ʾitpeʿel* form (compare the *haʾfel* conjugation, which sometimes weakens into *ʾafʿel*).

אִנִּין (verse 17) literally means _____; in this sentence, it functions as a copula, as pronouns often do in Aramaic and later Hebrew.

קַדִּישֵׁי (verse 18) is a term with a long and important history. In ancient Canaanite texts it refers to gods; however, the Hebrew Bible uses it primarily for angels (e.g., Psalm 89:6 and Job 15:15). Jews later applied it to themselves. In the Middle Ages, the Latin equivalent (*sanctus*) was used for "saints." (The English word is derived from the same Latin root.) For further reading on this term, see "The Saints of the Most High and Their Kingdom" by C. H. W. Brekelmans in *Oudtestamentische Studiën* 14 (1965) 305–29, and "The Identity of 'the Saints of the Most High' in Daniel 7" by G. F. Hasel in *Biblica* 56 (1975) 173–92.

(19) אֱדַיִן צְבִית לְיַצָּבָא עַל חֵיוְתָא רְבִיעָיְתָא דִּי הֲוָת שָׁנְיָה מִן כָּלְּהֵן דְּחִילָה יַתִּירָה שִׁנַּיהּ דִּי פַרְזֶל וְטִפְרַיהּ דִּי נְחָשׁ אָכְלָה מַדֲּקָה וּשְׁאָרָא בְּרַגְלַיהּ רָפְסָה. (20) וְעַל קַרְנַיָּא עֲשַׂר דִּי בְרֵאשַׁהּ וְאָחֳרִי דִּי סִלְקַת וּנְפַלָה מִן קֳדָמַיהּ תְּלָת וְקַרְנָא דִכֵּן וְעַיְנִין לַהּ וּפֻם מְמַלִּל רַבְרְבָן וְחֶזְוַהּ רַב מִן חַבְרָתַהּ. (21) חָזֵה הֲוֵית וְקַרְנָא דִכֵּן עָבְדָה קְרָב עִם קַדִּישִׁין וְיָכְלָה לְהוֹן. (22) עַד דִּי אֲתָה עַתִּיק יוֹמַיָּא וְדִינָא יְהִב לְקַדִּישֵׁי עֶלְיוֹנִין וְזִמְנָא מְטָה וּמַלְכוּתָא הֶחֱסִנוּ קַדִּישִׁין.

Translate into English:

דְּכֵן (verse 20) is what part of speech: _____

       gender _____

       number _____

What form are the following verbs:

	Root	Conjugation	Tense	Person	Gender	Number
צְבִית						
שָׁנְיָה						
דְּחִילָה						
מַדַּקָה						
סִלְקַת						
נְפַלָה						
מְטָה						

The subject of נְפַלָה is _____.

NOTE that the description of the fourth beast in verse 19 includes the phrase טִפְרַיה דִּי נְחָשׁ ("claws of bronze"), which is not found in verse 7 where it may, therefore, have been accidentally omitted.

(23) כֵּן אֲמַר חֵיוְתָא רְבִיעָיְתָא מַלְכוּ רְבִיעָאָה תֶּהֱוֵא בְאַרְעָא דִּי תִשְׁנֵא מִן כָּל מַלְכְוָתָא וְתֵאכֻל כָּל אַרְעָא וּתְדוּשִׁנַּהּ וְתַדְּקִנַּהּ. (24) וְקַרְנַיָּא עֲשַׂר מִנַּהּ מַלְכוּתָה עַשְׂרָה מַלְכִין יְקֻמוּן וְאָחֳרָן יְקוּם אַחֲרֵיהוֹן וְהוּא יִשְׁנֵא מִן קַדְמָיֵא וּתְלָתָה מַלְכִין יְהַשְׁפִּל. (25) וּמִלִּין לְצַד עִלָּיָא יְמַלִּל וּלְקַדִּישֵׁי עֶלְיוֹנִין יְבַלֵּא וְיִסְבַּר לְהַשְׁנָיָה זִמְנִין וְדָת וְיִתְיַהֲבוּן בִּידֵהּ עַד עִדָּן וְעִדָּנִין וּפְלַג עִדָּן. (26) וְדִינָא יִתִּב וְשָׁלְטָנֵהּ יְהַעְדּוֹן לְהַשְׁמָדָה וּלְהוֹבָדָה עַד סוֹפָא. (27) וּמַלְכוּתָה וְשָׁלְטָנָא וּרְבוּתָא דִּי מַלְכְוָת תְּחוֹת כָּל שְׁמַיָּא יְהִיבַת לְעַם קַדִּישֵׁי עֶלְיוֹנִין מַלְכוּתֵהּ מַלְכוּת עָלַם וְכֹל שָׁלְטָנַיָּא לֵהּ יִפְלְחוּן וְיִשְׁתַּמְּעוּן.

Translate into English:

NOTICE the difference between אָחֳרָן ("another") and אָחֲרֵיהוֹן ("after them") in verse 24, which are comparable to the Hebrew pair אַחֵר ("other") and אַחֲרֵי ("after").

לְצַד (lit. "to the side of") apparently means "against" in verse 25.

עִדָּן וְעִדָּנִין וּפְלַג עִדָּן (verse 25) refers to the three and one half units of time (1 + 2 + 1/2) which are also mentioned in Daniel 8:14 and 9:27.

What form are the following verbs:

	Root	Conjugation	Tense	Person	Gender	Number
תֶּהֱוֵה						
יִתְיַהֲבוּן						
יְהִיבַת						
יְהַשְׁפִּל						

NOTICE that the ה is retained in this last form, as in the grammatically similar יְהַעְדּוֹן (verse 26).

To what conjugation does each of the following verbs belong:

יְמַלִּל

יְבַלֵּא

יִסְבַּר

What is the root of:

לְהַשְׁנָיָה

לְהַשְׁמָדָה

לְהוֹבָדָה

All three of these words are _____.

What are the root and the conjugation for each of the following verbs?

	Conjugation	Root
יִפְלְחוּן		
יִשְׁתַּמְּעוּן		
יְהַעְדּוֹן		

(28) עַד כָּה סוֹפָא דִי מִלְּתָה אֲנָה דָנִיֵּאל שַׂגִּיא רַעְיוֹנַי יְבַהֲלֻנַּנִי וְזִיוַי יִשְׁתַּנּוֹן עֲלַי וּמִלְּתָא בְּלִבִּי נִטְרֵת.

Translate into English:

NOTICE the similar phrase near the end of Ecclesiastes (12:13).

List all the verbs in this verse and give the form of each:

Verb	Root	Conjugation	Tense	Person	Gender	Number

Chapter 28

INSCRIPTIONS

The oldest surviving texts in Aramaic are inscriptions. We will consider three of these, one from the language's earliest known period, another that was found in a modern collection so that its original date and location are unknown, and a third that comes from a seventh-century synagogue.

The following words are common in inscriptions and should be learned:

brother	אח
evil (sometimes באש)	ביש
remember	דכר
see	חמה
direct object marker	ית
thus	כן
is not	לישה
open	פתח

Our earliest evidence of Aramaic's long history comes from a series of inscriptions which were found in northern Syria and had been written during the time of Israel's divided monarchy.* Several of these are from the rulers of a country known as Samʾal, a petty kingdom of the ninth and eighth centuries, a time during which the Arameans established several small countries in this region. (The Bible mentions Damascus, Zobah, Beth Rechob, and Maacah.) The example which follows is by one Barrakib, who apparently ruled Samʾal towards the end of the eighth century, about the same time that Amos, Hosea, Micah, and Isaiah were active in Israel. It was found at Zinjirli in northwest Syria at the end of the last century. A relief with his picture (see p. 168) is inscribed with the words אנה בר רכב בר פנמו at the top. This same phrase opens the much longer inscription which we will read here.

---

*These are conveniently collected in H. Donner and W. Röllig's *Kanaanäische und Aramäische Inschriften* (Wiesbaden: Otto Harrassowitz, 1966).

אנה בר רכב בר פנמו מלך שמאל עבד תגלתפליסר מרא רבעי ארקא.

בצדק אבי ובצדקי הושבני מראי רכבאל ומראי תגלתפליסר על כרסא אבי.

ובית אבי עמל מן כל. ורצת בגלגל מראי מלך אשור במצעת מלכן

רברבן בעלי כסף ובעלי זהב. ואחזת בית אבי והיטבתה מן בית חד

מלכן רברבן. והתנאבו אחי מלכיא לכל מה טבת ביתי. ובי טב

לישה לאבהי מלכי שמאל הא בית כלמו להם פהא בית שתוא להם

והא בית כיצא. ואנה בנית ביתא זנה.

Vocabulary

settle (H)	יִשׁב	desire (Htn)	אבה
summer	כיץ	grasp	אחז
middle	מצעת	*dialect form of* בית	בי
exert oneself, toil	עמל	wheel	גלגל
and	פ-	behold	הא

Vocabulary (cont.)

righteousness	צדק	gold	זהב
quarter	רבע	this	זנה
run	רוץ	goodness	טבה
winter	שתו	be pleasing (H)	יטב

Use the biblical vowel system to vocalize the above text.

Translate it into English:

Proper Names

בר רכב — This name is pronounced Barrakib according to an inscribed Hittite seal, where it is spelled out syllabically (*Orientalia* 20 [1957] 345).

פנמו — Pronounced Panamuwa according to cuneiform inscriptions from several Assyrian rulers (e.g., Tiglath Pilesar III; see James Pritchard, *Ancient Near Eastern Texts Relating to the Old Testament*, pp. 282 and 283); *-muwa* was a common ending for names in Asia Minor (see כלמו below).

שמאל — The ancient name of the land in which Zinjirli is located; it may also have been called Yaudi.

תגלתפליסר — Tiglath Pilesar III, who is mentioned several times in the Bible (2 Kings 15:29; 16:7, 10; 1 Chronicles 5:6, 26; 2 Chronicles 28:20); he is called by the Babylonian throne name Pul in 2 Kings 15:19.

רכבאל — The patron god of Samʾal.

כלמו — An earlier ruler of Samʾal from the ninth century, who is apparently the author of another inscription found in Zinjirli (see H. Donner and W. Röllig, *Kanaanäische und Aramäische Inschriften,* no. 24, and James Pritchard, *Ancient Near Eastern Texts Relating to the Old Testament,* p. 654).

NOTICE that we have already encountered ארקא in Jeremiah 10:11, where it is juxtaposed with the more common form ארעא, demonstrating two different realizations of the Semitic consonant *ḍ*, which appears as צ in Hebrew (i.e. ארץ).* The title רבעי ארקא מרא is a translation from Assyrian (*shar kibrat arbaʾi*).

מצעת (middle) can be compared with mishnaic אֶמְצַע; the second section of the talmudic tractate נְזִיקִין is called בָּבָא מְצִיעָא (the first section is בָּבָא קַמָּא and the last section בָּבָא בַּתְרָא, as explained on p. 153).

התנאבו appears to be a *hitnafʿal* form from a root related to אבה and יאב (wish); its meaning would be something like "envy" or "be jealous."

The most conspicuous features of this early inscription are the number of forms which agree with Hebrew, rather than biblical Aramaic:

הושבני contrast the form הותב (e.g., Ezra 4:10) from the root יתב.

לישה corresponding to the Akkadian *lā išu,* comes from the words לא יש ("it is not"); however it appears as לית in other Aramaic sources, including the massoretes' marginal notes to the biblical text, where its abbreviation ל is used to identify forms that are spelled uniquely in the Hebrew text (see p. 55).

זהב is common in the Aramaic sections of the Bible, but appears there as דְּהַב (e.g., Ezra 5:14; 6:5, and often in Daniel 2, 3, and 5).

אחז usually spelled אחד in Aramaic.

זנה typically דְּנָה (but compare Hebrew זֶה).

*The two forms are juxtaposed in the Elephantine letter (Cowley 6) presented in chapter 29.

רצת appears as רהט in Aramaic (compare Targum Onkelos with the original Hebrew in Genesis 24:27, 20, 28, and 29).

These are all cases in which original Semitic sounds that came to be realized differently in Hebrew and in Aramaic (e.g., *t* as שׁ or ת, *t* as ט or צ, and *d* as ז or ד) here follow the "Hebrew" (really Canaanite) spelling. This inscription may, therefore, have been written before these two branches of Northwest Semitic had fully separated. Thus the original *t* appears as שׁ in הושב and ליש, *t* as צ in רץ and כיץ, and *d* as ז in זהב, אחז, and זנה.

כיצא   spelled קיט in biblical Aramaic (Daniel 2:35), but קיץ in Hebrew. The use of כ instead of ק may reflect a certain fluidity in spelling (so also שׁתו appears as סְתָו in Song of Songs 2:11). However, since the same spelling is found in several other inscriptions, it is more likely that dissimilation caused the ק to shift to כ, inasmuch as the word already had one sharpened letter (צ) in it.

Several other features in this inscription are characteristically Aramaic:

SOUNDS: The *â* sound is evident in אנה (as opposed to Hebrew אֲנִי) and words like טב, where it shifted to *ô* in Hebrew.

WORDS: בר חד כרסא מרא רברבן

FORMS: The determined state (ארקא, ביתא, מלכיא);

         masculine plural suffixes ending with *nun* (e.g., מלכן);

         perfect, 1st person singular forms ending with *-ēt* rather than *-tî* (e.g., בנית and אחזת).

The next inscription was found on a stone plaque in a nineteenth-century collection of antiquities at the Russian convent on Jerusalem's Mount of Olives. It mentions Judah's King Uzziah, who reigned during the early part of the eighth century; however, its "Aramaic style" script was not adopted by Jews until the Babylonian Exile, when it replaced the "Phoenician" (Paleo-Hebrew) script that had been used during the monarchy period. The inscription itself was probably written sometime around the first century.

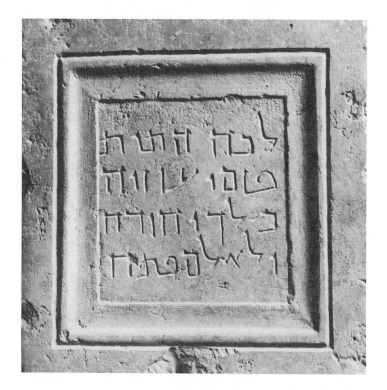

לכה התית טמי עוזיה מלך יהודה ולא למפתח.

Vocabulary

bones . . . . . . טם

here . . . . כה

Use the biblical vowel system to vocalize the above text.

Translate it into English:

התית   is an H passive form of the common root אתה ("come," cf. Daniel 6:18).

טמי   is equivalent to the Hebrew word עֶצֶם ("bone"). The loss of the ע suggests that it was not pronounced in this period; there are several reports in the Talmud indicating that the letters ע and א were often not distinguished in pronunciation during the early centuries of this era (*j. Berakhot* 2:4, *b. Berakhot* 32a, *b. Megillah* 24b, *b. Erubin* 53b).

למפתח   the מ in this word is shaped like the form (ם) which is used today at the end of words (see the illustration on p. 172). Apparently, the two shapes we use for the letter מ were originally interchangeable (see Isaiah 9:6); over time, one of them (ם) was reserved for the end of words, probably on the basis of analogy with other letters in which medial (כ, נ, פ, צ) and final forms (ך, ן, ף, ץ) had come to be distinguished. Thus ם is the only final form that does not have a tail.

The prohibition against opening the vessel containing Uzziah's bones is typical of many inscriptions (for several Phoenician examples, see James Pritchard, *Ancient Near Eastern Texts Relating to the Old Testament,* pp. 661–62). 2 Chronicles 26:23 reports that King Uzziah, who suffered from leprosy, was buried in a special location outside Jerusalem's city wall (cf. Josephus, *Antiquities* 9:10.4 §227 and Nehemiah 3:15). This inscription, then, attests to his bones' having been moved some time after their initial burial.

A final inscription comes from the mosaic floor of a seventh-century synagogue located in ʿEin Gedi, along the western coast of the Dead Sea between Qumran and Masada. (An earlier, Hebrew section of the inscription lists several ancient biblical luminaries and the signs of the zodiac.)

דכירין לטב יוסה ועירון וחזיקיו בנוה דחלפי. כל מן דיהיב פלגו בן גבר לחבריה

הי אמר לשן ביש על חבריה לעממיה הי גניב צבותיה דחבריה הי מן דגלי רזה

דקרתה לעממיה דין דעינוה משוטטן בכל ארעה וחמי סתירתה הוא יתן אפוה

בגברה ההו ובזרעיה ויעקור יתיה מן תחות שומיה. וימרון כל עמה אמן ואמן

סלה. רבי יוסה בן חלפי חזקיו בן חלפי דכירין לטב דרגי סני

אנון עבדו לשמה דרחמנה שלום.

Vocabulary

selah *(liturgical term)* . . סלה	amen *(liturgical term)* . . . . . אמן
hidden thing . . . . סתירה	nose . . . . אף
uproot . . . . עקר	between (בין) . . . . בן
discord . . . . פלג	steal . . . . גנב
property . . . . (ת)צבו	of . . . . -ד
Merciful One . . . . רחמן	stair . . . . דרג
wander . . . . שטט	seed . . . . זרע

Proper Names

חזיקיו — This form conforms to a normal northern pattern for spelling the divine element at the end of names rather than the more familiar (southern) יהו-.

חלפי

יוסה

עירון

Use the biblical vowel system to vocalize the above text.

Translate it into English:

NOTICE the phrase דין דעינוה (lit. "This one, which his eyes,"
i.e. "the one whose eyes . . .").

Several features of this inscription are familiar from other Aramaic texts we have studied. For example, תחות occurs in the book of Daniel (also Jeremiah 10:11), as does the direct object marker ית (Daniel 3:12) in contrast to biblical Hebrew's את. דכירין and ארעה also reflect common Aramaic forms (contrast the Hebrew words זכרן and ארץ), as does דין. Surprisingly, זרע is closer to the Hebrew form of the word for "arm" (זְרוֹעַ) than biblical Aramaic's (אֶ)דְרַע; note also שלום rather than שְׁלָם. Other notable spellings include:

בן for בין (between)

שומיא for שמיא (sky)

ימרון from the root אמר (say)

סני for שגיא (much)

The last two examples, along with הי rather than the more common היא, suggest that the pronunciation of several consonants was becoming weaker. (See p. 70 regarding שׁ becoming ס; other examples are mentioned on pp. 171 and 206.)

On the other hand, this inscription contains several unfamiliar phenomena:

— passive participles (גניב and יהיב) used in apparently active contexts.

— the particle דְּ where biblical Aramaic uses דִּי.

— final י in words the Bible spells with ה (e.g., גלי and חמי).

— the determined suffix marked with ה rather than the biblical א.

Chapter 29

LETTERS

Several Aramaic letters have survived from various periods of antiquity. Although our interest here is linguistic, they provide important evidence for understanding the nature of ancient letters in general.

Vocabulary To Be Learned

women . . . . נשין	fire . . . . אש
burnt offering . . . עלוה/עלתה	donkey . . . . חמר
compassion . . . . רחמן	month . . . . ירח
break . . . . תבר	to, with . . . . לות
here . . . . תנה	altar . . . . מדבח
	self . . . . נפש

The first letter was written in the fifth pre-Christian century at a Jewish settlement on the island of Yeb (Elephantine), which is north of the first cataract of the Nile, where the Aswan Dam is located today. The Persian Empire, which had conquered Egypt in 525 B.C.E., supported Jewish mercenaries in this military colony on the southern frontier of ancient Egypt. Their writings, on papyri, were discovered in the early part of the twentieth century. The following letter gives us a fair amount of information about the colony's history.

Lines 1–3

אל מראן בגוהי פחת יהוד. עבדיך ידניה וכנותה כהניא זי ביב בירתא:

שלם מראן אלה שמיא ישאל שגיא בכל עדן ולרחמן ישימנך קדם דריוהוש מלכא

ובני ביתא יתיר מן זי כען חד חד אלף. וחין אריכן ינתן לך וחדה ושריר הוי

בכל עדן.

Vocabulary

long	אריך
fortress	בירתה
who, which	זי
happiness	חדה
life	חין
prosperous	שריר

Use the biblical vowel system to vocalize the passage above.

Translate it into English:

Proper Nouns

בגוי — governor of Judah, apparently after Nehemiah

ידניה — son of Gemariah, priest and leader of the Jewish community

דריהוש — Darius II, who ruled Persia from 423 to 403. The letter ends with the author's statement that he wrote this in the 17th year of Darius' reign, i.e. 407 B.C.E.

חד אלף — 1000 times; compare the phrase חַד שִׁבְעָה in Daniel 3:19 (see p. 90)

Lines 4–13

כען עבדך ידניה וכנותה כן אמרן: בירח תמוז שנת 14 דריוהוש מלכא כזי ארשם

נפק ואזל על מלכא כמריא זי אלהא חנוב אלהא זי ביב בירתא המונית עם וידרנג

זי פרתרך תנה הוה. לם אגורא זי יהו אלהא זי ביב בירתא יהעדו מן תמה.

אחר וידרנג זך לחיא אגרת שלח על נפין ברה זי רבחיל הוה בסון בירתא לאמר:

אגורא זי ביב בירתא ינדשו אחר נפין דבר מצריא עם חילא אחרנן. אתו לבירת

יב עם תליהם עלו באגורא זך נדשוהי עד ארעא ועמודיא זי אבנא זי הוו תמה

תברו המו. אף הוה תרען זי אבן 5 בנין פסילה זי אבן זי הוו באגורא זך נדשו

ודשיהם קימן וציריהם זי דששיא אלך נחש ומטלל עקהן זי ארז כלא זי עם שירית

אשרנא ואחרן זי תמה הוה כלא באשה שרפו. ומזרקיא זי זהבא וכסף ומנדעמתא

זי הוה באגורא זך כלא לקחו ולנפשהום עבדו.

Vocabulary

roof	מטלל	temple	אגורא
anything	מנדעם	cedar	ארז
destroy	נדש	beams	אשרן
pillar	עמוד	lead (D)	דבר
wood	עק	door	דש
cut stone	פסיל	in agreement with ...	המונית עם
governor	פרתרך	that	זי, זך
pivot (of a door)	ציר	army	חיל
standing	קים	when (cf. כדי)	כזי
general	רבחיל	priest	כמר
burn	שרף	evil	לחיא
remainder	שירי	surely	לם
weapon	תלי	take	לקח
gate	תרע	basin	מזרק

Use biblical vowels to vocalize the passage above.

Translate it into English:

Proper Nouns

ארשם — Persian satrap over Egypt

חנוב — a male Egyptian god at Elephantine

וידרנג — commander of the Persian garrison at Elephantine and later *frataraka* ("foremost"), a position with judicial and military authority

יהו — the God of the Jews

נפין — son of Vidranga

מצריא — Egyptians

סון — Syene (ancient name of Elephantine); cf. Ezekiel 29:10 and 30:6

תמוז — a late summer month

רבחיל — the Bible includes several titles which are similarly constructed: רַב שָׁקֵה and, רַב סָרִיס, רַב מַג, רַב טַבָּחִים, רַב הַחֹבֵל

Lines 13–17

ומן יומי מלך מצרין אבהין בנו אגורא זך ביב בירתא. וכזי כנבוזי על למצרין

אגורא זך בנה השכח. ואגורי אלהי מצרין כל מגרו ואיש מנדעם באגורא זך

לא חבל. וכזי כונה עביד אנחנה עם נשין ובנין שקקן לבשן הוין וצימין ומצלין

ליהו מרא שמיא זי החוין בוידרנג זך. כלביא הנפקו כבלא מן רגלוהי וכל נכסין

זי קנה אבדו וכל גברין זי בעו באיש לאגורא זך כל קטילו וחזין בהום.

Vocabulary

be lost	אבד
chain	כבל
dog	כלב
throw down	מגר
property	נכס
fast	צים
buy	קנה
sackcloth	שקק

Use the biblical vowel system to vocalize the passage above.

Translate it into English:

Proper Nouns

כנבוזי — Cambyses, son of Cyrus; ruled Persia from 530 to 522 B.C.E. He apparently found the Jewish temple already standing when he conquered Egypt in 525 B.C.E. His destruction of Egyptian temples while letting the Jewish one stand may have contributed to tension between Jews and Egyptians.

Lines 17–22

אף קדמת זנה בעדן זי זא באישתא עביד לן אגרה שלחן על מראן ועל יהוחנן

כהנא רבא וכנותה כהניא זי בירושלם ועל אוסתן אחוהי זי עני וחרי יהודיא.

אגרא חדה לא שלחו עלין. אף מן ירח תמוז שנת 14 דריהוש מלכא ועד זנה יומא

אנחנה שקקן לבשן וצימין. נשיא זילן כארמלה עבידן. משח לא משחין וחמר לא

שתין. אף מן זכי ועד יום שנת 17 דריהוש מלכא מנחה ולבונה ועלוה לא עבדו

באגורא זך.

Vocabulary

incense	לבונה		also	אף
grain offering	מנחה		widow	ארמלה
oil	משח		our	זילן
anoint	משח		that	זכי
until	עד		this	זנה
			noble	חרי

Proper Nouns

יהוחנן — the high priest, mentioned also in Nehemiah 12:22 and 13:28

אוסתן — a Jew, brother of Anani

עני — scribe and chancellor to Arsame; 1 Chronicles 3:24 mentions a descendant of David who bore the same name

Use the biblical vowel system to vocalize the passage above.

Translate it into English:

This passage demonstrates that there were ties between the Jews of Elephantine and those in Jerusalem, an impression supported by the analogous links with those in Babylon described in the books of Ezra and Nehemiah.

Lines 22–30

כען עבדיך ידניה וכנותה ויהודיא כל בעלי יב כן אמרין. הן על מראן טב

אתעשת על אגורא זך למבנה בזי לא שבקן לן למבניה. חזי בעלי טבתך ורחמיך

זי תנה במצרין. אגרה מנך ישתלח עליהום על אגורא זי יהו אלהא למבניה

ביב בירתא לקבל זי בנה הוה קדמין. ומחתא ולבונתא ועלותא יקרבון על

מדבחא זי יהו אלהא בשמך ונצלה עליך בכל עדן אנחנה ונשין ובנין ויהודיא

כל זי תנה. הן כן עבדו עד זי אגורא זך יתבנה וצדקה יהוה לך קדם יהו אלה

שמיא מן גבר זי יקרב לה עלוה ודבחן דמן כדמי כסף כנכרין אלף ועל זהב.

על זנה שלחן הודען. אף כלא מליא באגרה חדה שלחן בשמן על דליה ושלמיה

בני סנאבלט פחת שמרין. אף בזנה זי עביד לן כלא ארשם לא ידע.

ב־20 למרחשון שנת 17 דריהוש מלכא.

Vocabulary

1000	אלף	*a coin*	כנכר
sacrifice	דבח	grain offering (cf. מנחה)	מחתא
price	דמי	intend (Gt–be thought)	עשת
gold	זהב	merit	צדקה

Use the biblical vowel system to vocalize the passage above.

Translate it into English:

Proper Nouns

שלמיה and דליה — sons of Sanballat (people with the same names are mentioned in Ezra 2:60; 10:39, 41; and Nehemiah 3:30 and 13:13, supporting the picture of post-exilic Jewry presented both in this document and the Bible)

סנאבלט — (Akkadian Sin-uballiṭ)—governor of Samaria (cf. Nehemiah 2:19; 3:33; 6:1; etc.)

מרחשון — month in late fall

The most conspicuous linguistic feature in this letter is its use of ז where biblical Aramaic uses ד, especially for the demonstrative elements זנה, זך, and זכי as well as זי (cf. זיל). Note also זהב (biblical Aramaic has דהב). On the other hand, the spelling עק for "tree" contrasts with the Hebrew עץ; biblical Aramaic uses אע. (Compare the word ארקא that is found in Jeremiah 10:11 for the Hebrew ארץ, which Aramaic elsewhere presents as ארע.)

The redundant syntax of the phrase אחוהי זי ענני (lit. "his brothers of Anani") is comparable to that found in biblical Aramaic, as described in chapter 16.

From almost six centuries later come a series of letters written by Simon bar Kosiba, who led a Jewish revolt against the Romans. He is better known by his title Bar Kochba (lit. "son of the star," based on Numbers 24:17). These documents, written in Hebrew, Aramaic, and Greek, were found in caves near those which produced the famous Dead Sea Scrolls. The following example raises interesting possibilities about his religious views:

שמעון ליהודה בר מנשה לקרית ערביה: שלחת לך תרי חמרין די תשלח עמהן

תרי גברין לות יהונתן בר בעין ולות מסבלה די יעמרן וישלחן למחניה לותך

ללבין ואתרגין. ואת שלח אחרנין מלותך וימטון לך הדסן וערבין. ותקן יתהן

ושלח יתהן למחניה הוא שלם.

Vocabulary

citron	אתרג
myrtle	הדס
palm	ללב
camp	מחנה
load	עמר
willow	ערבא
prepare	תקן

Use the biblical vowel system to vocalize the passage above.

Translate it into English:

Proper Nouns

יהודה בר מנשה

יהונתן בר בעין — with Masabala, apparently Bar Kochba's military commander of Ein Gedi, to whom most of Bar Kochba's letters are addressed

מסבלה — son of Shimon

קרית ערביה — lit. "town of the Arabs" or "willows," where Judah was posted between Ein Gedi and Bar Kochba's main camp (presumably at Betar)

The preposition לות is a compound made of up -ל and ות (from ית, which occurs in Daniel 3:12); in other words, it is a double direct object marker, which appears once (מלותיך) with an additional preposition (-מְ).

The reference to the palm (ללב), citron (אתרג), myrtle (הדס), and willow (ערבא) is reminiscent of the holiday of Sukkot (see traditional Jewish interpretations of Leviticus 23:40, as found in Targum Onkelos and *Mishnah Sukkah* 3–4, for example), at which time these four species are to be waved in celebration of a successful harvest.

Chapter 30

DEAD SEA SCROLLS

Several of the famous Dead Sea Scrolls, which were discovered during the 1940's and 1950's, are written in Aramaic. Many of these are the writings of a religious community that settled alongside the Wadi Qumran during the Hasmonean period (2d century B.C.E.), probably in order to avoid the wrath of the governing party in Jerusalem; other documents found there may have been the community's copies of more widely known writings.

The selections that follow are from a scroll called the Genesis Apocryphon (1QapGen) because it expands on passages in the book of Genesis. The sections here are based on Genesis 12, which describes Abraham and Sarah's visit to the land of Egypt. According to the Bible, Abraham was worried that the Pharaoh might have him killed so that he could have the beautiful Sarah for himself. In this passage, Abraham describes a dream he experienced as he entered Egypt, which foreshadows what he expected would happen there.

Vocabulary To Be Learned

face	אנף
wife	אנתה
companion	חבר
lovely	יא
take	נסב
eye	עין
love	רחם

19:14–17

וחלמת אנה אברם חלם בלילה מעלי לארע מצרין. וחזית בחלמי והא ארז חד

ותמרא חדא יאיא שגיא. ובני אנוש אתו ובעון למקץ ולמעקר לארזא ולמשבוק

תמרתא בלחודיהה. ואכליאת תמרתא ואמרת אל תקוצו לארזא. ארי תרינא

מן שרבא חדא. ושביק ארזא בטלל תמרתא ולא אתקץ.

186

Vocabulary

singly	לחוד	human	אנוש
uproot	עקר	cedar	ארז
cut down	קצץ	dream	חלם
family	שרב	shadow	טלל
date	תמר	remonstrate (*af'el*)	כלא

Use the biblical vowel system to vocalize the above text.

Translate it into English:

מעלי — the G infinitive of עלל; other G infinitives in this passage are מעקר, משבוק,
  and מקץ.

ל- — marks the direct object (ארזא).

אכליאת — a perfect form from the root כלא, which must, therefore, belong to the
  ʾaf'el conjugation.

אל — introduces a negative command.

The next column of the scroll describes Sarah in a way that justifies Abraham's con-
cern (Genesis 12:11), albeit one that seems more suitable to the Song of Songs than the book
of Genesis:

20:2–8

כמה נציח ושפיר לה צלם אנפיהא . . . . . וכמא רקיק לה שער ראישה כמא יאין להין

לה עיניהא ומא רגג הוא לה אנפהא וכול נץ אנפיהא . . . . . כמא יאא לה חדיה וכמא

שפיר לה כול לבנהא דרעיהא מא שפירן וידיהא כמא כלילן וחמיד כול מחזה

ידיהא. כמא יאין כפיה ומא אריכן וקטינן כול אצבעת ידיהא. רגליהא כמא

שפירן וכמא שלמא להן לה שקיא. וכל בתולן וכלאן די יעלן לגנון לא ישפרן

מנהא. ועל כול נשין שופר שפרה ועליא שפרהא לעלא מן כולהן ועם כול

שפרא דן חכמא שגיא עמהא ודלידיהא יאא.

Vocabulary

radiance, bloom	נץ		long	אריך
splendid	נציח		virgin	בתולה
form	צלם		bridal chamber	גנון
delicate	קטין		*possessive (cf.* זיל)	דיל־
pleasant	רגג		arm	דרע
soft	רקיק		breast	חדה
beauty	שׁוּפָר		attractive	חמיד
perfect	שׁלם		bride	כלה
beautiful	שׁפיר		perfect	כליל
be beautiful	שׁפר		hand	כף
leg	שׁק		whiteness	לבן
			appearance	מחזה

Use the biblical vowel system to vocalize the above text.

Translate it into English:

דן is equivalent to the biblical demonstrative דְּנָה.

Although Abraham's statement about Sarah's beauty is surprising in light of the Bible's reference to her as having been 90 at the time Isaac was conceived (Genesis 17:17, cf. 18:12) and having lived in Canaan less than 25 years (cf. Genesis 12:4 and 17:1), her beauty was often noted in post-biblical literature. For example, the rabbis say that she lit up the entire land of Egypt (*Genesis Rabbah* 40:5).

20:8–11

וכדי שמע מלכא מלי חרקנוש ומלי תרין חברוהי די פם חד תלתהון ממללין שגי

רחמה ושלח לעובע דברהא וחזהא ואתמה על כול שפרהא ונסבהא לה לאנתא.

ובעא למקטלני ואמרת שרי למלכא דאחי הוא כדי הוית מתגר על דילהא.

ושביקת אנה אברם בדילהא ולא קטילת. ובכית אנה אברם בכי תקיף אנה ולוט

בר אחי עמי בליליא כדי דבירת מני שרי באונס.

Vocabulary

force	אונס
cry	בכה
lead (away)	דבר
haste	עובע
wonder	תמה

Use the biblical vowel system to vocalize the above text.

Translate it into English:

Proper Nouns

חרקנוש—an Egyptian noble, not mentioned in any other traditions about this incident.

לוֹט — Abraham's nephew

NOTICE that שׂגי is spelled both with and without א.

אנתה corresponds to the Hebrew word אִשָּׁה (woman), with *t* realized as ת in Aramaic (it is שׁ in Hebrew) and the root's נ retained.

This document includes both די (the relative pronoun found throughout biblical Aramaic and at Elephantine in the form זי) and the particle דְ־, as in the synagogue inscription from Ein Gedi.

מתגר ("benefit") is apparently an *'itpaʿal* of either אגר or תגר, both of which can mean "earn, gain."

Chapter 31

MIDRASH

Numerous passages in rabbinic literature are written in Aramaic, although not all texts use the same dialect and the language frequently shifts back and forth into Hebrew. The passage below is from *Genesis Rabbah,* a collection of rabbinic lore which was probably compiled in Palestine during the fifth century. It is arranged as a commentary on the book of Genesis. The following selection relates to the Bible's statement that Abraham's brother Haran died עַל פְּנֵי their father Terah (Genesis 11:28). That phrase is usually translated "in the presence of"; however, the rabbis understood it to mean that Haran had died "on account of" his father.

Vocabulary To Be Learned

place	. . . .	אתר
bring (H)	. . . .	יבל
when	. . . .	כיון
die	. . . .	מות
deliver	. . . .	מסר
human	. . . .	נש

תרח עובד צלמים הוה. חד זמן נפק לאתר הושיב אברהם מוכר תחתיו. הוה אתי

בר נש בעי דיזבון. אמר ליה: בר כמה שנין את? אמר ליה: בר חמשין. אמר

ליה: ווי להדוא גברא דאת בר חמשין ותסגוד לבר יומא. והוה מתבייש והולך לו.

Vocabulary
(Words marked with an asterisk are Hebrew.)

set (H)	. . . .	ישב	embarrass (Dt)	. . . .	בוש *
how many	. . . .	כמה	that	. . . .	ההוא
sell	. . . .	מכר *	woe!	. . . .	ווי
instead of	. . . .	תחת *	buy	. . . .	זבן
			fifty	. . . .	חמשין

191

Use the biblical vowel system to vocalize the passage above.

Translate it into English:

NOTICE the intermingling of Hebrew and Aramaic. Forms like צלמים, and תחת are clearly Hebrew (perhaps הושיב, too, although it also occurs in the Barrakib inscription presented in chapter 29; the form הותיב is found throughout the book of Daniel); however, בר, נפק, זמן, חד, and לאתר are Aramaic, as is the particle ־ד.

בר is often used to indicate a quality, as in the phrase בר נש (human being). With a time span, it indicates age:

בר כמה שנין	how old
בר חמשין	fifty years old
בר יומא	one day old

סגד ("bow down") also occurs in Arabic, where it provides the root for the word *masjid,* which designates a place of worship, just as מַדְבַּח designates a place of sacrifice, i.e., an altar, and מִשְׁכַּב a place of lying, i.e., a bed. The Arabic word has come into English in the form "mosque."

חד זמן אתת איתתא טעינא חד פינך דסלת. אמרת ליה: הא לך קרב קדמיהון.

קם נסיב בוקלסה ותברהון ויהב ההוא בוקלסה בידוי דרבה דבהון. כון דאתא

אבוה אמר ליה: מה עבד להון כדין? אמר ליה: מה נכפור לך? אתת חדא איתתא

טעינא חד פינך דסלת ואמרת לי: קרב קדמיהון. דין אמר: אנא אכיל קדמאי

ודין אמר: אנא אכיל קדמאי. קם הדין רבה נסיב בוקלסה ותברהון. אמר ליה:

מה את מפלה בי ידעין אינון. אמר ליה: ולא ישמעו אזניך מפיך.

Vocabulary
(Words marked with an asterisk are Hebrew.)

how	* מה		ear	* אזן
flour	סלת		eat	אכל
mouth	* פה		club	בוקלסא
plate	פינך		this	דין
trick	פלא		that	ההוא
first	קדמאי		carry	טען
sacrifice (D)	קרב		deny	* כפר

Vocalize the passage above using biblical vowels.

Translate it into English:

NOTICE the use of ׳ as a vowel marker (*mater lectionis*), particularly in the participles (נפיק and טעין).

איתתא (woman) is the determined form, although its sense is indefinite (see p. 25). Its root is אנת, as shown by the form אנתה in the Genesis Apocryphon (chapter 30). In the Hebrew form of this word (אִשָּׁה) the נ has assimilated to the שׁ, as it does to the ת here. In the Genesis Apocryphon either the נ had not assimilated or the double ת dissimilated (like the H infinitive הנעלה, which comes from the root עלל; see p. 119).

נסתיה ומסרתיה לנמרוד. אמר ליה: נסגוד לנורא. אמר ליה: נסגוד למייא

דמטפין לנורא. אמר ליה: ונסגוד למיא. אמר ליה: נסגוד לעַנְנֵי דטעני מיא.

אמר ליה: ונסגוד לעננא. אמר ליה: נסגוד לרוחא דמובלי עננא. אמר ליה:

ונסגוד לרוחא. אמר ליה: נסגוד לבר נשא דסביל רוחא. אמר ליה: מלין את

משתעי. לא נסגוד אלא לאור. הריני משליכך בו ויבוא אלהיך שאתה משתחוה

לו ויצילך ממנו.

Vocabulary
(Words marked with an asterisk are Hebrew.)

prostrate self	משתחוה *	flame	אור
lift	נסה	except	אלא
save (H)	נצל *	god	אלוהים *
endure	סבל	behold	הרי *
cloud	ענן	carry	טען
throw (H)	שלך	extinguish (ʾafˁel)	טפה
talk (Gt)	שעה	water	מייא

Use the biblical vowel system to vocalize the passage.

Translate it into English:

The rabbis regarded Nimrod, who is mentioned in Genesis 10:8–10, as having been a powerful but wicked ruler who tried to impose his form of idolatry on all the ancient peoples under his control.

הוה תמן הרן קאים פליג. אמר: מה נפשך? אם נצח אברם אנא אמר מן דאבים

אנא אם נצח נמרוד אמר אנא מנמרוד אנא. כיון שירד אברם לכבשן האש ונוצל

אמרין ליה מן דמן את? אמר ליה: מן דאברם. נטלוהו והשליכוהו באש ונחמרו

מעיו ויצא ומת על פני אבוו. הדא הוא דכתיב וימת הרן על פני תרח אביו.

Vocabulary
(Words marked with an asterisk are Hebrew.)

belly	מעין		parch	חמר
win	* נצח		go out	* יצא
be saved (N)	* נוצל		descend	* ירד
divided	פליג		furnace	* כבשן
			will	נפש

Use the biblical vowel system to vocalize the passage above.

Translate it into English:

הדא הוא דכתיב (this is what is written)—introduces a biblical quotation, in this case the passage from Genesis (11:28) that the preceding story is intended to explain.

NOTICE the interweaving of Hebrew and Aramaic in this selection. The verbs נוצל and נחמרו are *nifʿal*, a conjugation which does not occur in biblical Aramaic. The following phrases are pure Hebrew:

הושיב אברהם מוכר תחתיו

ולא ישמעו אזניך מפיך

הריני משליכך בו ויבוא אלהיך שאתה משתחוה לו ויצילך ממנו

ויצא ומת על פני אביו

Chapter 32

Targum

With the spread of Aramaic among Jews after the Babylonian exile, the Hebrew Bible became increasingly inaccessible. It was, therefore, translated into Aramaic. Reciting such a translation was even required as part of liturgical Scripture reading (*Mishna Megillah* 4:4, cf. *Babylonian Talmud Berakhot* 8a). Several different translation traditions developed, some of which were eventually written down in what have come to be known as targumim (the root first occurs in Ezra 4:7, where it introduces the Aramaic section of that book). The most important of these are a translation of the Pentateuch attributed to Onkelos and one of the Prophets attributed to Jonathan. (These names may be related to Aquila and Theodotion, who were considered the authors of ancient Greek translations of the Bible; the latter means "God gives" in Greek, just as Jonathan does in Hebrew, while Aquila and Onkelos are phonetically close.) Although these versions tend to follow the original Hebrew rather closely, other Aramaic translations expand on the biblical text. Among these is a targum to the Pentateuch which appears to have reached its present form in Palestine sometime after the seventh century and has traditionally come to be ascribed to Jonathan (hence scholars' reference to it as Pseudo-Jonathan). Its rendering of the biblical text is considerably more expansive than that of Onkelos, as demonstrated by its translation of Genesis 22 (the binding of Isaac):

Vocabulary To Be Learned

inherit	ירת	after	בתר *
high	מרום	behold, how	האנא
slaughter	נכס	lift	זקף
on	עילוי	instead of	חולף
place	שוה	young servant	טליה

---

*From באתר; see p. 62 and Daniel 2:29 (p. 80) and 7:6–7 (pp. 152–54).

(1) והוה בתר פיתגמיא האילין מן דינצו יצחק וישמעאל. ישמעאל הוה אמר:

לי חמי למירות ית אבא דאנא בריה בוכרייא. ויצחק הוה אמר: לי חמי למירות

ית אבא דאנא בר שרה אינתתיה ואנת בר הגר אמתא דאימי. עני ישמעאל ואמר:

אנא זכאי יתיר מינך דאנא איתגזרית לתלסירי שנין ואין הוה צבותי למעכבא

לא הוינא מסר נפשי לאתגזרא. ואנת אתגזרת בר תמניא יומין אילו הוה בך מנדעא

דילמא לא הוית מסר נפשך לאתגזרא. מתיב יצחק ואמר: האנא יומנא בר תלתין

ושב שנין ואילו בעי קודשא בריך הוא לכולי איבריי לא הויתי מעכב. מן יד

אישתמעו פיתגמיא האילין קדם מרי עלמא ומן יד מימרא דייי נסי ית אברהם

ואמר ליה: אברהם.

Vocabulary

immediately	מן יד	organ	איבר
understanding	מנדע	if	אילו
test	נסי	if	אין
quarrel	נצה	mother	אם
refuse	עכב	handmaid	אמתא
wish	צבו	senior	בוכריא
holy	קודשא	perhaps	דילמא
seven	(ע)שב	worthy	זכאי
thirteen	תלסירי	today	יומנא
thirty	תלתין	word	מימרא
eight	תמניא	after	מן די

Use the biblical vowel system to vocalize the passage above.

Translate it into English:

ייי is the way God's name is presented in this manuscript.

NOTE: (a) the use of י as a vowel letter (*mater lectionis*) in:

nouns – אינת, אימי, מימרי, פיתגם

Gt verbs – איתגזר, אישתמע

final ה verbs – עני

(b) that the passive participle of חמי ("see") means "fitting," as does the passive form of the Hebrew verb ראה (ראוי)

(c) the Hebrew definite article on the demonstrative element in the phrase פיתגמיא האילין

(d) characteristically Aramaic features such as the direct object marker ית and the particle ד־.

ואמר ליה: האנא. (2) ואמר: דבר כדון ית ברך ית יחידך דאת רחים

ית יצחק ואיזל לך לארע פולחנא ואסיקהי תמן לעלתא על חד מן טורייא

דאימר לך. (3) ואקדים אברהם בצפרא וזריז ית חמריה ודבר ית תרין טלייוי

ית אליעזר וית ישמעאל עימיה וית יצחק בריה וקטע קיסין דזיתא ותאנתא ודיקלא

דחזיין לעלתא וקם ואזל לאתרא דאמר ליה יי. (4) ביומא תליתאה וזקף

אברהם ית עינוי וחמא ענן איקרא קטיר על טוורא ואשתמודעיה מן רחיק

(5) ואמר אברהם לעולימוי: אוריכן לכון הכא עם חמרא ואנא ועולימא נתמטי

עד כא לבחוני אין יתקיים מה דאתבשרית כדין יהון בנך ונסגוד למרי עלמא ונתוב

לוותכון. (6) ונסיב אברהם ית קיסי דעלתא ושוי עילוי יצחק בריה ונסיב בידיה

ית אישתא וית סכינא ואזלו תרוויהום כחדא. (7) ואמר יצחק לאברהם אבי

ואמר: אבא. ואמר: האנא. ואמר: הא אישתא וקיסין והאן אימרא לעלתא?

(8) ואמר אברהם: יי יבחר ליה אימרא לעלתא ברי: ואזלו תרויהום בלב שלים

כחדא.

Vocabulary

wait (ʾafʿel)	אוריך	here	כא
lamb	אימר	now	כדון
if	אין	here	כה
glory (יקר *with prosthetic* א)	איקרא	knife	סכין
recognize	אשתמודע	youth	עולימו
examine	בחן	cloud	ענן
choose	בחר	worship	פולחן
announce (Gt)	בשׂר	morning	צפרא
seize, take	דבר	do early (H, ʾafʿel)	קדם.
palm	דיקלא	Dt (התקיים) be fulfilled	קום
behold	הא	cut	קטע
here	הכא	rise in circle	קטר
olive	זית	wood	קיסא
hasten	זרז	perfect	שלים
only	יחיד	fig	תאנה

Use the biblical vowel system to vocalize the passage above.

Translate it into English:

כדין יהון בנך is the targum's rendering of the biblical phrase כֹּה יִהְיֶה זַרְעֶךָ in Genesis 15:5, where God promises Abraham that his descendants will be as numerous as the stars.

The spelling עים and אישתא further demonstrate the generous use of vowel letters in this text.

אסיק is an *ʾafʿel* form of the root סלק (cf. הַסִּקוּ in Daniel 3:23; see p. 119); note also אתבשר, which is *ʾitpeʿal* (the form is 3d person masculine singular perfect), and אשתמודעין, which is a verb based on the noun מודע (in the "*ʾishtafʿal*"). נתמטי is *nitpaʿel,* a mixture of *hitpaʿel* and *nifʿal.*

חזי (fitting) is a passive participle of חזה (see), providing yet again an example of a verb which means "to see" being used for "fitting" in the passive (others are Aramaic חמי and Hebrew ראוי).

(9) ואתו לאתרא דאמר ליה ייי ובנא תמן אברהם ית מדבחא דבנא אדם ואיתהפכר במוי דטובענא ותב נח ובנייה ואיתהפכר בדרא דפלוגתא. וסדר עילוי ית קיסיא וכפת ית יצחק בריה ושוי יתיה על מדבחא לעיל מן קיסין. (10) ופשט אברהם ית ידיה ונסיבת סכינא למיכס ית בריה. עני ואמר יצחק לאבוי: כפת יתי יאות דלא נפרכס מן צערא דנפשי ונדחי לגובא דחבלא וישתכח פסולא בקרבנך. עינווי דאברהם מסתכלן בעינווי דיצחק ועינווי דיצחק מסתכלן למלאכי מרומא. יצחק הוה חמי יתהום ואברהם לא חמי יתהום. עניין מלאכי מרומא: איתון חמון תרין יחידאין דאית בעלמא חד נכיס וחד מתנכיס. דנכיס לא מעכב ודמתנכיס פשיט צווריה. (11) וקרא ליה מלאכא דייי מן שמיא ואמר ליה: אברהם אברהם. ואמר: האנא . (12) ואמר: אל תושיט ידך לטלייא ולא תעביד ליה מידעם ביש. ארום כדון גלי קדמי ארום דחלא דייי אנת ולא עכיבתא ית ברך ית יחידך מיני. (13) וזקף אברהם ית עינוי וחזא והא דיכרא חד דאיתברי ביני שימשתא דשכלול עלמא אחיד בחרישותא דאילנא בקרנוי. ואזל אברהם ונסיב יתיה ואסיקהי לעלתא חולף בריה.

Vocabulary

arrange	סדר	catch	אחד
knife	סכין	*plural participle of* אתה	איתון
look (Dt)	סכל	behold	ארום
above	עיל	create	ברי
refuse	עכב	thrust	דחה
destroy	פכר	ram	דיכרא
division	פלוגתא	destruction	חבלה
blemished	פסול	thicket	חרישותא
struggle	פרכס	flood	טובען
extend	פשט	well	יאות
neck	צוור	only	יחיד
pain	צער	stretch forth (H)	ישט
wood	קיסא	now	כדון
offering	קרבן	slaughter	כסס
place	שוה	water	מוי
sun	שמש	anything	מידעם
twilight	ביני שימשתא	(*see* מנדעם *on p. 178*)	
completion	שכלול	banish	נדח

Use the biblical vowel system to vocalize the passage above.

Translate it into English:

פלוגתא (division) is a traditional term for the dispersion which took place after the confrontation with God involving the Tower of Babel.

בנא must be understood as "rebuild" in this context.

עינוי דאברהם is a redundant construction, which literally means "his eye of Abraham," i.e., "Abraham's eye" (see p. 85).

איתברי — this Gt form is based on the root ברי (create), which corresponds to the Hebrew root ברא; note the convergence of final א and final ה verbs in Aramaic.

ביני שימשתא — "twilight"; according to rabbinic tradition, God created several important things just before sunset during the week of creation (e.g., *Mishna Avot* 5:6).

(14) ואודי וצלי אברהם תמן באתרא ההוא ואמר: בבעו ברחמין מן קדמך ייי גלי

קדמך דלא הוה בלבבי עוקמא ובעית למיעבד גזירתך בחדווא. כדין כד יהון

בנוי דיצחק ברי עליין לשעת אניקי תהוי מידכר להום ועני יתהום ופריק יתהום.

ועתידין הינון כל דריא דקימון למהוי אמרין בטוורא הדין: כפת אברהם ית יצחק

בריה ותמן איתגליית עילוי שכינתא דייי. (15) וקרא מלאכא דייי לאברהם
תנינות מן שמיא (16) ואמר: במימרי קיימית אמר ייי חולף דעבדת ית פיתגמא
הדין ולא מנעת ית ברך ית יחידך (17) ארום ברכא אברכינך ואסגא אסגי ית בנך
ככוכבי שמיא והי כחלא דעל כיף ימא. ויירתון בנך ית קוריי שנאיהון. (18)
ויתברכון בגין זכוות בנך כל עממי ארעא חולף דקבילתא במימרי. (19) ודברו
מלאכי מרומא ית יצחק ואובלוהי לבי מדרשא דשם רבא והוה תמן תלת שנין.
ובההוא יומא תב אברהם לות עולימוי וקמו ואזלו כחדא לבירא דשבע. ויתיב
אברהם בבירא דשבע. (20) והוה בתר פתגמיא האילין מן בתר דיכפת אברהם
ית יצחק ואזל סטנא ותני לות שרה דאברהם נכס ית יצחק. וקמת שרה ופננת
ואשתנקת ומיתת מן אניקא.

Vocabulary

word	מימרא		anguish	אניקה
angel	מלאך		behold	ארום
withhold	מנע		on account of	בגין
multiply (H)	סגי		son	בן *
Satan	סטנה		school house	בי מדרש
youth	עולימו		petition	בעו
trickery	עוקמא		blessing	ברכה
cry out	פגן		decree	גזירה
save	פרק		innocence	זכו
city	קורא		joy	חדווא
swear	קיים		sand	חל
hate	שנא		praise (H/ʾafˁel)	ידה
Divine Presence	שכינתא		sea	ים
choke (Gt)	שנק		dwell	יתב
tell	תני		now	כדון
second	תנינות		star	כוכב
			shore	כיף

Use the biblical vowel system to vocalize the passage above.

Translate it into English:

סני — This word is consistently spelled שַׂגִּיא in the Bible, but סגי at Ein Gedi (p. 173). The letter שׂ came to be written ס in post-biblical Aramaic. Two examples of this which can be found already in the Bible are the spelling of the name אַרְתַּחְשַׁסְתָּא in Ezra 7:21 and of כַּסְדָּי in Ezra 5:12 (see p. 38).

שכינה — is a hypostasis of God's presence, as is God's מימרא (cf. the end of verse 1; the term is used more literally in verse 18).

בי — from בית

בריא דשבע — "the well of seven," a literal translation of the name Beer-sheba in accordance with the explanation of it given in Genesis 21:25–31.

AFTERWORD

The biblical readings in this book have covered the substance of the entire Aramaic corpus in the Hebrew Bible; however, these passages have been abridged and simplified to fit the levels appropriate to the individual chapters in which they are found. Now that you are familiar with the language's grammar, you can read all of these texts in the original. The vocabulary is readily available in most standard biblical dictionaries, including:

> *A Hebrew and English Lexicon of the Old Testament* by Francis Brown, S. R. Driver, and Charles A. Briggs (Oxford: Clarendon Press, 1907).

> *Lexicon in Veteris Testamenti Libros* by Ludwig Koehler and Walter Baumgartner (Leiden: E. J. Brill, 1958).

> *Hebräisches und Aramäisches Lexikon zum alten Testament,* Aramaic section ed. Johann Jakob Stamm and Benedikt Hartmann (Leiden: E. J. Brill, 1995), currently being translated into English under the supervision of M. E. J. Richardson as *The Hebrew and Aramaic Lexicon of the Old Testament.*

In addition, Ernestus Vogt's *Lexicon linguae aramaicae veteris testamenti documentis antiquis illustratum* (Rome: Pontifical Biblical Institute, 1971) is devoted solely to biblical Aramaic. The standard biblical concordances (by S. Mandelkern, E. Lipinski, and A. Even-Shoshan) also include Aramaic sections.

There are several valuable commentaries on the biblical books which contain passages in Aramaic. The most useful ones on Ezra are by Loring Batten (International Critical Commentary), Jacob Myers (Anchor Bible), and H. G. M. Williamson (Word Biblical Commentary). For Daniel, see those by James Montgomery (International Critical Commentary), John Collins (Hermeneia), and Louis Hartman and Alexander Di Lella (Anchor Bible).

207

The following tools will prove helpful for grammatical questions that may arise as you read selections from the Bible or investigate specific problems:

Franz Rosenthal, *A Grammar of Biblical Aramaic* (Wiesbaden: Otto Harrassowitz, 1963).

Hans Bauer and Pontus Leander, *Grammatik des Biblisch-Aramäische* (Halle/Saale: Max Niemayer Verlag, 1927).

Several other bodies of literature are written in Aramaic. The best sources for ancient Aramaic inscriptions are:

Herbert Donner and Wolfgang Röllig, *Kanaanäische und Aramäische Inschriften* (Wiesbaden: Otto Harrassowitz, 1971–76).

John C. L. Gibson, *Textbook of Syrian Semitic Inscriptions,* vol. 2, "Aramaic Inscriptions" (Oxford: Clarendon Press, 1975).

Joseph A. Fitzmyer and Daniel J. Harrington, *A Manual of Palestinian Aramaic Texts* (Rome: Biblical Institute Press, 1978).

Arthur E. Cowley, *Aramaic Papyri of the Fifth Century B.C.* (Oxford: Clarendon Press, 1923).

Emil G. Kraeling, *The Brooklyn Museum Aramaic Papyri* (New Haven: Yale University Press, 1953).

G. R. Driver, *Aramaic Documents of the Fifth Century B.C.* (Oxford: Clarendon Press, rev. ed., 1965).

Bezalel Porten and Ada Yardeni, *Textbook of Aramaic Documents from Ancient Egypt* (Jerusalem: Hebrew University, 1986–).

In addition to the glossaries in these works, the following dictionaries may prove helpful:

Charles-F. Jean and Jacob Hoftijzer, *Dictionnaire des inscriptions de l'ouest* (Leiden: E. J. Brill, 1965).

Jacob Hoftijzer and Karel Jongeling, *Dictionary of the North-West Semitic Inscriptions* (Leiden: E. J. Brill, 1995).

Several of the Dead Sea Scrolls, more and more of which are becoming available, are in Aramaic. Many of these texts are collected in:

B. Jongeling, C. J. Labuschagne, and A. S. van der Woude, *Aramaic Texts from Qumran* (Leiden: E. J. Brill, 1976–).

Klaus Beyer, *Die Aramäischen Texte vom Toten Meer* (Göttingen: Vandenhoeck & Ruprecht, 1987).

The diversity of rabbinic literature, much of which is written in a mixture of Aramaic and Hebrew, and the targumim makes it impossible to provide a definitive list of the material available. Most of the targumim are published in:

Alexander Sperber, *The Bible in Aramaic* (Leiden: E. J. Brill, 1959–73).

E. G. Clarke, *Targum Pseudo-Jonathan of the Pentateuch* (Hoboken, NJ: Ktav Publishing House, 1984).

Michael L. Klein, *The Fragment-Targums of the Pentateuch According to their Extant Sources* (Rome: Biblical Institute Press, 1980).

Alejandro Díez Macho, *Neophyti I* (Madrid: Consejo Superior de Investigaciones Científicas, 1968).

The best available tools for working with this material are:

Marcus Jastrow, *A Dictionary of the Targumim, the Talmud Babli and Jerusalmi, and the Midrashic Literature* (New York: G. P. Putnam's Sons, 1903; reprinted often).

Michael Sokoloff, *A Dictionary of Jewish Palestinian Aramaic of the Byzantine Period* (Ramat Gan: Bar-Ilan University Press, 1990).

The Syrian church and its adherents also produced a vast literature in the Syriac dialect. The best available dictionaries for this dialect are:

C. Brockelmann, *Lexicon Syriacum* (Hallis: Saxonum, 1928).

R. Payne Smith, *Thesaurus Syriacus* (Oxford: Clarendon Press, 1879; supplement by J. P. Margoliouth, 1927).

Reference tools for other dialects of Aramaic include:

Friedrich Schulthess, *Lexicon Syropalaestinum* (Berlin: Georg Reimer, 1903).

Ethel Drower and R. Macuch, *A Mandaic Dictionary* (Oxford: Clarendon Press, 1963).

J. A. MacLean, *A Dictionary of the Dialects of Vernacular Syriac* (Oxford: Clarendon Press, 1901).

Gotthelf Bergsträsser, *Glossar des neuaramäischen Dialekts von Maʾlūla* (1921).

Helmut Ritter, *Tūrōyo: Die Volkssprache der syrischen Christen des Tūr ʾAbdîn* (Beirut: Orient-Institut der Deutschen Morgenländischen Gesellschaft, 1976).

Rudolf Macuch, *Grammatik des samaritanischen Aramäisch* (Berlin: De Gruyter, 1982).

In recent years, scholars have begun to compile a Comprehensive Aramaic Lexicon, which will embrace the entire language. As work proceeds on this project, a variety of tools and reference works are being generated; already available is the first part of *An Aramaic Bibliography* by Joseph A. Fitzmyer, S.J., and Stephen A. Kaufman (Baltimore: The Johns Hopkins University Press, 1992). You may also wish to read some general descriptions of the Aramaic languages. Broad surveys of this type include:

Eduard Yechezkel Kutscher, "Aramaic" in *Current Trends in Linguistics,* ed. Thomas A. Seboek (The Hague: Mouton, 1970), vol. 6, pp. 347–412.

Eduard Yechezkel Kutscher, "Aramaic," *Encyclopedia Judaica* (Jerusalem: Keter Publishing, 1972), vol. 3, pp. 259–87.

Joseph A. Fitzmyer, S.J., "The Phases of the Aramaic Language" in *A Wandering Aramean: Collected Aramaic Essays* (Chico, CA: Scholars Press, 1979) pp. 57–84.

Stephen A. Kaufman, "Languages (Aramaic)" in *The Anchor Bible Dictionary* (New York: Doubleday, 1992), vol. 4, pp. 173–78.

With these tools and the grammar you have already learned, you can begin to explore any part of the huge corpus of Aramaic literature. Good luck!

PARADIGMS

Nouns and Adjectives

		Masculine	Feminine
Singular	Absolute	מֶלֶךְ	מַלְכָּה
	Construct	מֶלֶךְ	מַלְכַּת
	Determined	מַלְכָּא	מַלְכְּתָא
Plural	Absolute	מַלְכִין	מַלְכָן
	Construct	מַלְכֵי	מַלְכָת
	Determined	מַלְכַיָּא	מַלְכָתָא

Pronouns

Independent Pronouns	Possessive Suffixes			
	Singular Nouns		Plural Nouns	
Singular	Masculine	Feminine	Masculine	Feminine
אֲנָה	פִּשְׁרִי	מַלְכוּתִי	פִּשְׁרֵי	מַלְכְוָתִי
אַנְתְּ (or אַנְתָּה)	פִּשְׁרָךְ	מַלְכוּתָךְ	פִּשְׁרָיךְ	מַלְכְוָתָךְ
אַנְתִּי	פִּשְׁרֵכִי	מַלְכוּתֵכִי	פִּשְׁרַיְכִי	מַלְכְוָתֵכִי
הוּא	פִּשְׁרֵהּ	מַלְכוּתֵהּ	פִּשְׁרוֹהִי	מַלְכְוָתֵהּ
הִיא	פִּשְׁרַהּ	מַלְכוּתַהּ	פִּשְׁרַיהּ	מַלְכְוָתַהּ

Plural				
אֲנַחְנָה	פִּשְׁרַנָא	מַלְכוּתַנָא	פִּשְׁרַינָא	מַלְכְוָתַנָא
אַנְתּוּן (אַנְתֹּם)	פִּשְׁרְכֹם	מַלְכוּתְכֹם	פִּשְׁרֵיכֹם	מַלְכְוָתְכֹם
אַנְתֵּן	פִּשְׁרְכֵן	מַלְכוּתְכֵן	פִּשְׁרֵיכֵן	מַלְכְוָתְכֵן
הִמּוֹ (אִנּוּן or הִמּוֹן)	פִּשְׁרְהֹם	מַלְכוּתְהֹם	פִּשְׁרֵיהֹם	מַלְכְוָתְהֹם
אִנִּין	פִּשְׁרְהֵן	מַלְכוּתְהֵן	פִּשְׁרֵיהֵן	מַלְכְוָתְהֵן

211

Demonstratives

		Singular	Plural
Near (this, these)	*Masculine*	דְּנָה	אִלֵּין *(also* אֵל *and* אֵלֶּה*)*
	Feminine	דָּא	
Far (that, those)	*Masculine*	דֵּךְ	אִלֵּךְ
	Feminine	דָּךְ	
Masculine and Feminine		דִּכֵּן	

Numerals

	CARDINAL		ORDINAL
	Masculine	*Feminine*	
1	חַד	חֲדָה	קַדְמָי
2	תְּרֵין (תְּרֵי)	תַּרְתֵּין (תַּרְתֵּי)	תִּנְיָן
3	תְּלָתָה	תְּלָת	תְּלִיתָי
4	אַרְבְּעָה	אַרְבַּע	רְבִיעָי
5	חַמְשָׁא	חֲמֵשׁ	
6	שִׁתָּה	שֵׁת	
7	שִׁבְעָה	שְׁבַע	
8	תְּמָנְיָה	תְּמָנֵה	
9	תִּשְׁעָה	תְּשַׁע	
10	עֲשְׂרָה	עֲשַׂר	
20	עֶשְׂרִין		
30	תְּלָתִין		
100	מְאָה		
200	מָאתַיִן		
1,000	אֲלַף		
10,000	רִבּוֹ		

Verbs

	G	D	H
PERFECT			
Singular			
1	כִּתְבֵת	קַבְּלֵת	הַשְׁלְטֵת
2 Masculine	כְּתַבְתְּ (or כְּתַבְתָּ)	קַבֵּלְתְּ	הַשְׁלֵטְתְּ
Feminine	כְּתַבְתִּי	קַבֵּלְתִּי	הַשְׁלֵטְתִּי
3 Masculine	כְּתַב	קַבֵּל	הַשְׁלֵט
Feminine	כִּתְבַת	קַבְּלַת	הַשְׁלְטַת
Plural			
1	**כְּתַבְנָא**	**קַבֵּלְנָא**	**הַשְׁלֵטְנָא**
2 Masculine	כְּתַבְתּוּן	קַבֵּלְתּוּן	הַשְׁלֵטְתּוּן
Feminine	כְּתַבְתֵּן	קַבֵּלְתֵּן	הַשְׁלֵטְתֵּן
3 Masculine	כְּתַבוּ	קַבִּלוּ	הַשְׁלִטוּ
Feminine	כְּתַבָה	קַבִּלָה	הַשְׁלִטָה
IMPERFECT			
Singular			
1	**אֶכְתֻּב**	**אֲקַבֵּל**	**אֲהַשְׁלֵט**
2 Masculine	תִּכְתֻּב	תְּקַבֵּל	תְּהַשְׁלֵט
Feminine	תִּכְתְּבִין	תְּקַבְּלִין	תְּהַשְׁלְטִין
3 Masculine	יִכְתֻּב	יְקַבֵּל	יְהַשְׁלֵט
Feminine	תִּכְתֻּב	תְּקַבֵּל	תְּהַשְׁלֵט
Plural			
1	נִכְתֻּב	נְקַבֵּל	נְהַשְׁלֵט
2 Masculine	תִּכְתְּבוּן	תְּקַבְּלוּן	תְּהַשְׁלְטוּן
Feminine	תִּכְתְּבָן	תְּקַבְּלָן	תְּהַשְׁלְטָן
3 Masculine	יִכְתְּבוּן	יְקַבְּלוּן	יְהַשְׁלְטוּן
Feminine	יִכְתְּבָן	יְקַבְּלָן	יְהַשְׁלְטָן

	G	D	H
PARTICIPLE			
Singular			
Masculine	כָּתֵב	מְקַבֵּל	מְהַשְׁלֵט
Feminine	כָּתְבָה	מְקַבְּלָה	מְהַשְׁלְטָה
Plural			
Masculine	כָּתְבִין	מְקַבְּלִין	מְהַשְׁלְטִין
Feminine	כָּתְבָן	מְקַבְּלָן	מְהַשְׁלְטָן
IMPERATIVE			
Singular			
Masculine	כְּתֻב	קַבֵּל	הַשְׁלֵט
Feminine	כְּתֻבִי	קַבְּלִי	הַשְׁלֵטִי
Plural			
Masculine	כְּתֻבוּ	קַבְּלוּ	הַשְׁלֵטוּ
Feminine	כְּתֻבָה	קַבְּלָה	הַשְׁלֵטָה
INFINITIVE	מִכְתַּב	קַבָּלָה	הַשְׁלָטָה

Passives

	G	D	H
PERFECT			
Singular			
1	כְּתִיבֵת	קַבְּלֵת	הֻשְׁלְטֵת
2 Masculine	כְּתִיבְתְּ	קַבַּלְתְּ	הֻשְׁלַטְתְּ
Feminine	כְּתִיבְתִּי	קַבַּלְתִּי	הֻשְׁלַטְתִּי
3 Masculine	כְּתִיב	קַבַּל	הֻשְׁלַט
Feminine	כְּתִיבַת	קַבְּלַת	הֻשְׁלְטַת
Plural			
1	כְּתִיבְנָא	קַבְּלְנָא	הֻשְׁלַטְנָא
2 Masculine	כְּתִיבְתּוּן	קַבֶּלְתּוּן	הֻשְׁלַטְתּוּן
Feminine	כְּתִיבְתֵּן	קַבֶּלְתֵּן	הֻשְׁלַטְתֵּן
3 Masculine	כְּתִיבוּ	קַבְּלוּ	הֻשְׁלַטוּ
Feminine	כְּתִיבָה	קַבְּלָה	הֻשְׁלַטָה
PARTICIPLE			
Singular			
Masculine	כְּתִיב	מְקַבַּל	מְהֻשְׁלַט
Feminine	כְּתִיבָה	מְקַבְּלָה	מְהֻשְׁלַטָה
Plural			
Masculine	כְּתִיבִין	מְקַבְּלִין	מְהֻשְׁלְטִין
Feminine	כְּתִיבָן	מְקַבְּלָן	מְהֻשְׁלְטָן

Prefix-t Conjugations

	Gt	Dt
PERFECT		
Singular		
1	הִתְקְטֵלֵת	הִתְחַבֵּל
2 Masculine	הִתְקְטֵלְתְּ	הִתְחַבַּלְתְּ
Feminine	הִתְקְטֵלְתִּי	הִתְחַבַּלְתִּי
3 Masculine	הִתְקְטֵל	הִתְחַבֵּל
Feminine	הִתְקְטְלַת	הִתְחַבְּלַת
Plural		
1	הִתְקְטֵלְנָא	הִתְחַבַּלְנָא
2 Masculine	הִתְקְטֵלְתּוּן	הִתְחַבַּלְתּוּן
Feminine	הִתְקְטֵלְתֵּן	הִתְחַבַּלְתֵּן
3 Masculine	הִתְקְטְלוּ	הִתְחַבְּלוּ
Feminine	הִתְקְטְלָה	הִתְחַבְּלָה
IMPERFECT		
Singular		
1	אֶתְקְטֵל	אֶתְחַבֵּל
2 Masculine	תִּתְקְטֵל	תִּתְחַבֵּל
Feminine	תִּתְקַטְלִין	תִּתְחַבְּלִין
3 Masculine	יִתְקְטֵל	יִתְחַבֵּל
Feminine	תִּתְקְטֵל	תִּתְחַבֵּל
Plural		
1	נִתְקְטֵל	נִתְחַבֵּל
2 Masculine	תִּתְקַטְלוּן	תִּתְחַבְּלוּן
Feminine	תִּתְקַטְלָן	תִּתְחַבְּלָן
3 Masculine	יִתְקַטְלוּן	יִתְחַבְּלוּן
Feminine	יִתְקַטְלָן	יִתְחַבְּלָן

	Gt	Dt
PARTICIPLES		
Singular		
Masculine	מִתְקְטֵל	מִתְחַבַּל
Feminine	מִתְקַטְלָה	מִתְהַבְּלָה
Plural		
Masculine	מִתְקַטְלִין	מִתְחַבְּלִין
Feminine	מִתְקַטְלָן	מִתְחַבְּלָן
INFINITIVE	הִתְקְטָלָה	הִתְחַבָּלָה

Irregular Verbs

Hollow Roots

	Perfect	Imperfect	Participles Active	Passive	Imperative
Singular					
1	שָׂמֵת	אֲשִׂין	שָׂאֵן שִׂין	שִׂין	שִׂין
2 Masculine	שָׂמְתָ	תְּשִׂים	שָׂיְמָה	שִׂימָה	שִׂימִי
Feminine	שָׂמְתִּי	תְּשִׂימִין	שָׂיְמִין שִׂימִין	שִׂימִין	שִׂימוּ
3 Masculine	שָׂם	יְשִׂים	שָׂיְמָן שִׂימָן	שִׂימָן	שִׂימָה
Feminine	שָׂמַת	תְּשִׂים			
Plural					*Infinitive*
1	שָׂמְנָא	נְשִׂים			
2 Masculine	שָׂמְתוּן	תְּשִׂימוּן			מְשָׂם
Feminine	שָׂמְתֵּן	תְּשִׂימָן			
3 Masculine	שָׂמוּ	יְשִׂימוּן			
Feminine	שָׂמָה	יְשִׂימָן			

Final-ה

G

	Perfect	Imperfect	Participles Active	Passive
Singular				
1	בְּנֵית	אֶבְנֵא	בָּנֵה	בְּנֵה
2 Masculine	בְּנַיְתָ	תִּבְנֵא	בָּנֵיְה	בַּנְיָה
Feminine	בְּנַיְתִי	תִּבְנֵין	בָּנְיָן	בְּנֵין
3 Masculine	בְּנָה	יִבְנֵא	בָּנֵין	בְּנֵין
Feminine	בְּנָת	תִּבְנֵא		

	Perfect	Imperfect	Imperative	Passive Perfect
Plural				
1	בְּנֵינָא	נִבְנֵא		
2 Masculine	בְּנֵיתוּן	תִּבְנוֹן	בְּנִי/בְּנֵא	3 ms בְּנִי
Feminine	בְּנֵיתֵן	תִּבְנְיָן	בְּנוֹ	3 mpl בְּנִיו
3 Masculine	בְּנוֹ	יִבְנוֹן		
Feminine	בְּנָה	יִבְנְיָן	*Infinitive* מִבְנֵא	

	היה	D	H
PERFECT			
Singular			
1	הֲוֵית	——	——
2 Masculine	הֲוֵיתָה	מַנִּיתָ	——
3 Masculine	הֲוָה	מַנִּי	הַגְלִי
3 Feminine	הֲוַת	——	——
Plural			
3 Masculine	הֲווֹ	מַנִּיו	הַגְלִיו
IMPERFECT			
Singular			
1	——	אֲמַנֵּה	——
2 Masculine	תֶּהֱוֵה	תְּמַנֵּה	——
3 Masculine	לֶהֱוֵא	יְמַנֵּה	יְהַגְלִי
Plural			
1	——	נְמַנֵּה	נְהַגְלִי
2 Masculine	——	——	תְּהַגְלוֹן
3 Masculine	לֶהֱוֹן	יְמַנּוּן	יְהַגְלוֹן
3 Feminine	לֶהֱוְיָן	——	——
PARTICIPLE (active)			
Masculine singular	——	מְמַנֵּא	——
IMPERATIVE			
Masculine singular	——	מַנִּי	——
plural	הֲווֹ	——	הַגְלוֹ
INFINITIVE	——	——	הַגְלָיָה

NOTE that 3d person forms of היה begin with ל in the imperfect.

GLOSSARY

Numbers in parentheses are the chapters in which these words are first assigned. Hebrew words which appear in the texts presented in this book are also listed here (marked with an asterisk).

א

אַב	father (14; *plural* אֲבָהָת)
אבד	perish, be lost
	H—destroy, kill (14)
אבה	desire (Htn)
אֶבֶן	stone (15)
אגורא	temple
אִגְּרה	letter (3)
אֱדַיִן	then (5)
אונס	force
אור	flame
אזה	heat (18)
אזל	go (7)
אֹזֶן *	ear
אַח	brother (28)
אחד	grasp
אֲחַז *	grasp
אַחֲרֵי	after (12)
אָחֳרִי	another (16)
אָחֳרֵין	last
אָחֳרָן	another (13)
אֲחַשְׁדַּרְפַּן	satrap (25)
איבר	organ
אִילוּ	if
אִילָן	tree (20)
אימר	lamb
אֵימְתָן	frightful

אִין	if
אִיקְרא	glory
אִיתַי	there is (9)
איתתא	woman (*see* אנתה)
אכל	eat
אלא	except
אֵלֶּה	these (14)
אֱלָה	god (3)
אֲלוּ	behold (20)
אלוהים *	god
אִלֵּין	these (14)
אִלֵּךְ	those (7)
אֲלַף	thousand
אֵם	mother
אֻמָּה	nation
אמן	be faithful (H) (24)
	passive participle—מְהֵימָן
אמן	amen
אמר	say (6)
אמתא	handmaid
אֲנָה	I (10)
אִנּוּן	they (11)
אֱנוֹשׁ	human
אֲנַחְנָה	we (4)
אִנִּין	they, those (*fem.*) (11)
אניקה	anguish
אנס	trouble (G)

220

אַנְף	face (30)
אֱנָשׁ	man (10)
אַנְתְּ (אַנְתָּה)	you (*masc. sg.*) (11)
אנתה	wife (30)
אַנְתִּי	you (*fem. sg.*) (11)
אַנְתּוּן (אַנְתֹּם)	you (*masc. pl.*) (11)
אַנְתֵּן	you (*fem. pl.*) (11)
אָסְפַּרְנָא	exactly (11)
אֱסָר	prohibition (24)
אָע	wood
אַף	nose
אַף	also
אֶצְבַּע	finger (23)
אַרְבַּע	four (17)
אַרְגְּוָן	purple
אֲרוּ	behold
ארום	behold
ארז	cedar
אַרְיֵה	lion (25)
אריך	long
ארך	wait (*afʿel*—אוריך)
אַרְכָה	duration
ארמלה	widow
אֲרַע	earth (8)
אַרְעִית	bottom
אַרְקָא	earth
אֶשָּׁ(א)	fire (29)
אֻשִּׁין	foundations
אשרן	beams
אשתמודע	recognize
אָת	sign
אתה	come (G) (6); (H/A—bring, 18)
אַתּוּן	furnace (17)
אֲתַר	place (31) בָּאתַר after (12; *see* בתר)
אתרג	citron

ב

בְּ-	in (4)
באש	be evil
בגין	on account of
בהל	disturb (D) (20)
בוכריא	senior
בוקלסא	club
בוש *	embarrass (Dt)
בחן	examine
בחר	choose
בטל	stop (5) G—*intransitive* D—*transitive*
בי	*dialect form of* בַּיִת
בי מדרש	school house
בֵּין	between (12)
בִּירָה	fortress
בִּישׁ	evil (28)
בַּיִת	house (5)
בכה	cry
בלא	wear out (D)
בְּלוֹ	tax
בֵּן *	son
בנה	build (4)
בעה	seek, pray (14)
בָּעוּ	petition
בְּעֵל	master (5)
בקר	search (9—D)
בַּר	son (6; בְּנֵי—*pl. cstr.*)
בַּר	field (16)
ברי	create
ברך	bless (D) (22)
ברכה	blessing
בְּרַם	but
בשר	announce (Gt)
בְּשַׂר	flesh

בְּתוּלָה	virgin
בָּתַר	after (*from* בָּאתַר) (32)

ג

גַּב	side
גְּבוּרָה	power
גְּבַר	man (6)
גדד	cut down (21)
גַּו	interior (7)
	בְּגוֹא in the midst of (12)
גּוֹב	pit (25)
גוח	stir up (H)
גזר	cut, break off (15)
גְּזֵירָה	decree
גַּלְגַּל	wheel
גלה	reveal (14)
	H—take exile
גָּלוּ	exile (26)
גנב	steal
גנון	bridal chamber
גְּנַז	treasure (9)
גַּף	wing
גְּשֵׁם	body (19)

ד

דְּ-	which, that, of
דָּא	this (*fem.*) (14)
דֹּב	bear
דבח	sacrifice (*verb*)
דְּבַח	sacrifice (*noun*)
דבר	lead (away), take
דְּהַב	gold (9)
דּוּר	dwell (16)
דּוּשׁ	trample on
דחה	thrust
דחל	fear (20)

דִּי	which, of (3)
	כְּדִי when (26)
דִּיכְרָא	ram
דִּיל-	*possessive* (*cf.* -זִיל)
דִּילְמָא	perhaps
דִּין	this
דִּין	judgment (12)
דַּיָּן	judge (12)
דֵּךְ	that (*masc.*) (14)
דָּךְ	that (*fem.*) (4)
דִּכֵּן	that (4)
דכר	remember (28)
דְּכַר	ram
דָּכְרָן	memorandum
דלק	burn
דמה	resemble
דמי	price
דְּנָא/דְּנָה	this (3)
דִּקְלָא	palm (*also spelled* דִּיקְלָא)
דקק	be crushed (15; H—smash)
דָּר	generation (19)
דרג	stair
דְּרַע	arm
דשׁ	door
דָּת	law (12)

ה

הָא	behold
הָאנָא	behold, how (32)
הַדָּם	limb
הדס	myrtle
הוּא	he (11)
	ההוּא* that
הוה	be (8)
הִיא	she (11)
הֵיכַל	palace (8)
הכא	here

הֲלָא	is it not (*inter. particle*)		חֲדֵה	breast
הלך	go (12)		חדה	happiness
הִמּוֹ	they, them (5)		הֶדְוָה	joy
המונית עם	in agreement with		חוּד	singly (לַחוּד)
הֵן	if (9)		חוה	tell (13) (D/H)
* הרי	behold		חוה	prostrate self (Št—מִשְׁתַּחֲוֶה)
			חוּלָף	instead of (32)
	ו		חִוָּר	white
			חזה	see (15)
וְ	and			(*pass. part.*—proper)
ווי	woe!		חֵזוּ	vision
			חַי	living (26)
	ז		חיה	live
			חֵיוָה	animal (16)
זבן	buy		חַיִּין	life
זהב	gold		חַיִל	strength, army (22)
זי	who, which, of		חַכִּים	wise (13)
זִיו	splendor (23)		חָכְמָה	wisdom (14)
זילן	our		חל	sand
זית	olive		חלם	dream (G)
זך	who, which		חֵלֶם	dream (*noun*—13)
זכאי	worthy		חלף	pass by
זָכוּ	innocence		חֲלָק	portion
זכי	that		חמה	see (28)
זְמַן	time (14)			(*pass. part.*—proper)
זְמָר	music (17)		חֲמִיד	attractive
זַן	kind (17)		חמר	parch
זנה	this		חֲמַר	donkey (29)
זְעֵיר	small		חֲמַר	wine (23)
זקף	lift (32)		חֲמֵשׁ	five (17)
זרז	hasten		חמשין	fifty
זְרַע	seed		חֲנֻכָּה	dedication
			חַסִּיר	lacking
	ח		חסן	possess (H)
			חֲסַף	clay (15)
חבל	destroy (D) (10)		חַרְטֹם	magician (20)
חֲבָל	damage (19)		חֹרִי	noble
חֲבָר	companion (30)			
	(*fem.*—חַבְרָה)			
חַד	one (8)			

חֲרִישׁוּתָא	thicket
חֲרֹךְ	scorch (D)
חֲשַׁח	need (18)

ט

טָב	good (9)
טובה	goodness
טובען	flood
טוּר	mountain (15)
טַל	dew (21)
טליה	young servant (32)
טלל	seek shade (H)
טלל	shadow
טֵם	bone
טְעֵם	decree, taste (5; *see* שׂים)
טען	carry
טפה	extinguish (*ʾafʿel*)
טְפַר	claw
טרד	drive out (22)

י

יא	lovely (30)
יאות	well
יבל	bring (H) (31)
יַד	hand (18)
ידה	praise (H/A)
ידע	know (4; H—inform)
יהב	give (8)
יום, יומת	day (22)
יומנא	today
יחיד	only
יטב	be pleasing
יכל	be able, prevail (16)
יַם	sea
יעט	advise (Dt—take counsel)
יצא	go out
יצב	make certain (D)

יַצִּיב	surely (19)
יקד	burn (17)
יַקִּיר	difficult
יְקָר	glory (24)
ירד	descend
יְרַח	month (29)
יַרְכָה	thigh
ירת	inherit (32)
ישׁב	dwell (H—set)
ישׁט	stretch forth (H)
יַת	*direct object marker* (12)
יתב	dwell, sit
יַתִּיר	very (18)

כ

כ־	like, as (12)
כא	here
כבל	chain
כבשׁן	furnace
כדון	now
כְּדִי	when (26; *see* דִי)
כָּה	here
כהל	be able (21)
כָּהֵן	priest (11)
כוכב	star
כזי	when (*cf.* כְּדִי)
כיון	when (31)
כיף	shore
כַיִץ	summer
כֹּל	all (10)
	כֹּלָא everything
כלא	remonstrate (*ʾafʿel*)
כלב	dog
כלה	bride
כליל	perfect
כְּמָה	how (many) (19)
כמר	priest

כֵּן	thus (28)
כְּנָה	colleague (7)
כנכר	*coin*
כְּנֵמָא	thus (11)
כנש	gather
כסס	slaughter
כְּסַף	silver (9)
כְּעַן	now (4)
כַף	hand
כפר	deny
כפת	bind (D) (18)
כרה	become distressed (Gt)
כָּרוֹז	herald
כרז	proclaim (H)
כָּרְסֵא	throne (24)
כתב	write (3)
כְּתָב	writing (11)
כְּתַל	wall

ל

־לְ	to, for, *direct obj. marker* (3)
לָא	not (4)
לְבַב	heart (21)
לבונא	incense
לְבוּשׁ	garment
לבן	whiteness
לבש	wear (23)
לָהֵן	except, therefore (13)
לְוָת	to, with (29)
לחוד	*see* חוד
לחיא	evil
לְחֶם	meal (23)
לֵילִי	night (25)
לֵישָׁה	is not (28)
לֵית	there is not
ללב	palm

לם	surely
לקח	take
לִשָׁן	language

מ

־מ	from
מְאָה	hundred
מָאן	vessel (8)
מְגִלָּה	scroll
מגר	overthrow, throw down (D)
מַדְבַּח	altar (29)
מְדוֹר	dwelling (22)
מְדִינָה	province (7)
מַה	what(ever) (10)
מה	how
מוי	water
מות	die (31)
מָזוֹן	food
מזרק	basin
מחא	hit
מחזה	appearance
מחנה	camp
מַחְצְפָה	urgent
מחתא	grain offering (*cf.* מחתא)
מטא	reach (21)
מטלל	roof
מידעם	anything (*cf.* מנדעם)
מייא	water
מימרא	word
מכר	sell
מַלְאַךְ	angel
מִלָּה	word, thing (13)
מֶלֶךְ	king (3)
מַלְכוּ	reign (11)
מלל	speak (D) (26)
מַן	who(ever) (6)

מִן	from (9)		נְחָשׁ	copper (15)
	after, because מִן דִּי		נחת	descend (21)
	immediately מִן יָד			ʾafˁel (אַחֵת) deposit
מַנְדַּע	understanding		נטל	lift (22)
מנדעם	anything (*cf.* מידעם)		נטר	guard
מנה	count (G; D—appoint)		נכס	slaughter (32)
מִנְחָה	grain offering		נְכַס	property
מנע	withhold		נְמַר	panther
מסר	deliver (31)		נסב	take (30)
מְעֵה	belly		נסה	lift
מצעת	middle		נסי	test
מָרֵא	master (24)		נפל	fall (16)
מְרַד	rebellion		נפק	go out (8)
מָרָד	rebellious (4)		נִפְקָה	expenses
מרום	high (32)		נפשׁ	self (29), will
מרט	tear off		נִץ	radiance, bloom
משׁח	oil (*noun*)		נצה	quarrel
משׁח	anoint (*verb*)		נצח	win (D—distinguish self)
מִשְׁכַּב	bed		נציח	splendid
מִשְׁתֵּא	banquet		נצל	save (H)
			נְקֵא	pure
	נ		נשׁ	human (31)
			נְשִׁין	women (29)
נבא	prophesy (Dt)		נְשַׁר	eagle
נְבוּאָה	prophecy		נִשְׁתְּוָן	letter
נְבִיא	prophet		נתן	give (4)
נגד	flow			
נדב	be willing (Dt) (12)		**ס**	
נדד	flee			
נדח	banish		סבר	intend
נִדְנֶה	sheath		סגד	bow down (16)
נדש	destroy		סגי	multiply (H)
נַהִירוּ	illumination		סְגַן	prefect
נְהַר	river		סגר	close (26)
נוד	flee		סדר	arrange
נְוָלוּ/נְוָלִי	dunghill (10)		סוֹף	end
נוּר	fire (17)		סטנה	Satan
נזק	suffer damage		סכין	knife

סכל	look (Dt)	עַם	people, nation (12)
סלה	*liturgical term*	עמוד	pillar
סלק	go up (26)	עֲמִיק	deep
	הסיק (H) sacrifice	עמל	exert oneself, toil
סלת	flour	עמר	load
סְפַר	book (11)	עֲמַר	wool
סָפַר	scribe (3)	ענה	answer (13)
סָרַךְ	chief	עֲנַן	cloud
סתירה	hidden thing	עֲנַף	branch
סתר	tear down (G)	עֳפִי	foliage (20)
		עק	wood
ע		עקר	uproot (Gt—be uprooted)
		עָר	enemy
עֲבֵד	servant	ערבא	willow
עֲבִידָה	work, service (5)	עֲשַׂר	ten (17)
עבד	do, make (5)	עֶשְׂרִין	twenty
עַד	until (12)	עשת	intend
עדה	pass away (22; H—remove)		אתעשׁת (Gt) be thought
עִדָּן	time (13)	עֲתִיד	ready (18)
עובע	haste	עַתִּיק	old
עולימו	youth		
עוֹף	bird	**פ**	
עוקמא	trickery		
עֵילַּיי	on, above (32)	פ־	and
עַיִן	eye (30)	פגן	cry out
עכב	refuse	* פה	mouth
עַל	on, concerning, to, against (3)	פֶּחָה	governor (6)
עִלָּה	pretext (25)	פִּינַךְ	plate
עֵלָּה	above	פכר	destroy
עֲלָוָה	burnt offering (29)	פלא	trick
עִלִּי	Most High (21)	פְּלַג	half
עֶלְיוֹן	Most High	פלג	discord
עלל	enter (14)	פלוגתא	division (= Babel)
עָלַם	eternity (5)	פלח	worship, serve (17)
עֲלַע	rib	פָּלְחָן	worship
עלהא	burnt offering (29)	פְּלִיג	divided, undecided
עִם	with (12)	פֻּם	mouth (22)
		פַּס	palm

פְּסוּל	blemished	כָּל קֳבֵל דְּנָה	thereupon (14)
פְּסִיל	cut stone	קבל	receive (D) (25)
פַּרְזֶל	iron (15)	קַדִּישׁ	holy (20)
פרכס	struggle	קֳדָם	before (5)
פרס	divide	קדם	do early (H)
פרק	save	קַדְמָה	former time (26)
פַּרְתֹרֶךְ	governor	קַדְמָי/קַדְמָאי	first (17)
פשט	extend	קוּדְשָׁא	holy
פשר	interpret (23)	קוּם	arise, stand (G) (6)
פְּשַׁר	interpretation (13)		H—establish
פִּתְגָּם	message, word (10)	קִים D	D—swear
פתח	open (28)	התקיים Dt	Dt—be fulfilled
	צ	קוּר(א)	city
צבה	want (21)	קַטִּין	delicate
צְבוּ	wish, property	קטל	kill (G/D) (18)
צבע	be wet (Dt) (21)	קטע	cut
צְדָא	true	קטר	rise in circle
צדק	righteousness	קַיִט	summer
צִדְקָה	merit	קַיָּם	enduring
צוור	neck	קְיָם	statute (25)
צים	fast	קים	standing
ציר	pivot (of door)	קִיסָא	wood
צלה	pray (D) (10)	קָל	sound (17)
צלח	succeed, make prosper (H) (26)	קנה	buy, acquire
צְלֵם	statue, form (15)	קצף	be angry
צער	pain	קצץ	cut down
צפַּר	bird	קְצָת	end (22)
צפרא	morning	קרא/קרה	call, read (23)
	ק	קרב	approach (26) (D/H—sacrifice)
קֳבֵל	just as (11)	קְרָב	war
לָקֳבֵל	opposite, corresponding to (12)	קָרְבָּן	offering
כָּל קֳבֵל דְּ-	inasmuch as, because	קִרְיָה	city (4)
		קֶרֶן	horn (17)
		קְרַץ	piece
		אכל קְרַץ	accuse

ר

רֵאשׁ	head (chief) (7)
רֵאשׁ מִלִּין	complete account or essential contents
רַב	great (7)
רבה	grow (20)
רִבּוֹ	myriad, 10,000
רְבוּ	greatness (24)
רבחיל	general
רְבִיעִי	fourth (16)
רבע	quarter
רַבְרְבָנִין	chiefs
רגג	pleasant
רגז	anger (H)
רְגַז	anger
רְגַל	foot (15)
רגשׁ	assemble (25) (H)
רוּחַ	wind (20)
רוּם	rise (24)
רוּם	height
רוץ	run
רָז	secret (14)
רַחִיק	distant (10)
רחם	love (30)
רַחֲמִין	compassion (29)
רחמן	Merciful One
רמה	throw, impose (17)
רְעוּ	wish
רַעֲיוֹן	thought (23)
רפס	trample on
רקיק	soft
רשׁם	write (24)

שׂ

שָׂב	elder
שׂגא	grow great (19)

שׂ (cont.)

שַׂגִּיא	many (8)
שְׂטַר	side
שִׂים	issue, give (6)
שִׂים טְעֵם	issue decree or pay attention
שׂכל	consider (Dt)
שׂנא	hate
שְׂעַר	hair (19)
שׂקק	sackcloth
שׂרף	burn
שׂתו	winter

שׁ

שׁאל	ask (12)
שְׁאָר	remnant (11)
שׁבח	praise (D) (14)
שְׁבִיב	flame
שְׁבַע/שִׁבְעָה	seven (17)
שׁבק	leave alone, abandon (10) Gt—be transferred
שׁוה	be like (G) (24)
שׁוה	place (32)
שׁופר	beauty
שׁטט	wander
שֵׁיזב	save (18)
שֵׁיצִיא	finish
שׁירי	remainder
שׁכח	find (H) (23)
שׁכינתא	Divine Presence
שׁכלול	completion
שׁכלל	complete (11)
שָׁלוּ/שָׁלֵה	negligence (?)
שׁלח	send (3)
שׁלט	rule (16)
שָׁלְטָן	dominion (19)
שַׁלִּיט	authorized, mighty (12)
שׁלים	perfect

שְׁלַךְ	throw (H) (31)
שְׁלֵם	perfect
שְׁלֵם	be finished (24) (H—deliver)
שְׁלָם	peace (5)
שֵׁם	name (6) (*pl.* שְׁמָהָת)
שְׁמַד	exterminate (H)
שְׁמַיָּא	heavens (8)
שְׁמַם	be appalled
	אֶשְׁתּוֹמֵם *ʾitpolʿel*
שְׁמַע	hear, obey (17)
שְׁמַשׁ	serve (D)
שְׁמַשׁ	sun
	בֵּין שִׁמְשָׁתָא twilight
שֵׁן	tooth
שְׁנָה	change (D, H) (13)
שְׁנָה	year (8)
שְׁנָה	sleep
שְׁנַק	choke (Gt)
שְׁעָה	talk (Gt)
שָׁעָה	hour (18)
שַׁפִּיר	beautiful
שְׁפַל	be low (24)
שְׁפַר	please, be beautiful (25)
שָׁק	leg (29)
שְׁרַב	family
שְׁרָה	loosen (19)
שְׁרִיר	prosperous
שְׁרָשׁ	root
שֵׁת	six (11)
שְׁתָה (אֶשְׁתִּיו)	drink (23)

ת

תְּאֵנָה	fig
תְּבִיר	breakable
תְּבַר	break (29)
תּוּב	return (*intrans.*) (22)
	H—return (*trans.*), reply
תּוֹר	ox
תְּחוֹת	underneath (12)
* תחת	instead of
תְּלַג	snow
תְּלִי	weapon
תְּלִיתָי	third (16)
תלסירי	thirteen
תְּלָת	three (17)
תַּלְתִּי/תַּלְתָּא	ruler (24)
תְּלָתִין	thirty
תמה	wonder (G)
תַּמָּה	there (9)
תְּמָנֶה	eight (17)
תמר	date
תנה	here (29)
תני	tell
תִּנְיָן/תִּנְיָנוּת	second (17)
תַּקִּיף	strong (5)
תקל	weigh
תקן	prepare (H—restore)
תְּרֵין/תַּרְתֵּין	two (28)
תְּרֵי־עֲשַׂר	twelve (17)
תְּרַע	gate
תְּשַׁע	nine (17)

ERRATA

PAGE		CHANGE	TO
1	line 5 from bottom	Genesis (31:17)	Genesis (31:47)
3	right hand column	זְמָן	זְמָן
16	Vocabulary—to be learned	חוֹדַעְנָא	הוֹדַעְנָא
16	Vocabulary—to be learned	מהוֹדְעִין	מְהוֹדְעִין
16	Reference vocabulary	דְּכְרָנָיָה	דָּכְרָנַיָּא
16	Reference vocabulary שְׁלַחְנָא	שׁלה *perfect 3 m pl*	שׁלח *perfect 1 pl*
21	Vocabulary—to be learned	בַּטֵלַת	בְּטֵלַת
21	Reference vocabulary	day . . . יוֹמַת	days (pl. const.) יוֹמָת
26	line 5 from bottom of text	נָשִׁין	נָשִׁים
27	Reference vocabulary (לְכֹם)	to you	to you (*m pl*)
27	Next to last line of text	לחם	לְהֹם
27	Next to last line of text	דְנָה	דְּנָה
27	last line of text	וַעֵין	וְעֵין
29	first line		add נְבִיאֵי
33	Vocabulary—to be learned	כְּנָה	כְּנָת
33	chart—G conjugations	*peꜥal, peꜥil, hitpeꜥel*	*peꜥal, peꜥil, hitpeꜥel*
	D conjugations	*hitpaꜥꜥel*	*hitpaꜥꜥal*
	H conjugations	*hitapꜥel*	*hitafꜥal*
34	line 4 of text	שָׂם	שָׁם
38	line 2 of Aramaic text	כַּסְדָּיָה	כַּסְדָּיְא
38	line 5 of Aramaic text	וְיְהִיבוּ	וִיהִיבוּ
38	Next to last line	שֵׁשְׁבַּצַּר	שֵׁשְׁבַּצַּר
49	Reference vocabulary	need . . . חַשַׁח	needed thing . . . חַשְׁחָה
49	Reference vocabulary	*f pl* . . . מִתְיַהֲבָא	*f sg* . . . מִתְיַהֲבָא
52	line 1	עבר	עבד
54	3 m pl	הִמּוֹ	הִמּוֹ

231

56	6th line from bottom of text	שְׁתָר	שְׁתַר
57	Proper Names	פֶּרַס	פָּרַס
58	#8	שֻׁם	שָׁם
64	line 6 of text	עֲלָיִן	עֲלָךְ
66	3 f sg	־ַהּ	־ַהּ
67	3 f sg	מַלְכְוָתַהּ	מַלְכְוָתַהּ
67	1 pl	פִּשְׁרִינָא*	פִּשְׁרִינָא*
69	Reference Vocabulary	הוֹבָדָא	הוֹבָדָה
70	line 1 of Aramaic	מַלְכָה	מַלְכָּא
70	line 1 of Aramaic	. לָא	לָא
74	line 7 from bottom	מִן דִּי	מִן דִּי
75	Vocabulary—to be learned	בְעָה	בְּעָה
79	Reference vocabulary	דְּרַע	דְּרַע
79	Reference vocabulary	tell . . . חוא	tell (D) . . . חוה
87	line 6 of Aramaic	תֶּהֱוֵה תַּקִּיפָה	תֶּהֱוֵה תַּקִּיפָה
		וּמִנַּהּ תֶּהֱוֵה תְבִירָה	וּמִנַּהּ תֶּהֱוֵה תְבִירָה
89	3rd line of text	שֵׁת	שֵׁת
95	f sg	כְּתֻבִי	כְּתֻבִי
97	2nd line	הַשְׁחִין	חַשְׁחִין
107	imperative f sg	הַשְׁלֵטִי	הַשְׁלֵטִי
107	infinitive	הַשְׁלָטָה	הַשְׁלָטָה
114	Perfect 2 f sg	בְּנַיִתִי	בְּנַיִתִי
115	Vocabulary—to be learned	יִצְטַבַּע	יִצְטַבַּע
120	1st line of biblical passage	מְטָת	מְטָה
129	Passive participle, m sg	כְּתִיב	כְּתִיב
154	5th line	אֲנָשָׁא	אֲנָשָׁא
211	m pl nouns with		
	3 f sg pronominal suffix	פִּשְׁרַיהּ	פִּשְׁרַיהּ
217	Hollow roots		
	1 sg imperfect	אָשִׁין	אָשִׂים
	Active participle, m sg	שָׁאִן	שָׂאֵם
	Passive participle, m sg	שִׁין	שִׂים
	Imperative	שִׁין	שִׂים
222		דְּרַע	דְּרַע